Praise for
AFTER THE IDEA

"As a shark on *Shark Tank*, I've seen countless entrepreneurs light up when sharing their aha moment—only to falter when asked about execution. *After The Idea* focuses on the hidden challenges of the founder journey, offering guidance on everything from hiring the right team, to crafting go-to-market strategies and navigating the critical early decisions that make or break a startup. Julia Austin demystifies what happens after the lightbulb moment and gives aspiring founders valuable insights for the ever-evolving process of branching out of the status quo and building the future."

—Matt Higgins, author of *Wall Street Journal*
bestseller *Burn the Boats*

"So, you want to start a company or join a startup? Austin is the best guide imaginable for your journey. Insightful and generous with her knowledge, she will make sure you avoid common pitfalls and perils. She offers practical, tactical suggestions to help you find success. This book will become the go-to resource for anyone interested in the fast-paced world of startups."

—Kim Scott, author of *New York Times*
bestseller *Radical Candor*

"This terrific new book by seasoned startup operator and Harvard Business School professor Austin achieves that rare literary hat trick: it's insightful, riveting, and practical. If you want great storytelling and evidence-based advice for your next start up (whether brand new or underway), *After the Idea* is the book for you."

—Amy C. Edmondson, author of
Right Kind of Wrong

"Austin has crafted the manual every founder needs to read. In *After the Idea*, Austin merges her extensive experience with a clear passion for founders into a comprehensive guide that answers, in great detail, the question we whisper to ourselves every night: But how? With deep entrepreneurial insight, *After the Idea* delivers a road map for anyone determined to build and scale not just an idea, but a truly remarkable company."　　　　　　—Karen Young, founder, OUI the People

"Austin has distilled her decades of experience as an insider at a remarkable group of startups into a company-building manual that every founder can benefit from. Austin and I were colleagues at Akamai where her statement that 'Vision leads to execution' was on full display. She turned our deeply held vision into an execution road map. She came into an organization that was long on vision, passion, and culture, and honed all of those into an execution-focused machine. Her advice will help founders improve organizational stability, process, accountability, and good decision making without stifling the energy and passion that fuel the best startups in the world."

—Jonathan Seelig, cofounder,
Akamai Technologies

"Launching and scaling a startup can often feel like a high-stakes maze, full of challenges that test both your business acumen and your resilience. That's why *After the Idea* is a breath of fresh air. Austin offers more than just strategies to get from an idea to scale—she unpacks the emotional and psychological toll founders face, reminding us that sustainable success is built as much on self-awareness and alignment with purpose as it is on financial metrics."

—Jenny Fielding, cofounder and managing partner,
Everywhere Ventures

"*After the Idea* is a master class in intentional entrepreneurship. With wisdom born of experience and a genuine understanding of the emotional and operational complexities of startups, Austin provides a guide that is both practical and inspiring. For anyone seeking to build a sustainable, values-driven business, this book is indispensable. Every entrepreneur should read it."

—Jerry Colonna, author of *Reboot*

"*After the Idea* masterfully guides first-time founders through the labyrinth of building a startup. With its practical advice, thoughtful insights about founder psychology, and rich, real-world examples, this book is an indispensable resource for turning daunting entrepreneurial challenges into achievable milestones. A must-read for anyone embarking on a startup journey."

—Tom Eisenmann, author of *Why Startups Fail*

"In *After the Idea*, Austin maps a comprehensive blueprint that goes far beyond the typical startup manual, delving deep into the human element that is crucial for any founder to keep their sanity while facing the many perils of startup-building. Austin blends together personal anecdotes and practical advice, underscoring that building a company is as much about 'people stuff' as it is about product and fundraising. This book challenges founders and joiners to reflect on their 'why,' and to build a business that aligns with their true north, not just their financial goals."

—Eric Paley, managing director, Founder Collective

AFTER THE IDEA

AFTER THE IDEA

What It Really Takes to Create and Scale a Startup

JULIA AUSTIN

BASIC

VENTURE

New York

Basic Venture
Hachette Book Group
1290 Avenue of the Americas, New York, NY 10104
www.basic-venture.com

Printed in the United States of America

First Edition: June 2025

Published by Basic Venture, an imprint of Hachette Book Group, Inc. The Basic Venture name and logo is a registered trademark of the Hachette Book Group.

The Hachette Speakers Bureau provides a wide range of authors for speaking events. To find out more, go to hachettespeakersbureau.com or email HachetteSpeakers@hbgusa.com.

Basic Venture books may be purchased in bulk for business, educational, or promotional use. For more information, please contact your local bookseller or the Hachette Book Group Special Markets Department at special.markets@hbgusa.com.

The publisher is not responsible for websites (or their content) that are not owned by the publisher.

Print book interior design by Bart Dawson.

Library of Congress Cataloging-in-Publication Data
Names: Austin, Julia, author.
Title: After the idea : what it really takes to create and scale a startup / Julia Austin.
Description: First edition. | New York : PublicAffairs, 2025. | Includes bibliographical references and index.
Identifiers: LCCN 2024049123 | ISBN 9781541705272 (hardcover) | ISBN 9781541705296 (ebook)
Subjects: LCSH: Entrepreneurship. | New business enterprises. | Success in business.
Classification: LCC HD62.5 .A94 2025
LC record available at https://lccn.loc.gov/2024049123

ISBNs: 9781541705272 (hardcover), 9781541705296 (ebook)

LSC-C

Printing 1, 2025

To those who embrace the roller-coaster ride
and dare to change the world—this book is for you.

Be careful what you water your dreams with. Water them with worry and fear and you will produce weeds that choke the life from your dream. Water them with optimism and solutions and you will cultivate success. Always be on the lookout for ways to turn a problem into an opportunity for success. Always be on the lookout for ways to nurture your dream.

—LAO TZU, Chinese philosopher,
founder of Taoism (601–530 BC)

CONTENTS

CONTENTS

PART IV—WORKING AT SCALE

INTRODUCTION

WELCOME TO
STARTUP LAND

Early one Monday morning in 1999, while I was getting my kids ready for school before driving into the city for work, my pager started to go nuts. I was working at Akamai Technologies, a rapidly scaling business-to-business (B2B) startup that had a few hundred servers running a network service around the world that essentially made the internet experience faster for our customers' customers. I was the first and only release manager at Akamai at the time, a role that was sort of a hybrid of product manager, program manager, operations manager, jane-of-all-trades, and cat herder. It was a startup, after all, and we all did whatever we needed to do to keep the business going, regardless of who had what title. Since my role required me to be the glue between many different players that ran our business, I was on the front line when any major issue arose.

From the 911 messages I was seeing on my pager, I knew we were down. Not just a few regions of servers in a few countries, which happened sometimes due to situations out of our control, but the whole network was down. We were to use the 911 moniker only when the situation was dire, and this was my first time seeing it. It was an "Oh F-CK" moment. I hustled the kids into the car so I could put Dale, our systems operations lead, on speakerphone while we drove to school. "It's down, Julia. Like, totally dead," he said. While waiting for a stop light to turn green I tried to work through in my head what we had released the prior week that might have caused such a nightmare. Nothing came to mind. "Do we know if anything changed over the weekend that would have caused this?" I asked. He said, "All we know is that one of the engineers checked in some new code randomly yesterday. I think it was to fix a bug, but it looks like he did some other stuff while he was in there." This was a classic rookie mistake for our startup. We had no processes in place to prevent new code from being released onto our network without anyone's approval. One of our first hires, a bright MIT dropout who had just made millions on our IPO (startups went public weirdly early back then), decided to do some coding for fun on a Sunday. In doing so, he broke our network. And not just our network. Back then, our service was the backbone of most internet properties; we had basically broken most of the internet. It was *bad*.

We backed out the engineer's code, made many mea culpa calls to customers offering credits and apologies, and somehow avoided a PR nightmare—if X (née Twitter) or LinkedIn had been around back then, we would have been screwed. We thought we had things back on track by late Monday night, but still had another ugly day ahead as we realized on Tuesday that the mess the day before caused websites to load incorrectly—we're talking about clicking on a link on CNN.com and getting sent to a page on the Playboy.com site. Eek! Thankfully, one of our brilliant engineers figured out a way to fix this secondary issue, and by Tuesday night we were all feeling relieved.

Despite our great market success, we were still operating like a scrappy startup. It was time to grow up. We all felt terrible, and while it was just one engineer who caused this mess, we were all culpable; we let it happen. It was after this crisis, in the early days of Akamai, when everything began to turn around. I finally put the engineering and release processes in place that we had all resisted ("who needs processes, we're a startup!"), our network operations team put in better monitoring tools, and as a leadership team, we developed a planning and communication process that informed how the rest of the business would operate—from product prioritization to marketing and sales. It was the start of building a business that was poised to scale. Even when the internet bubble began to fracture and the industry seemed uncertain, the team hummed with such loyalty and camaraderie after that kerfuffle that we felt like nothing could stop us. Embracing more structure and organization shifted the already strong and supportive culture of the organization to one prepared for growth. We had reached the rocket-ship phase in a startup's life when you are scaling too fast to fly by the seat of your pants but not quite at the scale to operate with all the processes, policies, and procedures of a mature company.

I went on to join two more startups during their rocket-ship phases—VMware in 2005 and DigitalOcean in 2016. Most people know of these companies as massively successful businesses today, but, like Akamai, they were all fledgling businesses when I first came onto the scene. On one of my first days at DigitalOcean, an early hire with no prior startup experience complained about product priorities constantly changing and lots of people coming on board when it wasn't clear what their roles were. The employee asked me, "Is this normal startup crazy, or DigitalOcean crazy?" Simply telling this new hire that this was "normal startup crazy" reduced the stress they were feeling at the time. I had seen this movie before and knew what to expect, but most founders and often joiners of startups have no points of reference.

I was fortunate to land at three different technology startups that managed to figure out their operational issues and go public. At each company, I was able to both learn from others with more experience than me and offer my own experiences after several times at bat. That journey inspired me to pay it forward to support founders, joiners, and investors on their quest to build successful businesses. So, I started coaching, teaching, advising, and sitting on startup boards, and I founded a nonprofit organization for women founders. I joined the faculty of Harvard Business School (HBS) in 2016, where I developed and led several courses for students starting ventures while earning their MBAs. I am also a professionally certified executive coach working exclusively with startup founders. The Startup Operations course I created at HBS in 2021 specifically addresses how to build a startup with intention and is the inspiration for this book.

WORKING WITH INTENTION

It starts with an idea—there's a problem to solve and you're going to be the one to do it. And then before you know it, there's an OMG moment when you realize that you are not just building a product, fundraising, and selling, you are building a *company*. It may seem obvious, but it's always a shock when that moment comes in a founder's journey. In the early stages of a startup, you tend to focus on the immediate needs around creating a product and fail to take a more holistic view of what your operating business may look like months or years from now. It can be so much easier to focus on what's right in front of you when the big picture can be a daunting, and even potentially paralyzing, concept.

Founders are often portrayed to the outside world as "crushing it," but internally you may be filled with doubt, imposter syndrome, and fear, thinking *Does my idea suck and no one is telling me? Do I know anything about running a business or leading a team?* You may also struggle with balancing various roles when there's just a few people doing many things at your startup. This can cause you to lean toward tasks that are easier and quicker to do, saying to yourself *I have no idea where we're going and how to operationalize this business, but I know how to build a mobile app, so I'll just do that!* This can be a great attitude when raising capital early on and investors want evidence that you are not afraid to get your hands dirty. But those same investors will be on your back a year from now if you haven't stepped up and created a well-run business.

If every company founder could go back in time and rethink their startup plan, most would tell you that they wished they had been more intentional about the *operations* of their business. They've learned that it is never too early to be thoughtful about their culture and the people they hired, their brand, finances, legal considerations, and everything else beyond the product or service they offer. Most teams fail to get these tactics right at the start of a new venture, and not everyone has a coach or professor to show them the way throughout their journey.

That's why I wrote this book. This is the guide for you if you are a founder who is just getting started on your entrepreneurial journey or if you are already on your way and need to return to the basics. This book is primarily speaking to founders and startup joiners, but investors and startup advisors who read this book will get an insider's view of the pitfalls startups may run into and learn how to offer help to the founders they work with.

WHAT LIES AHEAD

Most founders know they need a more intentional operating system, but they stall for a simple reason: they don't know where to start. This is a super common roadblock because creating and growing a startup is a nonlinear process. It's a series of iterations and continuous learning that evolves an idea into a fully fledged business. It's freaking out about a delayed product release today, then about something else tomorrow. This book serves as a guide to that nonlinear process. While I won't offer every single how-to to run your business (that's a huge book!), I'll show you how to create an operational foundation for your company that keeps you out of common sticky startup situations—and prepares you to easily unwind messes that will inevitably show up.

When I work with my clients and students, I reach into the toolbox I've assembled from decades of experience and stories at my disposal and apply each as necessary depending on the situation. This book contains all those tools, and you can use them as needed. Basically, I am going to give you a tour of the gym and show you how all the equipment works. It's up to you to decide which tools to leverage, and when. But, just like you don't get a six-pack from one trip to the gym, you will need a few reps before you become adept at operating your venture. With the gym metaphor in mind, I'm going to start by asking you what your goals are, just like I do with my students. Why are you doing this? How do you define success? Just as fitness goals change, so may the goals of anyone on the startup journey. And I encourage you to return to these questions and tools as you traverse your startup path. I've designed this book so that you can read it from front to back to prepare you for the startup adventure, but it can also be a guide along the way. Pull it off the shelf and jump to a section when you can use a refresher on any topic you may be grappling with.

After exploring the foundational questions about why you're on this path and what your goals may be, I'll dive into the four main pillars that, together, form the basis of what ensures a successful startup: product, people, operations, and working at scale. I can't emphasize enough, however, that these areas interplay with each other all the time. As you create and run your startup, you will experience twists and turns based on all sorts of factors, from how you solve the problem, to the market and world events, to who the founders are, team dynamics, and even personal situations. Thus, you can't follow the advice in this book step-by-step and expect to end up with a wildly successful business. Instead, each pillar needs to be worked on in parallel, throughout your startup's journey, and will be covered in four parts of the book, as shown on the following page.

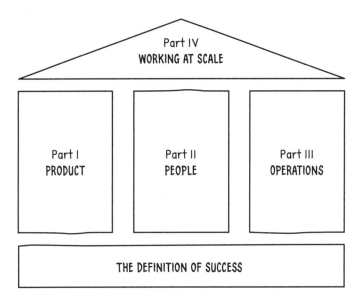

In **Part I: Product,** I provide a tool kit for proper problem and persona validation work (also known as "discovery") and equip those who already have products in the market with advanced techniques to ensure they're building the best new features and products as they scale.

Part II: People delves into the human aspects of growing a business, from deciding whether to have a cofounder to hiring, firing, and establishing a kick-ass organization from day one.

Part III: Operations breaks down the core elements of the business beyond the product and people stuff, such as legal, finance, marketing, and support. These can be seen as the more mundane elements of running a business, but without them, your business will not survive. Many founders and joiners miss this memo early on and feel gobsmacked when they realize how many operational activities they have to manage as they scale. Part III will prepare you for this if you're just getting started or reassure those already in it that it's totally doable with the right mindset and frameworks.

Finally, in **Part IV: Working at Scale,** I offer guidance on how to manage the business once you start operating at scale. Startups move fast, and the challenges that come from shifting from a tiny team to running a full organization with many moving parts can take you by surprise. I will also touch on the transitions and exit strategies many founders face as well as bring to light common struggles with mental health and stress management because these are core challenges in anyone's entrepreneurial journey.

I'll end the book with a glossary of common terms and a list of resources that complements the advice in this book.

There is no one perfect way to build a startup. Each experience is highly personal, and building a new business is hard, especially for those who don't come from privilege or have the good fortune of higher education. With this in mind, I have intentionally included many stories and examples about entrepreneurs and joiners in this book who you may not know of (yet). They haven't had their name in lights at TechCrunch Disrupt or their profile on the cover of *Forbes* magazine. These are founders who learned the hard way on their road toward success (or failure). My hope is that their stories will help you see around corners, make the process smoother, and set you up for success.

FOUNDATIONS

The four parts of this book are born from my years spent in the startup trenches helping companies navigate explosive growth. At the three startups I helped scale, I brought a method to the mess that allowed each company to flourish. I've seen what happens when founders take their company culture and operations seriously—and when they don't. And without both, something as small as a string of bad code can become a full-blown crisis that could implode your business. But with solid systems in place, your company can stay resilient even if a true catastrophe hits.

Now, to be clear, this is not a book about preparing for crises. It's just that disasters of one kind or another tend to crop up *a lot* when a company doesn't have a strong company culture and operational processes. The more effort that goes into building those systems, the less those disasters tend to be so . . . disastrous. To help you appreciate this point, let me share my first experience as a startup joiner.

In October 1999 I took a big career bet and left a cushy job with nine-to-five hours, decent pay, and very little stress to join Akamai Technologies. It was the middle of the internet bubble. Having loved the computer networking course I took in graduate school, I was fascinated by connected systems and the possibility of the internet becoming a ubiquitous solution to so many challenges from distributed teams to online shopping—both of which were in their earliest stages of development in the late 1990s.

Back then, internet companies were popping up and going public left and right with far fewer expectations on the scale and maturity of their businesses—very different from what's expected in today's market. From 1998 to 1999, there was an average of two IPOs a week and US stock prices were at a historical high. It was also the beginning of the startup boom that led to the era of hoodies, foosball tables, and unlimited snacks in the company kitchen. This was not our parents' corporate world. It was what I imagine the gold rush era was like, with lots of entrepreneurial pursuits and capitalistic optimism and droves of young professionals heading west to become internet millionaires—opting for stakes in the business such as equity and stock options over fat salaries and 401(k) plans. This was the internet startup boom, baby, and I wanted in.

With fresh capital from their most recent fundraise, the Akamai team—predominantly made up of academics and twenty-year-old grad students—was hiring like crazy. There was pressure from their investors to bring in "grown-ups" who had seen this movie before and could guide the company from a scrappy startup to a long-term, sustainable business post-IPO. After a long conversation with a friend who had recently joined Akamai, I became convinced that there was a great opportunity to get in early, be helpful, and possibly make a lot of money. I was the classic "startup curious" candidate with little tech startup experience but a ton of skills and eagerness to learn. So I scheduled an interview.

Through my interviews at Akamai I learned that these were my favorite types of humans. They were authentic, passionate, and brilliant. We instantly felt a connection, and my future boss offered me a job right then and there. Having been in corporate America for the past ten years, I was a bit taken aback by how loosey-goosey the whole hiring process was, but I was already starting to fall in love with this company. There were around fifty employees at Akamai that day, and they were adding ten to twenty new people a week to get us all in with a good strike price before the upcoming IPO. By the time I joined a few weeks later, I became employee number 289. On my first day, more than 80 percent of my coworkers had been at the business less than six weeks. It was *crazy*.

What became clear to me in the weeks that followed was that there was a huge gap between product success and the running of a successful startup. The day I interviewed, there was no product roadmap or release process—software updates and bug fixes were pushed out to our network all day, every day—and there were no quality standards for code or a clear internal communication strategy to keep our various work streams functioning well. We were in firefighting mode all the time. I became Akamai's first release manager—the job description of which I was told I could figure out once I got there. I spent my first few months getting up to speed not only on how the internet worked but also on how the business functioned. And as one of the few non-MIT, non–computer scientist (despite my technical master's degree) employees, with no one reporting directly to me, I was also trying to figure out how to gain credibility from my teammates to get shit done (GSD).

The most I was able to accomplish in my first six months, in addition to getting us over the Y2K hump, was to implement a weekly release process.[1] Akamai's cofounder and CTO Danny Lewin would, under no circumstances, let me devise a slower cadence like monthly or quarterly software releases. We developed a way to stagger new software releases on our live network to test that nothing broke and improvements worked, then, if that went well, we rolled out the software to the rest of the few thousand servers we had back then, aka "the world." It is a process that is still in place at Akamai twenty-five years later. It was like pulling teeth trying to get our engineers on board with having a regular release schedule. Even getting them to come to a weekly planning meeting was a big ask back then! Structure was not a popular concept, and there was an inherent fear that if we put in too much process, we'd slow down and lose our edge. However, once we recognized that the constant firefighting because of bad code began to dissipate with this release process in place, we embraced operational processes and began to bring some order to the chaos.

Then, tragedy struck.

11 P.M., SEPTEMBER 10, 2001

At nearly midnight, I found myself sitting in a boardroom with my company's leadership team discussing strategy with Danny. The room was littered with half-full Diet Cokes and empty takeout containers. We were overhauling the business in the face of the dot-com bubble burst. I had recently been promoted to be the company's vice president of engineering and was trying hard to keep the business afloat with my colleagues, hence the late-night strategy session. My kids were at home asleep in their beds, and, realizing how late it was, everyone agreed to break soon and pick things up in the morning.

Danny was flying to California the next day to meet with a prospective customer, and he encouraged us to continue the session without him in the morning. We wanted him to stay one more day and continue to hash this out, but he insisted that we take it from there. He trusted us to figure out how to execute our new plan. Earlier that evening, he had taken me aside during a meeting break to tell me he supported an engineering department reorganization that we had been arguing about for weeks. Even though it was my team to lead, and he wasn't technically my boss, his support as the CTO and company cofounder was critical to the success of this big change.

"Do it. You were right; I was being bullheaded," he said.

I was in shock—he rarely caved on disagreements. As a former captain in the Israel Defense Forces, he was intimidating. I was used to him shouting and saying I was being "obstreperous" (his favorite word). Past arguments usually resulted in me storming out of his office. As I would near the door, my back to him, he would throw a dry eraser with impeccable aim just past my ear—not to hit me, but to make sure I knew who was in charge. (Leaders would not get away with that behavior today. It was a different time!) I wasn't sure why he was suddenly agreeable on this particular night. I was happy to finally move on, but there was a nagging feeling in my gut about what made him pivot to all of this big decision–making and kindness in the past few days. The ambiguity in the air was palpable.

Driving into the office the next morning, September 11, the sun was shining, and I was feeling pretty inspired about the evening before. I was sitting in bumper-to-bumper traffic on Route 93 North heading from Boston's South Shore into Cambridge. But instead of my usual cursing out loud about why I chose this horrible commute and why I ever joined this crazy startup, I felt light and excited—he finally listened! I was thinking over how to implement the new organization plan and the new product roadmap. This was my jam—product and people stuff—and I couldn't wait to get to the office and dig in.

At approximately 8:00 a.m., back in the boardroom, the Akamai leadership team, minus Danny, picked up where we had left off the evening before. As we settled into our seats, our internal corporate lawyer was hanging up with Danny because the flight attendant had told him to turn off his cell phone.

About an hour into our meeting, one of my engineers came into the boardroom to tell us the internet was going wild because an airplane had hit one of the World Trade Center towers. In the early days of the internet, most Fortune 500 companies were on a mission to adopt the World Wide Web to reach their customers without website performance issues, and our service was critical to this mission. Since we ran a large portion of the internet back then and knew our customers would rely on us to keep their sites running during this situation, we immediately went into crisis mode, putting the strategy session on hold and reporting to our respective stations to ensure our teams were handling what we anticipated to be a very busy day.

We were unaware of what was about to unfold that day, but we knew much of the world would be getting their news on the web. It was critical that our service was 100 percent up and running and could handle the extra traffic. CNN, MSN, Yahoo! News . . . all the big players were running live streams on what was happening in New York City; Washington, DC; and Pennsylvania, and we were making sure that their services were fast and without interruption. It was a few hours into this crisis when the reality of the situation started to sink in and we understood that this was not an anomalous incident or FAA mishap but a terrorist attack on the United States.

It wasn't until that afternoon that we confirmed Danny was on American Airlines flight 11. He was in first class and likely the first victim as he attempted to prevent the terrorist attack.[2] Despite the gravity of the situation, we pressed on and continued to do so in his honor. It was the strong company culture our founders had built, combined with the excellent operating processes we had begun to put in place, that made it possible for us to get past that tragic moment in our company's history. It was the hardest day of my career, as it was for many, and although this was an extreme situation, it set me on a path to ensure that every business I worked for and with had the same strong company culture and operational structure to withstand the highest of highs and the lowest of lows. This event changed me and gave me a mission and purpose.

Akamai could have easily gone bust several times because of rookie errors we made or losing our CTO-founder on 9/11. But what kept us going when so many other companies wouldn't have made it? The answer isn't something magical—there wasn't just something in the water in early 2000s Cambridge, Massachusetts. It was something basic and fundamental, and yet something that I see so many promising startups lack: a strong operational foundation based on an incredible culture.

Our great culture and excellent operational processes—from our customer support team to my engineers who worked heroically to keep the internet alive that day and throughout the economic downturn when many startups were dropping like flies. Our strong foundation was the difference between us and ventures that were winging it without processes in place for hiring, managing, and revenue generating. I saw this again when I joined VMware as we successfully navigated tremendous growth and the 2008 financial crisis. The ride was a little bumpier when I first joined DigitalOcean, but today, all three ventures continue to thrive, and it's not just because they make great products and raised a lot of capital and went public. It's because they focused on execution as much as their products and took their operations and their culture seriously. This book will offer you opportunities to think about the operations and culture of the organizations you are building, joining, or investing in. Hopefully the lessons I impart in these pages will save you a lot of wasted time, money, and stress. But reader beware, not every startup is the same, and as stated prior, nuances will always arise depending on a multitude of variables, including but not limited to the people who start the company and their investors to market forces and world events. I also want to acknowledge that perspectives around the same situation can vary. How I remember an incident may be different from how my colleagues experienced it. The stories ahead represent my point of view, insights, and a lot of proven tools I've developed to guide you along the way. Enjoy!

1.

THE DEFINITION OF SUCCESS

Before we dive into the tactical stuff, let's get grounded on the concept of success and how I address it on day one of my course.

I open with my first cold call (a common teaching strategy at Harvard Business School where students are asked a question when they haven't been raising their hands) of the year: "Gio, what does success mean to you?" Giovanna "Gio" Abramo and her cofounder had ambitious plans for Plenna, which offers OB-GYN services to young women in Mexico City. Like many founders when posed this question, Gio's first response was to say, "We want to create a unicorn in Latin America." The term "unicorn" in startup land means a venture valued by the market at one billion dollars or more. That was a good start, but vague, so I pressed further. "OK, and when you look back on your venture once it becomes a unicorn, what do you want to say about the impact it's made? How will you feel about it?" This gave Gio pause. She hadn't thought much about what success would look like or feel like for *her*. After almost a full minute of contemplation—which can

15

feel like ages in a classroom of sixty people waiting for your answer—she said, "I want to feel proud that we brought access to high-quality health care for women in Latin America. That, with Plenna, women have a safe place to go for gynecological care. That we made a difference for women at scale." Then Gio gave one of her sharp, infectious smiles and said, "Oh, and I'd like to make enough money to retire early." Her fellow students smiled and nodded in agreement.

When I asked Gio if she and her cofounder were aligned on this vision for success, she proudly said yes and that they had even discussed what a successful outcome would be. Their "number," as some call it, is the exit valuation and desired path (acquisition versus, say, IPO) over a particular time frame. They had discussed ten years at most to reach their number, but this was of course dependent on how well the business scaled and their ability to build a team that allowed them to sustain their lifestyles outside of work. Both planned to raise families and work full time for the foreseeable future, but neither wanted to burn out by putting everything into their businesses. Gio and her cofounder are exceptions when it comes to this discussion so early in their journey. We'll talk more about this in Chapter 6 when we discuss the cofounder courtship.

I then ask my students to break out into their teams and discuss for ten minutes or so what success looks like to each of them. The teams are usually a mix of three to four student cofounders and joiners; the latter are students who are aspiring founders or will join a startup or be an investor after graduate school. Joiners take the course to build skills and deepen their understanding of startups by working on other students' startups. When we reconvene to debrief, I ask a few teams to share what they learned in their breakouts. A joiner on a team with two cofounders says, "I learned that these two cofounders have different ideas about success. Pat wants to turn around the business fast and exit to make enough cash to pay off school loans, and Mia is super passionate about the long-term potential of their idea and hopes to IPO someday and maybe get recognized for her thought leadership in

AI. It felt awkward when it was obvious they clearly haven't aligned on outcomes." The class gets a little uncomfortable in their seats realizing there are different expectations between their classmates and a joiner who may get stuck in the middle of this. Many of them experienced similar conversations in their breakout discussions—not an uncommon situation for startup joiners stuck between different cofounder mindsets and priorities!

Alignment around a shared vision for success and desired outcomes is tantamount to the long-term success of your startup—no matter what you build or how long it takes to reach some level of success. So, while everyone wants to jump into product discovery and solution building (it's coming in the next chapter, don't worry!), alignment on where your startup is heading is pretty darn important. Even if you are a solo founder, having that conversation first with yourself, then perhaps with a partner, mentor, or coach is an important grounding exercise before you get ahead of yourself.

My former student Sam Koch's company, Otto, is an enterprise sales software solution. After our classroom discussion about success, Sam was motivated to have an alignment conversation with his cofounder later that day. However, in that conversation, Sam shared that he and his cofounder only focused on what they each wanted in terms of financial achievements within a certain time frame and didn't get into their personal-outcome scenarios. This is common for many founders. It's much easier to center the success conversation on the growth of your product, types of customers and revenue, and it can be daunting to have vulnerable conversations and tie the success of the business to your personal goals and aspirations. It wasn't until an acquisition opportunity came up a year later that Sam and his cofounder were faced with the reality that they were not, in fact, aligned. Sam was open to the acquisition—success at a personal level for him meant proving to himself that he was able to start and build something on his own, as well as having the freedom to pursue another idea he'd been thinking about. His cofounder, on the other hand, wasn't a fan of the acquisition. He liked the independence of working on his own company, which was getting closer to profitability, and did not like the idea of becoming an employee at someone else's company. He wasn't that excited about the financial outcome and was perfectly happy living a modest lifestyle in favor of the autonomy of owning one's own venture. "We worked through the what-ifs and nonnegotiables for both of us. His was maintaining flexibility; for me it was returning cash to our investors." They ended up passing on the deal.

Even just getting clarity on why you want to start a new venture to begin with is important. Every aspiring entrepreneur or startup joiner I chat with has a different reason for why they want to get on this crazy ride. Some want the autonomy and control that comes from being their own boss (a myth if you take outside capital) or the ability to move fast to innovate (maybe, if it's tech, but that's not usually the part that will slow you down, although slowing down is what I will help you avoid in this book). Some want to prove themselves to their family and friends, and some, like Gio, want to make an impact on the world or in their community (and retire early!). However, it's hard to imagine what that path will look or feel like once a business is off and running or when it's time to pursue an exit or, for some, throw in the towel because they just can't get there for any number of reasons.

Whether a founder or a joiner, I encourage you to think about why you are jumping into startup land and what success means to you beyond just the possibility of a big financial outcome. And don't just think about it, record your thoughts in some way so you can reflect on this over time, because what success might look like today can change as you grow and mature throughout the journey. Choose a medium that works best for you to record these thoughts, such as a physical journal, an electronic document, or even a video recording of yourself answering the questions. Set a baseline before the business scales and life happens (marriage, family, relocation, etc.) and commit to revisiting the topic regularly. Consider using the design-thinking methodology of diverging and converging (diverge<>converge) with team members where you each consider your thoughts about success separately (diverge) and then come together (converge) to discuss each other's perspectives. Here are some prompts to help you get started:

- Why are you on this journey?
- Why are employees, coworkers, investors, and/or press bragging about your venture in the future?
- Postventure, what will be your proudest achievements? How did your business impact the world and/or communities you care about?

The diverge<>converge process is useful in many different scenarios and can help remove bias and influence that can happen with many voices in a room—especially if there is a very passionate team member who tends to dominate a conversation or is stubborn about their ideas. As you discuss each other's perspectives, work on building alignment in areas where you disagree, including how you might support each other in those areas. This exercise will allow you to set a solid foundation about where you hope to be in the future as you start your journey today.

Part I
PRODUCT

Investing the time to *validate the problem you are solving* and *for whom you are solving it* is vital to the long-term success of any venture. This may sound obvious, but it's a major blind spot for so many startups and a big reason why they fail. Everything from who you hire to how you operate your business will largely depend on the type of product you are building and who your buyers and users are. Hiring and operating a business is hard enough. Imagine how much harder these tasks would be if you are off the mark about what you're building and for whom. You may start on this journey with inspiration from your own experience—a pain point you have that you are almost sure others have, or perhaps a scientific invention that is looking for a problem to solve. Most startups will pivot a lot before they find a winning solution. Instagram began as Burbn, a location-based app cluttered with features that allowed friends to check in to venues and events and share plans with friends. The founders raised $500,000 in early funding, but the app never really took off until they noticed that users were not adopting Burbn's check-in features at all. However, they were posting and sharing photos all the time. With enough funding to keep going, they reduced the product to a bare minimum viable product (MVP), rebranded, and became a success. YouTube was a dating site before it was acquired by Google for $1.6 billion and became the ubiquitous video-sharing platform it is today, and even Uber, which began as a concept to offer a black car service to the average American, evolved to a consumer ride-sharing service that took the world by storm.

In all those cases, it took the companies years and many dollars—and sometimes luck, timing, and the good fortune of the privilege their founders were born into—to get where they are today. But knowing most entrepreneurs don't come from privilege, and most don't get it right on their first try, how do you set yourself up for success? I am a strong advocate for moving slowly, iterating (a trial-and-error process that involves creating, testing, and revising experiment and solution ideas until a desired outcome is achieved), and learning, versus moving quickly and breaking things. When you take the time to truly understand your target audience's pain points and who they really are, then you are more likely to end up on a path toward success. Getting this deeper understanding also helps you figure out how to build a business around the concept, because your product alone is not the venture.

In this first part of the book, I'll walk you through the important steps of discovery work and introduce you to tools that will allow you to clarify the problem you've set out to solve, your target personas, metrics of success, and how to develop a company roadmap to operationalize your venture.

With that, let's begin!

2.

WHY DISCOVERY MATTERS

These days, unless you are doing quantum physics or creating a new treatment for cancer, building a product, especially a software product, is pretty darn easy. From no-code solutions to having generative AI products at our disposal that can write code and even create marketing plans for you, it has never been easier to build software. Even consumer goods and brick-and-mortar ventures can be augmented with technology that can result in easier methods to build. So if it's so easy, why isn't everyone creating a unicorn company? Because building is not the hard part. What's hard is building the right thing, for the right people (and people and/or the companies they work for are complicated!), and then building the right operating model behind that thing. We'll break down the latter in Part III of this book, but before we get there, it's critical to understand why discovery is so important and then how to do that discovery work.

It is not uncommon for startups to jump to building their product right away. There are lots of reasons this might happen. Sometimes,

23

you are swept away by the desperate urge to bring an idea to life, especially when you feel you have personal experience or expertise that will give you an edge. Sometimes the urgency stems from the pressure to hit goals and deadlines set by investors. You may want to gain a competitive head start—worried that if you don't build it and get it out there fast, someone else will. Whatever the drive, it is so tempting to just get going. I get it. But remember, Google was not the first internet search tool, and Facebook was not the first social media app—it's all about execution (and a little bit of luck and timing)!

Chip Heath and Dan Heath, the Stanford professor and Duke Fellow, respectively, and bestselling authors of *The Power of Moments: Why Certain Experiences Have Extraordinary Impact*, say, "You can't appreciate the solution until you appreciate the problem." When you ramp up too fast and build too soon, it is likely you have not fully understood the problem and that you will fail at your first attempt at a solution, and fail fast. According to data from the US Bureau of Labor Statistics in 2023, 10 percent of startups fail within their first year, and unless you have unlimited access to cash, you will bail, and not start over, just as fast.[1] You can see this in the dotted line in the graph below. The research of my colleague Tom Eisenmann, the Howard H. Stevenson Professor of Business Administration at Harvard Business School, tells us that 35 percent of startups fail because of lack of product-market fit (PMF).[2] PMF is when customers are buying, using, and telling others about the company's product at a scale large enough to sustain that product's growth and profitability. I believe that this 35 percent failure rate can drop with proper discovery work *early on*—as shown with the solid line below. Proper discovery work, which I will break down in depth in this chapter, involves doing experiments that validate or invalidate hypotheses about problems and the people who have them. By slowing down to do this work you will not only prevent wasted precious time and money building the wrong thing, but you will likely begin to structure your business operations the right way.

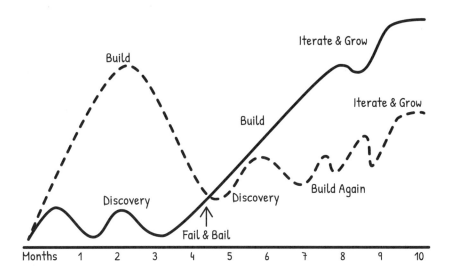

It is unlikely that a solution can reach PMF without information that comes from proper discovery work, but poor discovery work can also lead to you muddling along with modest PMF. A low- or slow-growth business may be a lifestyle choice for you, but the lack of growth may result in your inability to raise capital or have a reasonably successful exit that meets the expectations of your investors, if you have them. My former student Gabe Horwitz, chief product officer and cofounder of eqtble, an analytics tool for human resource professionals, lamented, "I wish that someone had given us the push in the early days to look for validation from customers instead of VCs [venture capitalists]. We were so desperate to chase the Tech-Crunch article that we changed our goal from closing customers in the early days to closing VCs. Customer validation equals momentum and sustainability." Gabe and his team's pursuit of venture capitalists' approval, press, and notoriety caused them to be several years behind on truly understanding their customers.

Gabe's startup has enough traction and capital in the bank to figure their challenges out, but you may not have that opportunity, and a swift build that misses the mark can cause your venture to fail. This can leave you feeling defeated or unmotivated to try again. You fail, and fail hard. You may pull up your bootstraps and go at it again—ideally with more time focused on discovery the second time around—but many founders at this point throw in the towel. They are embarrassed, out of cash, and need to support their lifestyle and/or families. I applaud each of them for even trying their hand at entrepreneurship, but the truth is that healing after a failed startup can be an emotional process. We'll talk more about that in the final part of this book when we get to "Exits and Transitions."

Finally, even if you are close to or have already reached PMF, it's possible that operational considerations were not factored into the plan, leaving you with an improperly configured organization set up to scale. Kait Stephens and her cofounder Zack Morrison, both former students of mine, would have made that mistake had it not been for their great early discovery work. Kait's inspiration for the first iteration of her venture, Found, came when she lost her engagement band at the gym. It was not only emotional for her to lose such a personal item, but it was also a diamond and was expensive to replace. Her early idea was a way for people to easily tag items of personal and/or monetary value using QR codes and provide a means for anyone who finds these tagged items to return them to their owner via a mobile app where these tagged items were tracked. Kait knew that a wedding ring was not the best form factor for QR codes at the time, but that emotional feeling of losing such a precious item was enough to light the fire and get her thinking about other items people may want to track. Zack had an engineering background and could have started to build a complete solution shortly after partnering with Kait. But these cofounders knew they had a lot to learn about both the profile of consumers who might tag items of value and about those who find lost items. They needed to understand whether their target demographic was aligned with a market segment worthy of going after. Also, they needed to learn how the "loser" and "finder" user behaviors played out in the real world to be sure that this was a realistic endeavor.

Regardless of demographics, the questions about users' behavior—will people know what to do with QR codes (this was 2018, just before the use of QR codes became ubiquitous) and how likely or motivated will they be to return the items?—were critical to defining what Found would need to build in their MVP. Kait and Zack's first set of experiments were simply tagging a bunch of random items—water bottles, headphones, backpacks—with self-made stickers with QR codes on them and strewing them around a few city parks, large building lobbies, and high-foot-traffic areas. The QR codes were linked to a very basic app Zack created using off-the-shelf software (he didn't do any significant coding) that sent texts to him and Kait as people scanned the QR codes on found items with their phones. From this experiment, they not only learned whether people understood the QR scanning process on their cell phones, but also gained dozens of other behavioral insights that informed their MVP. A key learning was that most "finders" didn't want to meet the owner of the lost item and instead wanted to leave it somewhere for retrieval like a lost and found or office building or hotel reception desk. This led to an operating model discussion on whether the cofounders wanted to partner with facilities that could install return boxes or employ a delivery service to manage the return process.

Kait and Zack also experimented with various ways to motivate returns of lost items by offering different incentives like cash rewards from the owner of the items, coupons for free coffee, donations to selected nonprofits, and even a gamified concept where one could earn badges for being a good citizen for some number of returns per month. All of these experiments not only informed the priority list of features for their future mobile app, but also allowed them to refine their business model, marketing strategy, and operating plan. They learned that their initial business idea could be an operational headache and very expensive when it came to actual returns of lost items. They also learned that printing QR code stickers was cumbersome and could be hard to monetize. Operating as a sticker sales business that might become an insurance company was going to be a complex business model, and it wasn't a very appealing concept to either founder. Not only did they learn a ton about their target audience and market segment, but a great additional outcome of their discovery work was to identify that—while entirely possible to create this type of business—this was not a business they were excited about. They were not thwarted, however. Instead, it became a stopping point for the team to step back and reassess.

What's noteworthy here is that their discovery work, before building a fully featured MVP, unlocked a whole new business idea. The stickers were a blocker so they explored whether products could be manufactured with preprinted QR codes. This led to shifting their focus from a business-to-consumer (B2C) brand to a business-to-business (B2B) brand and restarting their discovery work to learn about the pain points that consumer brands were experiencing. Remember, this was 2018 and QR codes were just starting to gain traction when Apple released their iOS 11 update that allowed consumers to scan the codes with their phones. Brand owners were frustrated that consumer data was lost in the retail process. Brands knew which retail channels worked well for them and had some demographic information about who was buying their products through credit card data. However, unless their customers opted into warranty programs, they lacked a way to stay in touch with their customers after the purchase experience for further engagement like upselling or to encourage repurchasing.

Armed with this insight from brands, Kait and Zack saw an opportunity to solve both the business and consumer pain points. Give consumers an easy way to scan QR codes on products to register warranties or to restock a favorite item, such as a beverage or beauty brand, and, by doing so, capture detailed buyer data for the brands. This led to their current business, renamed Brij ("bridge"), which allows brands to stay connected to their customers using an omnichannel approach with Brij's QR code integration technology—an entirely different type of business than what they intended to build, and one completely informed by extensive up-front discovery work.

Had Kait and Zack immediately started to build their B2C solution and marketed Found at inception, they would have structured the business in a very different way. They would have likely hired retail distribution and e-commerce specialists and invested heavily in consumer-brand marketing. Their technology would have focused on an insurance-type model and not have the marketing analytics capabilities it has today. Had they not done early discovery work, they may have never reached PMF or raised capital to fund the growth of their now thriving venture.

Whether building an app or creating the next hot beauty brand, it's critical that you know who your customers are and understand their pain points. You need to invest meaningful time to explore the following about your target customers:

- What makes them frustrated about this topic today?
- How do they solve their problem today?
- What is missing in their personal or work lives that they don't even realize will make them happier, healthier, save money, or be more productive?
- What are their behaviors today that you may improve or need to change for them to benefit from your product?

If you don't slow the freak down and explore these questions properly, you'll never get to the fun part, which is actually building and running a *company*! And this is an important additional point because part of your discovery work will also help identify whether you are building a *feature*, a *product*, or a *company*. Through experimentation efforts, it should start to become clear whether your idea is big enough that it constitutes an entire venture, which will be very important if you intend to raise capital. A founder building a widget to improve the use of the latest sales customer relationship management (CRM) tool, like Salesforce, may find this is a feature that Salesforce can build themselves and put the founder's venture out of business tomorrow. If it's a feature-rich product, the venture could be a ripe acquisition opportunity for Salesforce as a new product. However, if there is a roadmap that takes the widget from a feature to a whole new CRM solution that competes with or even disrupts Salesforce as a market leader, then there may be a company brewing. Discovery work can help a venture identify the pain points for that first MVP widget and who will buy it first (often called a "beachhead"), but it should also help you assess whether there's a big enough market opportunity to go from widget to company.

Understanding pain points is also important if your idea is to create a product that is not a medicine (essential to have), but rather a vitamin (nice to have). Examples of vitamin products are any number of social media apps like Facebook, Instagram, or TikTok, at least when they first entered the market. We could argue these apps solve other problems today (like marketing/advertising pain points for brands), but in the early days, these products were not going after a specific pain point. Or were they? We could assert that social media products solved the pain point of loneliness or feeling disconnected from friends and family. They certainly introduced a few new and controversial problems too, which is also worthy of assessing in the discovery process, albeit much harder since sometimes it's difficult to predict how humans will behave or, in the case of ChatGPT, how fast technology will evolve. However, even exploring these possibilities can help a venture avoid heading in the wrong direction. For example, a business leveraging generative AI (GenAI) today to augment video game development could learn from discovery work that the game industry itself will evolve via its use of GenAI, and as such video games with their game-creation challenges will be built in a completely different way. Thus, helping game developers today may be moot, and perhaps it's better to imagine a new set of problems the gaming industry will face once GenAI goes mainstream in that market.

Even when a venture already has a product in the market, the discovery work never stops; products and their users evolve, and so must your venture. In the remainder of Part I, I will not only provide a tool kit for proper discovery work but will also equip those who already have products in the market with techniques to ensure they're building the very best new features and new products as they scale.

DO YOU REALLY WANT TO DO THIS?

A deep discovery process not only lends tremendous insight into your future venture but will also offer personal insights. Consider what came out of Kait and Zack's early discovery work. They were able to validate that they wanted to be on the entrepreneurial path, but also learned that they did not want to create an insurance-tech business. This was just as important to discover as the insights about their products, customers, and how they might operate their business. A startup that gets to PMF will operate for an average of seven to ten years. That's a significant part of one's life and often occurs when founders and their teams are simultaneously going through personal transitions like partnering, raising families, empty nesting, or caring for elderly parents. These transitions are manageable in startup land thanks to fewer stigmas around working from home and flexible hours. But you need to be intentional about it. I was thirty-four years old with two kids under five when I joined Akamai in 1999 and would often commiserate with Danny about how we balanced our time with our kids while we ate, slept, and breathed Akamai. The great thing about early-stage ventures is you can decide what kind of culture you want to build to support work-life balance (Akamai let me work from home one day a week, which was a novel concept back then!), and as you work through the discovery process, it can be a great way to assess what that culture will need to be for you to feel good about riding this roller coaster. I'll cover this topic in more detail in Chapter 7.

Once you get past the question, *How will I do this for seven to ten years as I continue to mature and grow as an adult?*, the next fundamental question is, *Is this the particular roller coaster I want to get on?* or even, *Do I want to be on this roller coaster at all?* I once advised a founding team that was trying to solve the security deposit return problem for renters. They promised to get 100 percent of a tenant's security deposit returned at the end of a lease, and in their early experiments they were quite successful in doing so. However, like Kait and Zack, one thing became clear through their discovery work: they didn't like the market they found themselves in. They enjoyed working with the tenants themselves—often young adults with whom they could identify—but this team was spending a lot of time with landlords and lawyers. Not that there's anything wrong with this group of people, but this team felt disconnected and demotivated by their interactions with this side of the market, which was contentious and slow to adopt new technology. So, even though they were getting traction with their experiments, in the end their discovery work informed their decision to stop working on the idea because their hearts were not in it.

Finally, whether you are a founder or a joiner, you must get out there, make mistakes, and be vulnerable with total strangers. You cannot start a venture without interacting with all sorts of people you've never interacted with before. It can be exhilarating for some and terrifying for others. Discovery work can be an extremely humbling experience, but it can also be an incredible learning experience if you're open to the possibility that you are going to feel a little like one of those inflatable clown toys that gets punched and has to bounce back up . . . over and over again. It's getting a lot of "nos" and a lot of ghosting before you might get a "yes." And that's something you will have to deal with throughout the life of your startup, even at scale. The discovery process will either help you get comfortable with being vulnerable or inform your decision about whether the entrepreneurial journey is right for you.

3.

THE ART OF
DISCOVERY

Founders are very quick to qualify their discovery work with data from customer interviews. "I spoke to fifty people who said this is a problem for them." I always take these comments with a grain of salt because you must master how to interview and talk with customers to avoid bias and get to the source of truth. I recommend you read *The Mom Test*, which covers interview best practices.[1] I am also skeptical when I hear aspiring founders base their early solutions primarily on interviews, because interviews alone will not validate your hypotheses about the problem to solve and for whom. Interviews can at best validate interest versus actual intent and, at worst, lead to false positives. Customers simply saying they have the problem you imagine they have or that they would use your solution if you created it is not a guarantee that if you build it, they will actually adopt it. Similarly, putting up a website with a landing page to see who clicks to learn more about your imaginary solution or running an A/B test to see what concept is more appealing may help you get emails and gather data about prospective buyers, but these experiments also primarily gauge interest, not intent. Desk research can also offer insights into the market and people you are going after, but you'll have a far better shot at getting to PMF by performing deep discovery work in addition to these tactics.

Yinka Ogunbiyi is the founder of Halo Braid. As a British Nigerian woman, she has experienced firsthand the time and effort it takes to braid coarse hair. She learned through her desk research that consumers like her collectively invest over eight billion hours per year in this process! Her inspiration for Halo Braid came during the pandemic lockdown. Without access to a braiding salon, she attempted to braid her own hair. "Not only did it take me four days to braid my own hair, but my hands were stiff and painful by the time I was finished. If that was *my* experience, what was it like for stylists who do this full time?" She began to research the experience for stylists and learned that they suffered from chronic pain and had to minimize their practice (thus lower their income) to mitigate long-term damage to their hands. There must be a better way! As a second-time founder with an engineering degree, she set her mind on creating a braiding device that not only minimized the time impact for consumers getting their hair braided but also reduced the physical impact this work had on stylists.

Yinka felt it was important for her to develop a patentable hardware solution, but she also knew that her personal experience trying to braid her own hair did not necessarily answer many questions she had about the stylists who may use this product and how they might integrate a device like this into their practice. "When I first laid out my plan to do deeper discovery work, I wanted to understand everything from how their clients sit in the stylist's chair to determine the design of the device itself, to whether the stylists had adequate power supplies and storage spaces for the devices in their salons. I knew I would not understand these nuances just by interviewing stylists." The stylist was the primary "persona" for her MVP (I'll explain personas more on page 36). In addition to the dozens of stylists she interviewed to understand their pain points—both physical and as business owners and operators—Yinka leveraged ethnographic research techniques involving hours of observation of stylists braiding various clients' hair. Her secondary persona was the clients themselves, and she ran experiments to understand how they selected stylists as well as took note of their emotional responses while undergoing the braiding process, which was often a multisession activity. This research before building the first prototype of her future hair-braiding device gave her a better sense of how she would build a solution that satisfied both stylists and their clients' needs.

Once she had a working prototype created with a 3D printer, Yinka delved deeper into the discovery process to understand what stylists would do when presented with a proposed solution to their problem. Just presenting them with the prototype of the device and asking them to use it without instructions helped her understand how the device would be used in practice. "One thing that came up during these tests was that although hair braiding is physically demanding, it is mentally relaxing for stylists. So, we made the device as intuitive and 'mindless' as possible by minimizing steps in the braid setup process." Through her prototype experiments, Yinka was able to get further clarity on the problem, the target persona, and, like Kait and Zack, what her business model and operating plan might entail.

HYPOTHESIS EXPERIMENTS

The best approach for going beyond interviews and market research in discovery work is to run experiments designed to prove or disprove a hypothesis. Hypothesis experiments should be done (A) to validate the personas themselves (*Is this who I am building a solution for?*), (B) to understand personas' current problems and the market segment, and (C) to test prospective solutions. Early experimentation should lean more toward the current state (getting the facts right), and as personas, problems, and markets become clearer, your hypothesis experiments will evolve toward solution iteration. But remember, like almost everything in startup land, this is a nonlinear and highly iterative process and you may take two steps forward toward a solution and then have to take one step back before you start to get a good handle on the right problem to solve and for whom.

Kait, Zack, and Yinka all took the time to plan and conduct their early experiments to validate their personas, problems, and markets by first brainstorming their hypotheses about each using the four-step process below. This is another opportunity to diverge<>converge with your team. If operating solo, I recommend you bring a colleague or two into the process to help you look for gaps and biases—sometimes, when we're too close to or in love with our idea, we can miss obvious things!

Step 1: Brainstorm "I/we believe" statements about the following:

The persona(s): These are archetypal people who will most benefit from your product. They have pain points, goals, and motivations and are different than ideal customer profiles (ICPs), which focus on the characteristics of the ideal company or business you want to sell to. The personas are the individuals who will interact with and/or buy your solution. Clearly defined target personas will focus your ongoing discovery work and will align design teams, marketing, sales, and support, among others, as your venture starts to take root.

Three to five target personas are common for a typical product, and no more than two should be primary. Too many primaries can create an overly complex product—trying to be good for all may result in a solution good for none. Primary personas can represent each side of a marketplace or they could be buyers versus users of your product. More personas may arise once a product gains traction. It's good to identify antipersonas too—who does *not* have this problem or would never buy this product? Defining antipersonas will keep you focused when it comes to designing experiments and prioritizing what to build. It is through discovery work that personas are more clearly defined so that a solution can be developed for a broader market.

The problem: What pain points do you believe are out there that need solving? Are they different per persona or in certain markets or geographies? You may have different belief statements about problems for different scenarios, such as what a certain persona's pain points are for a ride-sharing service on a sunny day with no traffic versus on a rainy day during rush hour. And this same scenario could be very different for the rider (who wants a fast pickup) than for the driver persona (who wants to take advantage of surge pricing).

The market: What industry, geography, or other market segment are you going after? For both Yinka and the team trying to solve for getting security deposits back, it was urban cities in the United States. For Kait and Zack, it was the marketing departments of large brands worldwide.

Write as many detailed and specific belief statements as possible. Saying "We believe people who find lost items want to return them to their owners" is not specific enough to design an experiment. "People" and "items" need to be broken down into different types of tests to understand what types of people take the time to return a lost item. And then there's figuring out what types of items these people are motivated to return. Kait and Zack's lost-item tests included all sorts of low-cost and more expensive items and helped them learn that university students were more inclined to return someone's headphones than a lost stainless steel water bottle. A different test with different items in the same location or the same items in a new location may have resulted in different outcomes.

Yinka had a variety of belief statements for the stylists. For example, "I believe stylists working full time in salons will have storage space for a device at their stations." If she was going to sell her devices to salons, she wanted to run experiments to be sure that space constraints would not prevent adoption, because what good is a new device for hair braiding if her target personas have no place to store it? Sometimes it can be the little things that can prevent adoption, and one wrong assumption can throw off a whole business plan.

Step 2: Group similar hypotheses together and identify any new hypotheses that come up through this activity. If this was done as a diverge<>converge exercise, come together with your teammates and review each other's lists.

Step 3: Prioritize the hypotheses you decide are most important to focus on first. This can be challenging when there are so many things to discover and can lead to "peanut buttering"—spreading around too much stuff and causing a mess—if you are not careful! I discuss that concept more in Chapter 16. This prioritization will often be based on your access to certain audiences. Kait and Zack's first hypotheses were focused on college students on campuses because they themselves were graduate students on a college campus and students lose stuff, a lot! However, most hypotheses to be proven will require you to get out of your comfort zone and do a lot of cold calling before you can start. This is another reason founders tend to skip deep discovery work, because it can take a lot of time and effort to make these connections! Yinka prioritized her hypotheses around stylists at established salons—before focusing on "chair renters" who typically bring their own supplies—because it was important to understand more about what salon policies were if they were to be her primary buyer. This meant building relationships with many stylists and salons before she could run her experiments. There is no wrong answer on which hypotheses to start with, and sometimes you just have to go with your gut.

Step 4: Design experiments to prove/disprove each hypothesis that include:

The belief statement for each experiment

For whom and/or what (persona, problem, and/or market)

Experiment plan—*this should be as detailed as possible*: From when and where, to who will conduct the experiment and the materials needed (pen, paper, computer, table, test materials/ingredients, etc.). Make sure you have a script if several team members will be running these experiments. This ensures consistency when running the same experiment and you won't question if the results were skewed because one team member said or did something differently than the other. You may also include a postexperiment survey (see "Surveys" below) to capture impressions or data from your subjects.

Measures to assess the experiment outcomes: In early experiments, this will be more of a SWAG (a scientific wild-ass guess), when you just take a stab at a measurement based on assumptions drawn from your own experience or research data. An experiment based on a SWAG measurement will tell you if you're onto something or not. And *not* being onto something can be a great outcome because you just saved yourself a lot of wasted time and possibly money building the wrong thing. The Found team's early SWAG was frequency of lost items based on their own experiences losing items. They also relied on insurance data about the average retail value of items in filed claims as a SWAG to assess the value of items their target personas cared about having returned. You will shift away from SWAGs to a more concrete way to measure the results of your experiments as you run more and more tests.

39

SURVEYS

Unless you are a trained researcher with deep experience in the art and science of surveying, be careful about depending on surveys as a primary form of discovery work. Surveys should never be used to ask people to predict what they might do with your solution.

The best way to use surveys for discovery is to gather historical data about your hypotheses around the problem or after an experiment. Such as "When was the last time you planned a trip out of the country?" or "What is the average amount of money you spend a week on coffee?" Good survey answers should be binary (yes/no) or use scales or ranges such as, "Did you book the trip abroad that we recommended?" or "On a scale of 1 to 10, rate the accuracy of our data report." Data-centered responses like binary, scales, and range answers are easier to quantify, but they can also be very subjective such as if you were to ask someone to rate the spiciness of a salsa product as mild, medium, or hot—one person's hot could be another's mild.

Discovery survey best practices:

- Ten or fewer questions. Longer surveys can lead to higher drop-out rates.
- It should take no more than five to ten minutes to complete.
- Only ask must-needed demographic questions such as age, income, years on the job, etc. Get what you need to ensure you are comparing apples to apples, but don't use their interest in completing the survey to find out everything about each individual who answers. You can always get that later (next bullet).
- Always end with a final question that asks whether they are willing to (A) follow up if there are more questions and (B) recommend someone in their network for you to follow up with to garner more survey/test subjects (be sure to ask for name and contact information).

Like interviews, surveys are just one more set of data to contribute to the discovery process and you don't need hundreds of responses to a discovery process survey to get to your insights.

EXPERIMENTATION BEST PRACTICES

Before we get into examples of ways to conduct experiments in the discovery process, let's get clear about a few best practices.

- **Manage variables:** Each experiment should have as few variables as possible. There is empirical evidence that when we create discrete experiments with few variables, we only need to do five such experiments before the data starts to level out. It can feel incredibly tedious to break down every hypothesis, create tests to prove/disprove them, and then execute each experiment. However, each experiment will likely unearth critical insights that lead to higher success rates of early solutions.[2]

- **Avoid bias:** Experimenting with friends, family members, former coworkers, or even members of affinity groups can result in biased outcomes. You can never be sure that these close connections will openly share their fears, doubts, or emotional responses the way a stranger would. If you are building something you plan to sell to the masses, then strangers are your best subjects. So, roll up your sleeves and figure out where these people are and find ways to connect with them. This search can be an experiment itself both to locate personas (e.g., on social media groups or through certain venues or professional connections) and to get them to talk with you and be willing to participate in your experiments. My student Abdou Ndao sent many emails and posted and placed ads on different platforms before he found his target personas—DIY car repair enthusiasts on Reddit—to run experiments for his AI "car clinic" bot. Janvi Shah, Sylvan Guo, and Nicole Clay, founders of Hue, ran Facebook ads to gather their first test subjects—women of color struggling with finding makeup foundations that matched their skin tones. They offered gift cards to a beauty retailer in exchange for participation. Gift cards or other incentives like a free financial analysis to test your new budgeting app can be helpful to recruit participants, but hold off on these strategies unless you are really struggling to get your test subjects. That struggle itself could be telling—maybe these personas don't exist, or maybe their pain isn't as bad as you hypothesized!

Note: Some experiments may not be impacted by bias. For Yinka to experiment on friends' hair with her braiding device to assess its braiding capabilities would be fine, but to ask them whether they liked the resulting braids may have resulted in biased answers.

- **Beware of novelty experiments:** Running an experiment only once or over a short period of time risks a false positive or negative. Early experiments may show behaviors that suggest users' love for a solution or affect the way they do things, but if you ask them to keep doing it, will you get statistically significant results? A student team believed that families with children aged ten to thirteen struggled with planning weeknight meals. Their hypotheses were (1) these families wanted to eat meals together more often and (2) cooking together made families feel more inclined to sit down to dine together. After getting basic information from three different families about the contents of their pantries and the best day of the week to cook together, their first experiment was to text each of the family members a few meal-preparation options for their chosen cooking night. Each family member voted on their ideal meal plan for that night. Then, the team would text each family a shopping list and wait until the end of the week for the family to report back on their experience. Based on their feedback, the team would again send meal options and a shopping list. The first week, the families joyfully went grocery shopping and cooked together and reported how game-changing it was to have this push to cook and eat together. The second week, one family ghosted the team, and another said they were too busy to participate that week due to after-school activities and work demands. The remaining family followed the plan again, but now, a little more comfortable with the concept, they sent back a lot of harsh feedback about dietary requirements and the cost of the ingredients. Just by running the experiment for more than a week, the team was able to identify which type of persona may be more inclined to adopt a solution, e.g., not a family with busy schedules and work demands. But also, a few weeks of iterative work allowed the novelty of the experiment to wear off, and they got to the meat of what these families needed (pun intended), which turned out to be much more about managing budgets and shopping for dietary needs than it was about family time. This became a critical decision point for the team—do they continue to find other ways for families to engage and connect (like planning movie or game nights?), do they push harder to discover other ways to understand meal preparation? Or do they pivot and focus more on family budgets and/or dietary planning? I'll cover more about longitudinal experiments and measuring results in the next chapter. The point here, though, is to not rely on a short-term experiment to validate results. It usually takes many experiments, with minimal variables, over time before you will achieve deep insights.

EXPERIMENTATION TECHNIQUES

It is very easy to use low- or no-code solutions, high-fidelity proto-types, or 3D printers to whip up a solution experiment, but I beg you to resist going straight to investing in building a fully baked solution unless you are clear about the problem you wish to solve and the target personas. Yinka was very clear about the problem and who her persona would be, so the next logical step was to create a 3D-printed prototype of the device to start solution experiments. However, the team experimenting around family time was not clear on the problems around the family meal journey at all, so creating a software product too early to help families plan meals together would have been a waste of time and money. There are many ways to run handcrafted experiments that tell us what we need to know about the problems, personas, and proposed solutions without building too much, if anything. In fact, these scrappy experiments allow you to be quite close to the problem and the persona, giving you a deep, often personal, understanding of what's really going on. This increases the probability of building a much better solution for the right people and problems! Now let's break down the most common types of approaches you can use to run experiments beyond interviews and surveys.

Ethnographic Research

Ethnographic research is one of the most underutilized and often most valuable forms of experimentation. This is simply observing your target customer in the environment where you believe they are experiencing pain. Yinka's ethnographic research involved hours in salons to observe stylists braiding hair. You will likely see things through ethnography (also known as "observation tests") that no interview or survey will ever tell you. You will see emotional responses to challenges such as a frown on a subject's face when they get to a hard part of a process or a smile when they get the right result on a report. You may also see subtleties or work-arounds that your subjects don't even realize they have. I was once observing an engineering leader provision some virtual machines for one of her teams using a competitor's cloud product. She had everything configured, but before finishing the process, she opened a different tab in her browser and started looking up data in her company's financial system. When I asked what she was doing, she replied, "Before I hit save, I want to be sure this setup won't push our department over our budget for the month. The last thing I need is for my engineers to be midway through a project and then hit a wall because we are over budget." Had I just interviewed this subject, I may not have learned how sensitive budgeting was for her or that she had to go to a separate system to look up budget information. This was an important insight in terms of how we would price our product and also gave me an idea for a feature where users could monitor their expenses against their budgets in real time in our product.

Be the Bot

Before creating a product, try to insert yourself into a situation as closely as you can to truly get into the shoes of your audience. I call this "being the bot" (before building and then selling the bot) and there are generally two ways to do this: concierge and Wizard of Oz experiments.

Concierge experiments: Also known as "white glove" experiments, this is when the people you are interacting with are fully aware you are experimenting to learn about something. The students experimenting with the meal-prep idea mentioned earlier were fully transparent with the participants about what they were trying to learn and that they were going to do everything low-tech with their test subjects before creating any new software. Another student of mine, Ruben Ortega, was inspired by his and his husband's frustration with their inability to afford nice four- and five-star hotels when they each traveled solo. His hypothesis was that discerning solo travelers would be willing to share a high-end hotel room with a stranger instead of home sharing or couch surfing. With full transparency, he arranged for various travelers to share hotel rooms to learn everything from what it would take for them to agree to stay in a room together (cost, mutual friends, legal documents to mitigate risk, etc.) to how the hotels felt about this type of arrangement. Through these concierge tests, he learned a ton about all these things with only a few nights' stays with several willing participants.

Wizard of Oz (WoZ) experiments:[3] These experiments are as they imply—the target audience is unaware that there's no real system behind the "curtain." For example, my students Chris Abkarians and Nikhil Agarwal wanted to make student loan refinancing easier. Their early MVP was a simple WoZ-style experiment consisting of a website that asked a student loan holder to answer a bunch of questions about their current loan, financial profile, and refinancing objectives. The website appeared to "automagically" offer refinancing options within twenty-four hours, but in actuality, it was Chris and Nikhil behind the scenes researching options for each prospective customer. Not scalable by any means, but this WoZ test allowed them to learn what they needed about their customers and the refinancing process to create the right long-term solution, now Juno, which offers group bargaining power to over two hundred thousand members that have secured close to a billion dollars in loans.

Low-Fidelity Experiments

Low-fidelity (or "lo-fi") experiments can range from paper or digital prototypes for software ideas to handcrafting items as Yinka did before going into mass production. They tend to lean toward solutioning, but they should be designed to validate hypotheses before finalizing product plans. Chloe Bergson and Alison Evans are the cofounders of SAYSO, a craft cocktail company. Their early experiments were based on two problems they believed they could solve. First, that most consumers who enjoyed cocktails rarely had all the ingredients handy at home to prepare these beverages. For example, most consumers don't have all the necessary spices and limes in their pantry to whip up a spicy margarita on the fly. Second, that premade cocktail mixers were full of sugar and unhealthy ingredients, which excluded a market segment of those looking for better-for-you options. They wanted to bring health-conscious consumers a shelf-stable solution in the form of a tea sachet where one just adds water and alcohol (or not) to make a delicious cocktail in minutes. Chloe and Alison's lo-fi experiments involved steeping different healthy ingredients in their refrigerator to make a formula they, subjectively, felt met their taste criteria. They then handcrafted product samples at their dining room table, which taught them a lot about how different sachet materials, powdered and dried ingredients, would work. From there, they asked bars and restaurants to host events using their samples so they could observe the usability of the sachets. Through these lo-fi experiments, they learned what the right ingredients and portion sizes were for their product and how best to manufacture and market the product based on consumer behaviors. They went on to create multiple flavors of sachets and now sell their products through several different retail chains in hundreds of stores across the United States.

For those focused on software products, digital prototypes can offer valuable insights, but you need to be careful not to confuse a user experience (UX) test with a hypothesis validation experiment. A UX test is usually done once you are further along in the discovery process, and you are fine-tuning the navigation of a software product. Digital prototypes for hypothesis experiments, however, aim to unearth pain points or requirements. For example, if you were building a new platform to help consumers rent apartments, you may have a digital mock-up of the apartment search flow. If your prospective user is hovering their finger over a "search properties" button, but resisting a click, you can ask "What's causing you to pause?" They may say, "I was looking for a filter option." While also good information about the UX (filtering is important), this could also open a new line of inquiry about the personas you may serve. Further probing about why a filtering option would be helpful may lead to learning that monthly rent information is more important than amenities like on-site laundry or parking. What makes one user who cares about budgets different from one who cares more about certain amenities? Are there other considerations that renters care about? And so on.

I mention paper prototypes above—which are literally sketching out screens on paper to get quick feedback on key elements—because not everyone is tech savvy, and even if you are, sometimes a quick sketch is all you need to assess key elements in the customer journey. Another version of this type of experiment is a common product design method called "card sorting" and can be incredibly useful when you are trying to understand customer processes, pain points, and priorities. This can be done with index cards or using a software tool that allows someone to sort their order of priorities or even process flows. To demonstrate how this works, imagine you were thinking about ways to improve how someone books activities when they travel. To understand how a target persona approaches activity planning, you'd do the following:

- **Create a stack of index cards with various steps** that you imagine are part of a typical travel-planning process, such as "book flight," "book hotel," "internet search for activities," "ask friends for recommendations," "book activities," and "check into hotel."
- **Ask them to order the cards** according to how they typically plan a trip. It's important to not disclose what you are trying to understand about a process, so your subject is authentic instead of trying to tell you what they think you want to hear. You can tell them they can leave any tasks out that they don't do (maybe they are spontaneous and don't plan activities at all) and even give them blank cards to handwrite in options if you are missing a step in their process like "call hotel for suggestions."

Based on how they organize the cards, you will learn how they think about their planning process. If they put the "book activities" card after the "check into hotel" card, it signals that they plan activities once they arrive at their destination. So, creating a product that requires long lead times and coordination for activities may not be a great solution for this type of persona. If you continue to do this process with several more participants—remember, minimize variables and try to do this with similar personas to get clear results—you should start to see patterns, such as "the busy business traveler who tries to get an activity in when they are on the road tends to book it once they are at their destination," but "the couple planning their vacation tends to book activities after they book their hotel and ask their friends for recommendations weeks before they depart." These insights can help you determine both *who* you are building a product for and *how* they might use it.

You can also use cards or a software tool to do a "MaxDiff analysis" to identify the relative importance of different items.[4] In a MaxDiff analysis, participants are presented with a series of topics and asked to select which items they consider most and least important. The process is often repeated multiple times with different sets of items until you can identify the patterns that tell you the most or least important pain points. Using the activity-planning example, if most participants list "book hotel" most important and "book activities" least important, it can be an indication that booking activities is a lower priority than securing a hotel—this could lead you on a path to create a better hotel-booking system rather than an activity-booking system *or* look for a different target persona who cares more about activity planning when they travel. The MaxDiff analysis can also be a helpful tool for understanding buying preferences, such as features, price, quality, and other criteria. The card-sorting exercise and MaxDiff analysis tools are so basic and can be so useful, inexpensive, and easy to do!

Bootstrapping Technical Solutions

For the same reasons lo-fi experimentation can save time and money and prevent you from building the wrong thing, you can take advantage of tools already available in the market to do your discovery work and to start building your solution. My former student Angela Gu wanted to create a way for newly retired professionals to find part-time work and build community. To validate her hypotheses about these retirees and the problems she believed they faced, she bootstrapped a community-engagement experiment using the website Meetup. She ran a series of events—each growing in number of participants and referrals—until she not only had a better sense of what retirees wanted but also how they were likely to engage with a platform and each other. She eventually migrated these early adopters from Meetup to the technology solution she has developed for her business, Hively, a successful and trusted guide for seniors navigating their third chapter.

Another former student, Amelia Lin, did a similar experiment for her hypothesis that families wanted to share stories with each other, such as their parents' first date or grandparents' immigration journey. Amelia is an experienced programmer and could have created a solution on her own from the start. Instead, she leveraged existing products like Skype, SoundCloud, email, and Dropbox to patch together a solution that allowed her to validate her hypotheses about how families shared stories. Families were encouraged to record stories and upload them to Dropbox and then send the links of these stories to other family members to watch. Through these bootstrapped experiments she learned that while video made it a very engaging listening experience, vanity and insecurities became a barrier for family members telling their stories. She also learned that family members wanted to be able to comment on these stories and see others' comments securely on the platform. There was an emotional connection to these stories that Amelia hadn't anticipated. These experiments gave her the insight she needed to create an MVP to record, comment on, and share audio stories within one secure platform. Many insights and iterations later, this platform evolved to the first version of Honeycomb, a secure photo- and story-sharing platform for family and friends. In 2024, Honeycomb was acquired by Ello, a leading provider of AI education technology for children.

So, before you build anything, ask yourself what you can do to simulate what you hope to build by taking advantage of what's already out there. Further, it's never a bad thing to ask people to use an incumbent solution for you to see how people approach it, what they like and dislike, as I did with the ethnography experiment with the engineering leader provisioning virtual machines. Learning from current customers, even with consumer goods, can be incredibly insightful—especially if you yourself are a product user because you will get a more unbiased sense of how others feel about that solution today, and not just draw conclusions from your own personal experience.

WILLINGNESS TO PAY AND EARLY BUSINESS MODEL RESEARCH

There is a tendency for founders to assess customers' willingness to pay (WTP) and develop business models far too early in the life of a startup. A rough sketch of a business model can give you a sense of whether it's worth going forward on an idea. You can do research to assess the total addressable market (TAM) to ensure the market is worth pursuing and make assumptions about unit economics, but in the venture's earliest stages, you don't know what the business will ultimately be, and relying too much on early research can be a lot of wasted effort. Further, just like asking people if they like your idea or would use your product can lead to false positives based on interest rather than intent, asking people if or what they would pay for a way to solve their problem—especially early, when you don't even know what you are selling yet—is not the same as someone actually buying your product. WTP experiments should only be conducted once you have done the other experiments noted in this chapter and have developed a stronger conviction around personas and their problems. When you start iterating on solutions with customers you can then start experimenting with pricing (something I'll discuss in more detail in Chapter 13). That said, if you are running a lo-fi or concierge experiment for free with a customer prospect and suggest you will take the solution away unless they pay for it, it's a start to validating WTP. Even better is when your customers offer to pay before you ask for money. Airtable is a great example of this—they offered their early MVP to users for free so they could see who used it and for what use cases.[5] So many businesses started to rely on the product for their productivity that they asked Airtable's founders if they could start paying for it to ensure it didn't disappear. This kind of organic demand from users is also seen as a strong signal of PMF. It indicated that Airtable was addressing a real pain point.

VULNERABLE ASSUMPTIONS

Hypothesis experimentation will lead to the set of assumptions on which you will build your venture. You can't plan for every outcome, and focusing too much on a plan B if things don't go well can become a self-fulfilling prophecy, as my friend Matt Higgins, serial entrepreneur and investor, suggests in his book *Burn the Boats*. However, it is important to revisit these assumptions periodically to assess which may be most vulnerable; or, put another way, if the assumption proved wrong, it would create significant risk for the venture.

Gio and her cofounder had a vulnerable assumption that they would be able to hire an exclusive, full-time obstetrics team in each Plenna location in Mexico City. As they recruited their team for the first clinic, they learned that the doctors and nurses they wanted to hire preferred to work part-time without strings attached to pursue their independent practices. Gio and her cofounder had to adjust their business model to accommodate these requirements, including changing how they had budgeted for compensation of the team and how they thought about scheduling—changing from a fixed forty-hours-per-week schedule to a more flexible work schedule for each employee. While it was a change of plans and impacted their day-to-day operations by adding a scheduling component they hadn't anticipated, this new approach made their business more competitive in the talent market.

The Plenna team was able to make it work, but not every venture works out that well. Pets.com, which was a hot new startup in the early days of e-commerce, made a lot of bad assumptions about marketing-spend and business models, but one of their most vulnerable assumptions was that they could manage shipping and logistics efficiently and affordably. Whether it was lack of proper discovery work or just severely underestimating the cost of shipping bulky, heavy, low-margin items like pet food, this, coupled with several other operating missteps, led to the eventual demise of the venture.

Identifying and mitigating risks around vulnerable assumptions can be done by taking these three steps:

1. Identify no more than three assumptions that may make your venture vulnerable.
2. If you can't run an experiment (because of time, money, or other logistical challenges) to mitigate these vulnerabilities, sketch out a rough plan B for each if in fact the assumption turns out to be false or challenging to resolve quickly/at low cost.
3. Finally, have a metric in mind (we'll talk more about metrics in Chapter 5) and a timeline for what may cause you to go for plan B.

It is much better to take a few hours to think about this than have a moment of crisis and not have a plan to address it while you still have time/money. Startup advisors can be helpful here too—especially if they are domain experts and can help you explore assumptions in areas in which you may be less knowledgeable.

Whatever approach you decide to use to validate your hypotheses, focus on discovering the truth (or fiction) about what's really going on for your target personas and the problems you theorize they have. That being said, you don't want to get stuck in experimentation mode forever. "Perfect is the enemy of good" is an expression attributed to Voltaire that suggests aiming for perfection can be a barrier to progress. Determining that things are "good enough" can be both metric-driven and based on instincts. That said, it is the "founder's curse" to feel your product is never good enough, even at scale when customers love your product! Whether you are just getting started in discovery mode or you are iterating on a product already in-market, it is important to time-box experiments, especially if you are debating whether to pivot toward a new solution or problem to solve. Pick a time frame and decide what results must occur within it that will determine whether to keep marching or stop what you are doing and move on to the next thing. There is no exact science on how to do this, and it can take many experiments before you know what "good" looks like or find that you are chasing a red herring.

Finally, as my late father used to say, "People are funny." Human behavior is ultimately what you are trying to understand in almost every discovery scenario, and people do not always behave in expected ways. Experimentation is the only way to see what they actually do (not what they tell you they do or might do) in the problem state and what they will do as you iterate on solutions with them. Further, getting humans to change their behavior is hard. As compelling as a problem may be to solve, until you understand what humans are actually thinking, feeling, and *doing,* your efforts could be for naught.

4.

THE CUSTOMER JOURNEY

Y ou've been out there running your experiments and getting to know personas, problems, and markets, but how do you distill all that information so you can start to build a solution? I am a big believer in visualizing insights because they can help identify trends and patterns that might be difficult to see in raw data. Some of the best tools to do this are journey mapping and storyboarding. These tools not only allow you to flesh out the process your target audience goes through today, but also help you envision what the world might look like with your solution in play. They help you determine the customer's job to be done.[1] This is especially important when you are trying to determine if you are building a feature, a product, or a whole company. By breaking down problems step-by-step using these tools, you can begin to create your own story of what's possible (or not). Journey maps and storyboards developed over time can become the foundation of the company roadmap that we'll discuss more in Chapter 5. However, if you are finding it hard to break things down and imagine lots of possibilities, then you may not have something worth spending time on.

Like almost everything in startup land, journey mapping and storyboarding are iterative processes. You may start your first pass at these as part of the hypothesis-generation process, before you start your experiments, and then refine them as you learn along the way. Let's walk through a step-by-step guide on how to use these helpful tools.

JOURNEY MAPPING

The journey map is a step-by-step visual representation of an individual's experience. An "as-is" journey map plots out how a prospective customer handles a specific scenario today. A "to-be" journey map plots out what the scenario might be like if you were to improve their journey with your solution. Both types of journey maps should have the following key components for each step of the process:

- Touchpoints (a phone call, a google search, a car ride . . .)
- Emotional responses—neutral, happy, frustrated, super annoyed . . .
- Opportunities where you could minimize the frustration or eliminate particularly challenging steps

The trickiest part of starting any journey-mapping process is deciding the beginning and end of a journey. For example, if you are trying to solve a problem in the travel space, the journey could start when a traveler decides to go on a trip and end when they book their flights and hotel—to focus on planning and itineraries—or it could start with their departure date through their return—to focus on sharing trip details with friends. A travel-related journey map could also be for an avid traveler who wants to catalog all their trips over their lifetime. It's common to have many journey maps for different problems to solve within a complex scenario, for different target personas, different use cases, and so on.

To demonstrate how to create an as-is journey map similar to the simplified example below, let's say you're hoping to build an app to ease the pain that twentysomethings face when they are searching for an apartment. First, you would write the belief statement for a particular persona—Renter Reagan in this example—who you think struggles with the time and complexity of finding and applying for an apartment. Next, you plot Renter Reagan's process from the moment they decide to look for a new apartment until they apply for a desired unit. There could be other journeys like finding roommates or movers, but this journey is just one focus area. Each step is informed either from your own experiences, through discovery work you've already completed, or can be theoretical and will need to be validated through your discovery work. Further, each of these steps may require maps themselves, and there could be different types of journeys depending on renter demographics, budgets, and cities they want to live in, but let's keep it simple here. Once the steps are laid out, you would then identify the touchpoints for each, such as using spreadsheets, web searches, different methods to communicate with landlords and their brokers, etc. From there, you note Renter Reagan's emotions at each step (smiley, sad, and mad faces are best!). Visual representations of emotions are critical here because these are the pain points that drive experiments and identify opportunities, which is the last part of the process: write where there may be an opportunity under each step.

The process of creating a journey map can be as powerful as identifying the opportunity itself! By walking through each step, you may realize you missed an important aspect of the persona's journey and/or identify a new hypothesis to validate. It can also help you prioritize experiments or even what solution to build first. In this example, there are lots of opportunities to address pain points for Renter Reagan. However, just because there are lots of possibilities doesn't mean you should or *can* fix all of them. That's another benefit of

PROBLEM STATEMENT: We believe that finding and applying for a new rental apartment is time-consuming and cumbersome

PRIMARY PERSONA: Renter Reagan

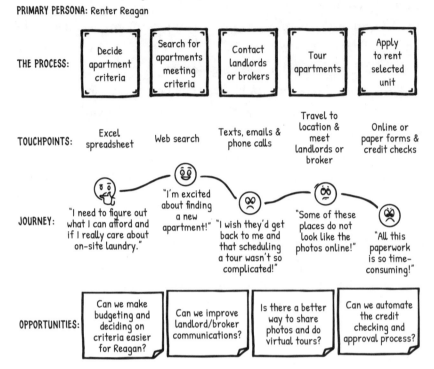

THE PROCESS:
- Decide apartment criteria
- Search for apartments meeting criteria
- Contact landlords or brokers
- Tour apartments
- Apply to rent selected unit

TOUCHPOINTS:
- Excel spreadsheet
- Web search
- Texts, emails & phone calls
- Travel to location & meet landlords or broker
- Online or paper forms & credit checks

JOURNEY:
- "I need to figure out what I can afford and if I really care about on-site laundry."
- "I'm excited about finding a new apartment!"
- "I wish they'd get back to me and that scheduling a tour wasn't so complicated!"
- "Some of these places do not look like the photos online!"
- "All this paperwork is so time-consuming!"

OPPORTUNITIES:
- Can we make budgeting and deciding on criteria easier for Reagan?
- Can we improve landlord/broker communications?
- Is there a better way to share photos and do virtual tours?
- Can we automate the credit checking and approval process?

journey mapping—it will help you visualize not only what needs to be improved but also whether you want to improve things or if it's even possible to do so. In this example, trying to fix everything at once can result in an overly complex MVP that's hard to build and use (sometimes referred to as "boiling the ocean"). Further, by seeing it all laid out like this, you may decide changing how landlords/brokers communicate could be challenging or that automating credit checks is a whole other business you don't want to get into.

As you start to develop solution ideas based on your experiments, you can once again draft a journey map to visualize how your solution may change all or part of the customer journey. This second journey map (below) visualizes what it might look like if we start to address the first set of problems, figuring out Renter Reagan's budgets, finding appropriate units, and scheduling tours. This is the beginning of a feature list for a solution. However, I would encourage more low-fidelity experiments before heading straight to app building in this case. Consider concierge or WoZ tests to help renters figure out their budgets and apartment criteria, do their searches for them, and serve as the go-between with the landlords/brokers. This is a way to "be the bot," as noted in Chapter 3, to be sure you really understand what's painful in the process. For example, if you offer to help renters with their budgets by asking them to share income information and they refuse to do so because of privacy concerns, how will you mitigate that with a software solution? Or, what mitigation will you put in place if you try to get brokers to use an online scheduling form but they refuse because they prefer texts and phone calls to schedule tours? These insights can lead to new journey maps, and you can keep

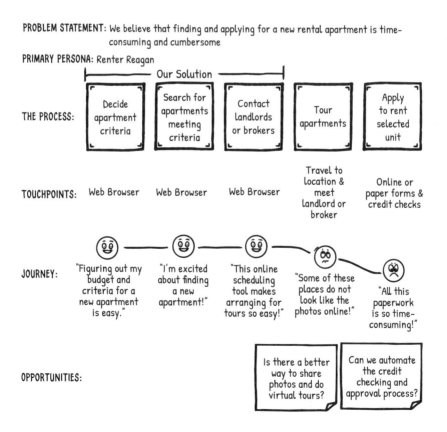

PROBLEM STATEMENT: We believe that finding and applying for a new rental apartment is time-consuming and cumbersome

PRIMARY PERSONA: Renter Reagan

THE PROCESS:
Our Solution
- Decide apartment criteria
- Search for apartments meeting criteria
- Contact landlords or brokers
- Tour apartments
- Apply to rent selected unit

TOUCHPOINTS: Web Browser | Web Browser | Web Browser | Travel to location & meet landlord or broker | Online or paper forms & credit checks

JOURNEY:
"Figuring out my budget and criteria for a new apartment is easy."
"I'm excited about finding a new apartment!"
"This online scheduling tool makes arranging for tours so easy!"
"Some of these places do not look like the photos online!"
"All this paperwork is so time-consuming!"

OPPORTUNITIES:
Is there a better way to share photos and do virtual tours?
Can we automate the credit checking and approval process?

iterating until you feel you have resolved enough concerns that you are ready to build.

Journey maps are useful for every startup—regardless of the type of product or industry you are in. It's guaranteed that each experiment and each iteration of a solution will likely shift the persona's journey or lend insight into new problems or market conditions. Having clarity by using this tool along the way will not only support the evolution of your venture but will also serve as an alignment tool for team members who will appreciate understanding the customer journey for their own work. And you don't just use a tool like this early on when you're deep in discovery mode. As you scale, all business functions, such as marketing, sales, and support, also benefit from creating journey maps to visualize where their touchpoints are for anything from ad campaigns to support calls. Even in mature businesses, journey maps are invaluable when you are trying to prioritize features and ensure you are creating the best product you can offer.

STORYBOARDS

Storyboards are a level deeper than journey maps. They further visualize what's really happening with your customers as you imagine their lives today versus what their experiences could be. The quick and dirty way to do this is to create a six- or eight-frame cartoon-style drawing of the as-is process. You don't need to be an artist; stick figures are fine! Start with distilling the basic steps that you believe a target persona follows today to achieve their goal—e.g., Renter Reagan applying to rent a unit they've already toured. This is represented in the drawing with the six frames.

Then, repeat the process with a new storyboard and try to eliminate at least two frames from your first drawing to imagine a to-be process. For example, what if Renter Reagan was already preapproved for the apartment unit based on their search criteria earlier in the process?

Below, we see that instead of filling out paperwork, they can easily complete a form online (and we have assumed all the data they need is easy to upload instead of sorting through papers). Renter Reagan still needs the guarantor information, but the parent can do that themselves instead of sharing all their personal and financial information with their adult child. They also still have to wait to hear about getting the unit, but with the preapproval process, now they are just waiting for the landlord to confirm they have all the information they need to rent them the unit.

As with journey maps, storyboards offer the opportunity to visualize the world for your target personas in a way that evokes a deeper understanding and empathy for their pain points. I've seen many aha moments from these exercises that have changed the trajectory for both new and mature businesses. At DigitalOcean, we were exploring a team-collaboration feature for managing cloud infrastructure. Our journey map and storyboards visualized how we believed a team of engineers struggled to communicate about their various technical needs for cloud infrastructure and how that would improve with our new features. We assumed there was a lot of back-and-forth between team members. However, our ethnographic research taught us that it was more common for one engineer—or their manager—to solicit each team member's needs and manage resources for the group. This completely changed our view of the as-is process and resulted in a to-be storyboard that would streamline requests to one person instead of creating a collaboration tool. This process saved us from building the entirely wrong thing!

DISCOVERY IS FOREVER

Founders are usually the first product managers of a startup. Product managers (PMs) define and coordinate product priorities between various functions of the venture, like engineering and design or manufacturing and distribution. They serve as the voice of the customer and are in constant discovery mode. Even when founders let go of day-to-day product-management activities, continuously learning from customers remains critical. In all my leadership roles at startups, even with teams of PMs working for me, I routinely conducted "listening tours" with our customers as well as with those who did not use our products to understand how they used competitors' products. Each of these discussions gave me tons of insights. In one such situation, an engineering leader at a startup took out her phone to show me the invoice she got from a competitor. It was complicated, and she wasn't sure what she was paying for or how to optimize expenses with her limited budget. This led me to ask more leaders of engineering teams to show me their invoices from various providers, including from our own customers. From this exercise, I learned how complicated the monthly bills were for a cloud service—including ours! This led to improvements at the end of the customer journey that we hadn't considered early on when we were more focused on getting them on board and using our product.

The conclusion here is to never lose touch with your customers and to take the time to truly understand their journeys and unmet needs. Even in the later stages of a new venture, a week (which is a long time in startup land!) should never pass without having at least one interaction with a customer or prospect to stay fresh and keep learning. I recommend that all startup teams have a tracking method—which could be as simple as a spreadsheet—to stay on top of who is talking with whom and the learnings from each interaction. And don't just track it, set up times to discuss patterns and create journey maps and storyboards to turn these insights into improvements and opportunities for your business.

5.

SETTING THE VISION AND A PLAN

In the earliest stages of validating your hypotheses and assumptions, you are not fully a company . . . yet. In this stage, there are still unknowns about the persona, problem, and market, and, as discussed in Chapter 3, business models and long-term strategies can be a bit fuzzy. When startups start to get some traction with repeatable use of a solution and/or revenue coming in the door, even if not at PMF yet, it is critical for the team to step back and consider where they are headed. This is when it's time to establish the vision and purpose of your venture, also known as its true north. It's when to define a roadmap that directs how the overall success of the business will operate and be measured. The true north and roadmap will evolve as you continue efforts to get to PMF, but by at least taking a first pass at these early on, you can minimize the stress that comes with moving fast without a clear direction.

When I first met the DigitalOcean team they were under significant pressure from their investors because the tremendous growth they had experienced in their first three years was starting to level out. Their defensibility strategy (often referred to as a startup's "moat") was racing to market with a basic cloud offering with limited features that was fast and easy to use. The product appealed to developers who were doing side projects at work where they needed virtual machines for experimentation, or they were working on personal projects at home and needed an inexpensive cloud solution to host simple websites for content sharing and e-commerce transactions. The product also appealed to the startup community, but with less than 10 percent of startups surviving after their first year, there was tremendous churn as startups shut down. The low-cost and simplicity model was defensible in the early days. But a lack of additional cloud capabilities that bigger cloud solutions like Amazon's AWS or Microsoft's Azure provided, such as load balancing and object storage, prevented Digital-Ocean from reaching the revenue goals they had pitched in their most recent series B fundraise.

TRUE NORTH

In my first month working with the company as a consultant, it became clear that DigitalOcean had lots of metrics to track new users and several new features and products in the works, but there was no clearly defined true north, nor was there a roadmap with a plan to reach broader goals for the business. Further, the rest of the organization was out of sync with the product team, thus unprepared for marketing, selling, supporting, or even billing for these new features. Resolving these challenges became my first order of business when I joined the company several months later as their full-time CTO. I dove headfirst into a true north vision-setting exercise that then led to a roadmapping and prioritization process across the organization. These activities not only aligned the leadership team on a strategy and execution plan but also gave clarity to the whole organization on what we were doing, why, and how we would get there. This alignment led to us shipping seven new products and features in less than eighteen months. It also allowed us to move upmarket—beyond hobbyists and startups—and go after larger revenue opportunities, and positioned us to prepare for an IPO.[1]

When the fog of what you are doing starts to lift after deep discovery work and you are becoming clearer about the business you are building (such as when Kait and Zack realized they were building a marketing-technology company and not an insurance business) it is time for you to craft a true north statement—this can also be referred to as a mission statement, and it is not a one-hour exercise. Some organizations take weeks and hire consultants to get this right. When you are a small venture and low on cash, it's fine to carve out a few hours with cofounders, early team members, advisors, and so on to draft a broad, *impact-focused* vision for the business. This is usually something bold like Google's "To organize the world's information and make it universally accessible and useful." A broad, impact-focused statement like this gave Google the latitude to expand in new areas like creating productivity applications or even self-driving cars—not just stay a search tool. Not only does a statement like this offer opportunities for expansion, but it also provides guardrails for the organization. When a new idea or direction comes up, you can ask, "How does that idea or direction align with our true north?" Your true north does not have to be set in stone (it may change as your venture evolves), but it's a forcing function to ensure the team, investors, customers, and partners are all clear about the direction of the business.

True north statements take time and require a creative, iterative process. To start the process, in a group or by using the diverge<>converge process with key team members, it is important to brainstorm both the impact you envision your business will have and on which audience. Just aligning on "developers" as our target audience was an exercise in itself for the leadership team at DigitalOcean. We debated audiences ranging from software engineers at small-to-medium businesses to engineering leaders at larger enterprises. Some wanted our impact to be simplifying access to cloud technology, but others felt our impact was to make software development easy with or without the cloud. We eventually landed on "To empower developers to build great software," which allowed us to be more than just a cloud company; our impact would be focused on any developers, but we could extend into other tools or services so they could build great software. Most startups have several iterations of their true north statements—it's okay to try a few on before committing—but too much thrash and change in this statement can cause the same for the business. Try to have one that you can live with for a year or so or until critical growth or pivot point in the business. DigitalOcean revisited their true north statement years later and reverted to the focus on cloud technology with a new true north statement: "To simplify cloud computing so that developers and businesses can spend more time building software that changes the world."

VISION LEADS TO EXECUTION

A clear true north statement is the vision that leads to an execution plan for what you will be doing in the next twelve to eighteen months. To be clear, twelve to eighteen months is a *long* timeline for a startup. So much can change (the market, the product, the people, the world!) that it's hard to predict the next six months, never mind twelve to eighteen. So, while it's tricky to predict the future, laying out a strategy for the next twelve to eighteen months will at least give you a sense of what might be happening at the business in the near term, before getting into a detailed execution plan. Our true north statement at DigitalOcean allowed us to develop a high-level company roadmap to identify major workstreams over the coming eighteen months that would lead to achieving key business goals, such as an increase in revenue and the number of customers in new market segments.

Once you have clear business goals, the next step is to develop an operating plan to execute on those objectives and set clear measures to march toward that direction. The objectives and key results (OKR) method was first developed by Andy Grove at Intel. Google founders Larry Page and Sergey Brin adopted OKRs across their small thirty-or-so-person team in 1999, and OKRs remain an integral part of how Google operates. Some may consider the OKR process to be too heavyweight for early-stage ventures but there is a way to keep it light and useful early on. The trick is to narrow the scope to *no more than three* high-level goals that are most meaningful to the business in the near term, say less than twelve months for an early venture. Then, the person or team responsible for each functional area such as product, marketing, or support can write their own goals to align with these company goals.

The acronym SMART—specific, measurable, achievable, relevant, and time-bound—is often used in conjunction with OKRs to describe criteria for writing effective management goals.[2] For example, three high-level company goals for an early startup may be:

1. Ship a key feature in the second quarter (Q2)
2. Close six new customers who need these features by Q4
3. Attain end-of-year annual recurring revenue (ARR) goal by end of Q4

With these high-level goals in mind, a SMART goal for the product team may look like this:

Specific: Build product feature
Measurable: Shipped (and functional!)
Achievable: The discovery process is complete, the product has been specified, and we have the team to build it
Relevant: It's a must-have feature, not a "nice to have"
Time-bound: Must be done by Q2

And the marketing team's SMART goal may look like this:

Specific: Implement marketing plan

Measurable: Website updated, press notified, social media content prepared

Achievable: The right skills and resources are in place

Relevant: Customers and prospects need to know about the new feature

Time-bound: Must be done by Q2

Defining these high-level goals aligns the team and ensures everyone is working on the right things. It also provides clarity on what success looks like for the business. Because early-stage businesses are less predictable, I recommend that goals are set no more than four to six quarters out and that there is a diminishing degree of confidence as you look further out, as shown below.

Some organizations break their OKRs into more granular components using key performance indicators (KPIs). KPIs are usually more detailed metrics, which we'll discuss next, and can be helpful for some teams to ensure they are tracking month to month.

True North					
12–18 Month Vision					
Q1 (OKR/KPI)	Q2 (OKR/KPI)	Q3 (OKR/KPI)	Q4 (OKR/KPI)	Q5 (OKR/KPI)	Q6 (OKR/KPI)
90%+ Confidence		75–90%		<75%	
Product, Sales, Go-to-Market, Company Ops (HR, etc.)					

STRATEGIC

OPERATIONAL

METRICS THAT MATTER

KPIs are only useful if you're measuring the right things. Regardless of your personal measures of success that we discussed in Chapter 1, it's not just gut feel and intuition that signal the success of the business, but also specific metrics that allow you, your teams, and your investors to gauge whether you are making progress toward your goals. And progress can mean very different things depending on whether we're talking about product adoption versus other operational-success metrics like quality metrics for a consumer product venture managing their cost of materials, or employee satisfaction for a venture focused on building a strong company culture. Metrics can also evolve over time as a startup evolves.

So, how do you identify metrics to fairly evaluate your KPIs and OKRs? Measures like monthly or daily active users (MAUs and DAUs) are a common default for technology applications to track user engagement but may not make sense for certain use cases. And what does "active" mean, anyway? According to a 2022 study, Instagram users were active an average of twelve hours per month or thirty minutes daily, but this is a mature product where "active" could be anything from scrolling through one's feed to watching reels or liking posts.[3] For Instagram, hours on the app or "session length" is a critical KPI. The restaurant reservation application OpenTable's early KPIs[4] focused on getting as many restaurants as possible on the platform. Once they had established strong relationships with their restaurant customers, they shifted their KPI focus on speed and efficiency and how much time a consumer spent in the app to find a restaurant and book a table. Instead of caring about lots of time in the app like Instagram, OpenTable wants customers in and out of the app as fast as possible. That was their next job to get done, and they have since evolved to focusing on seated diners (people who followed through on their reservations) and other more relevant KPIs as the venture has scaled.

Sometimes you'll have both internal and external KPIs. The software product Tango creates how-to guides with screenshots in seconds. Each how-to guide is called a "Tango." A sales director might create a Tango to show new team members how to pull sales reports, or an administrative assistant might create a Tango to teach interns how to create a calendar event. An internal KPI for the Tango product team is the time it takes from signing up for the product to capturing their first Tango. "We call it 'time to magic moment,'" said their cofounder and CTO, Brian Shultz. However, because their product is sold as a productivity tool to enterprises, their external KPI focuses on how often Tangos are shared, or more importantly *used*, across their customers' organizations. By clearly defining these different KPIs, Tango centers all their non-engineering efforts—sales, marketing, support, etc.—around creation and use of Tangos.

Some KPIs are hard to track early on. Longitudinal KPIs for products that improve the health of customers or products that optimize business operations will rely on adoption, data collection, learning curves, and business-process changes, which can take months if not years before you know if your solution is having an impact. Yinka has short-term KPIs that track stylists' increased number of available hours to braid hair and the resulting additional customers and revenue for stylists. However, Yinka will not know whether her hair-braiding device will improve stylists' aches and pains in their hands (a very subjective thing to measure!) until they start to use the device often enough to relieve stress on their hands. And the device's impact on a long-time braider with existing hand pain may be different than a new braider who would have to be tracked over some extended period before Yinka could assess whether the device minimized or even eliminated hand pain. Even the impact on stylists' clients may take time to track, such as how satisfied they are with the long-term hold of the braids and whether they return to the stylist for new braids or refer friends to the stylist.

Sometimes, customers may not trust a startup to even allow you to measure these longitudinal KPIs. This is especially the case for technology products sold into large enterprises. In our early days at VMware, it was easy to measure how our desktop products improved productivity for developers; setting up a physical device, which used to take hours, was reduced to minutes or even seconds with our software solution. However, large enterprises that stood to gain substantial cost savings with our product implemented at scale in their data centers were hesitant to adopt this new technology for their critical applications. We had to convince these prospects to allow us to run proof of concepts (POCs) for months to prove to them that we could deliver a secure and reliable option that saved them money. We eventually won a few over, which led to our explosive growth. With a growing number of large enterprise customers using our product, our KPIs evolved to track not just cost savings for our customers but also security, performance, and reliability metrics.

BEST PRACTICES FOR VISION SETTING AND OKRS

When done well, OKRs and KPIs will keep your team grounded in your true north vision and focused on clear, actionable steps that move your startup toward your goals. Creating these metrics is a great exercise to do as a team and can be a valuable communication tool for key stakeholders, such as your investors and customers. As you start creating them, keep these two best practices in mind.

- **Set objectives that are not only SMART but also challenging.** Not achieving a goal isn't necessarily bad if you make good progress. In fact, most OKR practitioners say *not* to set goals that you know you'll easily achieve, because then what's the point? Some also say the *A* in SMART stands for aggressive, versus achievable.

- **Designate a DRI (directly responsible individual) to drive the OKR process.** Sometimes this is a founder or a chief of staff or someone with excellent project management skills to keep the process on track—they are not setting the goals themselves; rather, they are simply driving the process. DRIs are also important for each goal to ensure there is accountability and clear ownership. Some companies adopt the RACI model to do this. RACI stands for responsible, accountable, consulted, and informed, and the model helps teams prioritize their actions and makes it clear who is responsible for what.

Setting your true north, planning, goal setting, and metrics tracking are ongoing needs for any venture that is getting traction. It is important to be careful not to overdo it (spending too much time tracking and not enough time building and selling!), but not doing it at all is risky business. If you are raising capital, have a board of directors, and/or plan to hire employees, getting alignment on where you are going, measures of success, how you will get there, and by when is critical. Using a bus driver metaphor for a founder, you wouldn't pull up to a bus stop with a random vehicle and ask a group of people to come aboard to help you figure out how to get to an unknown destination. Having clarity on the destination and when you'd like to get there will determine what type of vehicle you will drive, who gets on it, and what their roles will be. And those are what we will discuss next.

PART I

PRODUCT TOOLBOX

Why Discovery Matters

- Slow down and do proper discovery work. This involves doing experiments that validate or invalidate hypotheses about the problem you have set out to solve.
- A deep discovery process will also offer personal insights into whether you want to be doing the kind of work your idea requires.

The Art of Discovery

- Craft "We believe" statements to identify hypotheses you need to test about your target personas, their problems, and the market.
- Go beyond the interview and conduct experiments to test your hypotheses:
  - o Ethnographic research (observation tests)
  - o Be the bot with concierge and Wizard of Oz tests
  - o Low-fidelity experiments and bootstrapping technical solutions

The Customer Journey

- Use journey mapping and storyboarding to distill the data from your discovery experiments and identify trends and patterns.
  - o An "as-is" journey map plots out how a prospective customer handles a specific process today.
  - o A "to-be" journey map plots out what the process might be with your solution.
- Storyboards further visualize what's really happening with your customers as you imagine their lives today versus what their experiences could be.

Setting the Vision and a Plan

- When you start to get traction with your product, step back and establish a true north statement and roadmap for the business for the next twelve to eighteen months.

- True north statements take time and require a creative, iterative process. To start the process, brainstorm both the impact you envision your business will have and on which target audience.

- It's okay to try on a few true north statements before committing. Have one that you can live with for a year or until critical growth or pivot point in the business.

- Once you have a true north statement, set SMART, high-level strategic goals and develop an operating plan.

- Measure your strategic goals with functional OKRs and KPIs that align with those high-level goals.

Part II
PEOPLE

I once had a CEO-founder of a startup say to me, "I wish people were like computers and you could just program them to do the work instead of dealing with all these softer issues." Gasp! While that sounds incredibly crass, I got what he meant. Even though artificial intelligence will likely supplant many of the mundane and even some of the more sophisticated roles of humans in a business, unless one attempts to fund and operate their company solo (or AIs become entrepreneurs), people will be involved, and as we learned in the chapters in Part I, people are complicated! You and the cofounders you might partner with, the employees you hire and work with, and even your investors and customers all bring their personal baggage to work every day. In addition to personal baggage, you and they are likely scarred from past bosses and coworkers (maybe even former teachers and professors). Unless everyone has done deep work with a therapist or coach, these aspects of our lives manifest in all sorts of ways within an organization. How people perform and behave at work as individuals is part of the challenge of leading a business and can be especially challenging as a startup evolves from a couple of founders to growing teams.

Our demons stay with us until we reckon with them and the result manifests in a number of common organizational and human resource challenges that—if not addressed—can be the death of a business. "I wish someone had warned me I'd spend this much time on people stuff" is the most common gripe I get from entrepreneurs. While they were busy getting to product-market fit and raising capital, the organization began to grow around them. Even when they did their best to be careful about establishing an inclusive culture and setting the bar high for top-quality hires, they rarely anticipated how many issues they'd be confronted with around the human aspects of their business. And while they are battling their own demons, they are grappling with the tension created when leaders try to delicately balance culture with productivity, all while the business continues to shift, pivot, and (ideally) scale. It can be brutal to contend with!

From whom we start the journey with to how the team evolves over time, it is the people in and around our business that are the most important asset. In the chapters ahead I'll delve into the key people areas that tend to trip up new ventures the most and are essential to prepare for when building a successful startup. I'll start with the topic of cofounders in Chapter 6. We'll explore whether you need one (if you don't have one already), how to go about finding one and managing that relationship if you decide to go that route, and an approach to finding advisors and other support systems if you decide to go it alone. Chapter 7 covers culture and organizational strategy, which we'll explore through the question, *What kind of organization do we want to be when we grow up?* I'll start by walking you through the process of creating a vision for your company culture including how to think about diversity, equity, and inclusion at the very start. With that piece in place, in Chapter 8 I'll help you develop a method for hiring the team that will help you grow into the company you strive to become. Hiring is one of the most challenging aspects of growing a business after your idea starts to take root. Writing job descriptions, sourcing candidates, interviewing, onboarding, and managing talent are all a part of startup life—and the stakes for getting them right are even higher in a small, growing company.

Finally, Chapter 9 covers separation because some hires won't work out. I'll show you how to develop the self-awareness to know whether the employee was the problem or the company failed to set that person up for success (and how to avoid repeating that mistake). I'll also cover how to separate from an employee so that everyone maintains grace and dignity.

6.

THE COFOUNDER COURTSHIP

One of the first and most important people decisions founders will make is whether to go it alone or to have cofounders. The answer isn't always obvious. Having cofounders can lower the risk of the business and allow for different skills that complement each other, but forcing these relationships can result in bad "marriages" that create more harm to a business than help. When a great match happens it can be magic, but, just like any marriage, one should not enter the relationship rashly. Time and again, I have observed founders pressured into finding their technical or business cofounder before investors will give them a term sheet. Although not the only data point that may lead to unicorn status, there is some evidence[1] that unicorn ventures (those valued at a billion dollars or more) are slightly more successful with two or three cofounders. Further, investors sometimes worry about the risk associated with a solo founder if they were to burn out or bail on the business. However, these same investors tend to confuse the need to augment a skill set with the need for a full partner. In their haste to satisfy investors' demands (and keep their businesses afloat!), solo founders often rush to fill that gap without considering whether their cofounder is truly a good match. I have seen just as many startup failures due to bad cofounder relationships as I have due to a solo founder lacking the support of a cofounder. I've worked both for and with hundreds of entrepreneurs in the last few decades, and my observation is that each cofounder situation is highly dependent on chemistry, the experience each brings into the relationship, leadership styles, and many other factors that can be easily overlooked.

Lizzie's original cofounder, Paul, was a longtime close friend from college. Paul had a business-operations background and Lizzie had an engineering background. She was passionate about uncovering bottlenecks in technical teams, and because he was working at LinkedIn at the time, he was passionate about helping people love their careers. They experimented and pivoted multiple times on their company—originally called Pathlight—which was a two-sided software solution using AI to match technical job seekers to the right roles based on skills, instead of credentials. Lizzie pushed the product more toward supporting engineering teams because that was her passion, but Paul struggled to build the conviction he needed to commit to an engineering-centric business. Lizzie and Paul made the common mistake of assuming a friendship and general common interest was enough for them to start a business together. They did not align on the type of business they would build and what success might look like. The cofounders amicably parted ways, and he's still involved as a product resource as her business evolves, but it was a regrettable divorce. "I was ready to leap towards this idea, and he just couldn't get there," Lizzie said.

Months after Lizzie's split with her first cofounder, I introduced her to one of my former coaching clients, Joe, a seasoned startup CTO whose venture had recently had a successful exit. Joe was ready to go back to the beginning and work on another startup. Having learned many valuable lessons from her first attempt at cofounder relationships, Lizzie approached this next round of "cofounder dating" carefully. Joe, on the other hand, had just wrapped up an incredible ten-year run at his first startup with four of his dearest friends as cofounders and had a good sense of what it felt like to have a successful cofounding team. They were each coming into the situation with very different perspectives—not uncommon for most cofounding teams. Following many of the tips I will provide in this chapter, Lizzie and Joe—who each lived on the West and East Coasts, respectively—took great care in getting to know each other. They discussed everything from the product and the vision they had for the business to how they would support each other as partners, including the plan for when Lizzie took time off for her upcoming wedding and honeymoon and Joe's time off for the birth of his second child. They took turns traveling to each other's home cities to spend time face-to-face to test how that felt and had deep conversations about the road ahead. In other words, they didn't take the courtship process lightly.

Through their process, Lizzie and Joe worked hard to develop their true north and reach alignment on the direction of the business, which is now called Quotient and focuses on developer productivity using AI technology. They only decided to join forces once they felt they had spent adequate time truly building a partnership and reaching alignment on their true north. They went on to thrive as a team, successfully raised capital, and began to scale their venture as a solid cofounding team.

Reflecting on her yearlong cofounder courtship process, Hively founder Angela, whom we first met in Chapter 3, said, "One of the most important lessons I learned is that onboarding a cofounder and teammate takes time, patience, and a lot of communication. While having a partner can be energizing and motivating, it also requires a significant investment of time and energy to get them up to speed, align on decisions, and invest in the human relationship." In 2021, on his popular podcast, neuroscientist and Stanford professor Andrew Huberman interviewed Dr. David Buss, a founding member in the field of evolutionary psychology and professor of psychology at the University of Texas, Austin, whose research centers around partner selection and human relationships. In the interview, Dr. Buss describes his research on how people select mates and the dynamics of courtship. While the podcast was focused primarily on heterogeneous relationships, marriage, and monogamy, I couldn't help but notice the parallels with cofounder relationships as I listened. Both go through a courtship process in which each person assesses whether the other would be a good match for them in areas related to goals, ambition, emotional stability, and commitment. My brain is in the entrepreneurship space most of my waking hours, so as I listened to this podcast it made me think about how many entrepreneurs don't appreciate how similar these courtships are, and to Angela's point, how necessary it is to take the time and be patient through the process. Let's dig into how to think about this in more detail.

DO YOU NEED A COFOUNDER?

Before we get into courtship, let's first think about whether you need a cofounder at all. This question can come up at any point in your startup journey, whether it's early on as you are just thinking about a problem you want to solve; when you're already getting traction and feel the pinch for a cofounder, such as when you're missing a certain skill needed for the business; or if you're getting feedback from investors suggesting you should find a cofounder. You might even consider bringing in a cofounder if you're feeling lonely or crave a thought partner to work with. Whatever the drivers are, there are three lenses you can apply when evaluating whether you need a cofounder: partnership, expertise, and experience. Even if you have one or several cofounders already, it's worthwhile to apply these lenses to make sure you are aligned on what will keep ensuring a successful relationship.

Partnership

Consider past professional or educational situations in which you worked with a peer collaborator or team. Did you value partnership, shared risk, and collaboration with others? How did you handle conflict, resolve differences in opinions, or meet deadlines when the work was divided? How did you approach making big decisions together? If you look back on these experiences with fondness or even recall moments of growth from resolving a conflict, having a cofounder may be incredibly valuable to you. It can be great to have someone to brainstorm with, share the workload, and commiserate with during your journey. But having cofounders—like a committed personal partnership—is also a big test of your ability to be vulnerable and to handle conflict, and of your willingness to compromise. There will be many times a cofounding team will disagree on things—from product and hiring decisions to operating procedures and a fundraising strategy—and how you process these decisions together is fundamental to a healthy cofounding relationship. Self-awareness, a willingness to lean into conflict, and the ability to thrive together in ambiguous situations will be critical in a cofounding relationship. If you question whether you are up for sharing these experiences with one or more cofounders, you may need to do some introspective work before taking on a cofounder or, perhaps, go it alone.

I was involved in a cofounder courtship once with a serial entrepreneur who was a solo founder in their first startup and wanted to find a partner for their second. We had many lunches and coffees and discussed the pros and cons of the business we might build together. In one conversation, we discussed how we would handle critical decisions when we disagreed. Would we "disagree and commit" with each other or would we battle it out until we were fully aligned? To disagree and commit can be a good way to move forward if a topic isn't vital to the life of the startup, but we must make an urgent call. Interestingly, my potential cofounder saw the disagree-and-commit process as letting one of us "win" instead of viewing it as a compromise in the spirit of partnership. This gave me the "ick," among a few other things they said and did during our courtship. It told me this was not going to be a good cofounder for me, and that this person was probably better off being a solo founder.

Conversely, Brendan Schwartz and Chris Savage, who were college roommates and BFFs before starting Wistia, a video platform for marketers, are so aligned as cofounders that when a *significant* acquisition opportunity arose,[2] they spent a few days talking through the offer and what they would do next if they were to sell their business. They wanted to be sure they each understood each other's pros and cons and landed on a mutually agreeable outcome that didn't feel like one of them was compromising in any way. They wanted to be absolutely sure they prevented a decision that could have led to resentment or other fractures in their relationship. They ended up declining the offer because, despite the financial windfall such an acquisition would have been for both founders and for most of their employees, the reality was they loved their business and partnership and had no desire to be employees elsewhere. "We realized in the course of weighing that decision that our next venture would be to rebuild what we had built the first time, which seemed like a mistake," Chris, Wistia's CEO, said. "We also believed that we could take what we had already built a lot further if we didn't sell the business." Chris and Brendan also had the good fortune of having taken little outside capital, thus they felt no pressure to exit from investors. So, instead, they bought out their investors using debt financing, paid their longtime employees bonuses for sticking with them, and continued to run a profitable business.

Expertise

If considering a cofounder, self-awareness is so important when it comes to not only how you handle partnerships but also to assessing your technical and/or domain expertise. A technologist may lack management or operating skills like marketing or sales, and a sales leader may lack technical or strategic skills. Some skills can be learned on the job, but early-stage founders often underestimate how long these things can take to learn, and rookie mistakes can set back (or kill) a business before it's barely out of the gate. You might be able to teach yourself how to code, but your business may not have the time to wait for you to do that. Or, perhaps you are bringing a consumer product to market and you know nothing about manufacturing and distribution. If you have lots of time and money (and maybe some support from advisors, which we'll discuss further), you may figure these things out and be better for it by learning as you go, but most startups can't afford that time and expense.

In addition to technical, management, or operating expertise, you may require domain-specific expertise. Having domain expertise will not only inform the product strategy but will also help your startup gain credibility in the market and potentially open doors on the sales side. Investors may also expect or even require there be a domain expert on the team. Andrea, a tech-savvy former business consultant and the founder of HumanFirst, an insights and evidence platform for digital biomarkers, lacked the clinical expertise and network to gain credibility with the pharmaceutical companies and clinical teams to whom she aimed to sell her product. However, her cofounder, Dr. Sofia Warner, brought medical expertise and credibility into the startup. In addition, they engaged advisors who were pharmaceutical experts and researchers and who gave them all the knowledge, connections, and credibility needed to get their product off the ground.[3] Note that these experts do not necessarily have to be cofounders and can be first hires, like a chief scientist or medical officer. I'll touch more on this later in the chapter, but the point here is: know what you don't know!

Experience

You can have expertise in a particular area, like coding or clinical trials, but have limited real-world experience in operating businesses. Many founders worked at a mature company before their startup and got a taste of what a successful company feels like at scale, or they were a joiner at a startup that scaled. Maybe they got to experience a great company culture or maybe it was terrible and they learned what *not* to do. Even if they have prior work experience at a mature company or startup, unless they are serial entrepreneurs, most founders have never been managers or led entire functions of a company before. Christina Ross is an expert in financial systems, worked at several mature companies, and had been a joiner in three different startups as a head of finance before launching her own financial technology company, Cube. She had a deep understanding of the problems to be solved for finance leaders, but also had seen this movie before and had a sense of what startups are all about. It was both her professional experience and her domain expertise that built credibility with potential customers and investors. She was comfortable with the frenetic nature of the discovery work when she first got started and knew what a good (and bad) cofounder partnership looks like, having seen both in prior startups she'd joined. However, even though she had subject matter expertise and great work experiences, Christina was not an engineering expert who knew how to build software, so she recruited a seasoned technical cofounder who also had startup experience. Their collective subject matter and engineering expertise *and* experience allowed them to be nimble, raise a lot of capital, and scale fast over just a few years when others may have taken far longer or stalled taking on the same type of venture.

Applying the lenses of partnership, expertise, and experience can help you assess your blind spots. A seasoned cofounder with startup experience can offer perspective and be a calming force even if it's just acknowledging the craziness that is startup life. A prospective cofounder who has only worked at large companies may have great expertise, but could be used to leading and not doing and can hold some disdain for getting their hands dirty. One of my favorite early VMware stories happened on my very first day when I was settling into our mostly vacant office space that housed one talent recruiter and an IT guy. I was essentially the founder of our first remote engineering site. I was walking around looking for office supplies and asked the IT guy where one could find a pen and he said, "Oh, we were waiting for you to start and assumed you'd get the pens." Here I was, a head of engineering, hired to build a two-hundred-plus-person team, but also the de facto office manager. So off to the office supply store I went to get the pens! I had the experience to know we'd eventually hire an office manager to handle supplies and other facilities matters. It was not beneath me to get the pens or handle other basic things that just needed to get done, like figuring out seating plans and buying printers and other office necessities. In other words, just because you're experienced doesn't mean you should be above getting the pens! So be sure an experienced potential partner also has grit.

KNOWING WHAT YOU WANT

Once you have applied each of the lenses, you can decide whether the next step is to find a cofounder or go it alone. This is a highly personal choice, and it is important to be intentional about the process. I break down each scenario below:

- **No partnership—low expertise/experience:** If you decide you are better off going it alone without a lot of experience or expertise yourself, I suggest you plan to bring on experienced hires and advisors. This will offer you the freedom to make your own decisions without having to get buy-in from a cofounder and can be a great opportunity to learn and build expertise as you gain experience. However, it could take longer to get things done on your own and find the right team and advisors to work with before the venture starts to gain momentum. If you decide to try to raise venture capital, the expertise and experience of your team and advisors in this scenario will be very important.

- **No partnership—high expertise/experience:** If you decide you are better off going it alone and have a lot of experience and/or expertise, you may be able to do a lot on your own and bring on less experienced hires, contractors, and advisors as needed. According to research by venture capitalist and experienced startup founder Ali Tamaseb for his book *Super Founders*, one in five unicorn companies are founded by a single person, and a study done at the Wharton School of the University of Pennsylvania found that startups with single founders may last longer and achieve higher revenue.[4] Perhaps experience, expertise, and less time spent debating with cofounders led to these statistics. However, even if these are good reasons to be a solo founder, going solo will likely lengthen the time it takes to get to PMF and/or operationalize the business. Investors may see your business as risky as a solo founder, but the right team and/or advisors on board can allay these concerns.

- **Partnership—low expertise/experience:** If you decide you want to get on this roller coaster with a partner(s), I suggest you follow a proper courtship process as described in the second half of this chapter. Without much expertise or experience, you may consider a combination of one or more cofounders and a few experienced hires and/or advisors. Multiple founders can bring different skills and expertise to the table, which can lead to better decision-making, increased innovation, and improved overall performance.

- **Partnership—high expertise/experience:** Even with some experience and/or expertise, if you want a partner, I still suggest you follow a proper courtship process, as Lizzie and Joe did. You likely know what gaps you are missing and will need to test both partnership and skills and/or experience compatibility. When my dear friend Sophia Dominguez, second-time founder and augmented reality expert, was starting to think through her next venture, including who her ideal cofounder would be, she had a much better sense of what that would look and feel like. "In my first startup, the cofounder process was organic, and it turned out we were misaligned on a bunch of things from our vision for the company to what partnership meant. Things got ugly in the end when we had to shut down our startup. In this next go-round, I am being much more intentional about who I partner with."

According to Tamaseb, 36 percent of billion-dollar startups are founded by two people. The data suggests having a cofounder could lead to more financial success, but remember it takes time to find the *right* cofounder(s). Some founders forge ahead with their idea and even get to market before they find that ideal "someone." You don't have to wait to start the process, and sometimes a first hire, contractor, or advisor can become your cofounder. My client David Benhaim was hired in 2013 by solo founder and CEO Greg Mark as the first engineering hire at Markforged, a 3D carbon-fiber- and metal-printing startup. It was almost two years into his tenure at Markforged that David became a cofounder of the venture. "Greg and I were making every decision together, and we complemented each other in so many ways. He was focused on hardware materials, sales, and strategy, and I was all about software and engineering execution. It was a humbling experience when he invited me to be his cofounder, but it also made a ton of sense." David's equity was adjusted up to account for his cofounder status, and in 2017 he was promoted to be CTO of the company. Greg and David left Markforged shortly after the venture went public via a SPAC in 2021. After a well-earned break, the two cofounders went on to launch their second venture in 2023, Backflip AI, which raised a significant amount of venture capital right from the start because of the team's startup credibility and strong cofounder partnership.

Whether you've decided to go it alone or it's taking longer than ideal to find a cofounder(s), having a strong first hire who is a technical or domain expert instead of a cofounder can suffice; the same holds for someone with strong sales, marketing, or other operational skills. You might also consider a second-in-command (COO, CTO, etc.) who plays a key role in the business without the official cofounder title and compensation. These individuals can still receive founding team–worthy equity grants and, in earlier-stage businesses, could be anointed as "cofounder" down the road if the relationship blossoms over time, like David at Markforged. It is much easier to convert someone to a cofounder and give them more equity later than it is to demote or fire them and claw back equity.

THE COFOUNDER COURTSHIP

If you've decided that you're ready for a cofounder, you have basically decided to seek a mate for a long-term partnership. Just like a personal relationship may result in children, big financial decisions (like buying a house), and running a household, a cofounding relationship will force you to commit to how you will nurture employees, manage finances, and run your business. There are big decisions to make: "How will we educate our kids?" is like "What kind of company culture will we have?" There are philosophies on which to reach alignment: "Where will we raise our family?" is like "Will we have a home office or remote-friendly work environment?" You can't discover how you will answer these deeper questions with a prospective cofounder over a few coffee meetings. It's a courtship, and despite the urgency you may have to get going with the startup so you can raise money or hire people, I can't emphasize enough how important it is to nurture these prospective relationships as you would a personal relationship.

I suggest the following steps to court your cofounder(s). Even if you had a cofounder before in a previous startup, it can be a good way to assess what went well and what did not go well the last time to inform the next time, as Sophia did.

- **Conduct a listening tour** by meeting other startup cofounders. Talk with them about their own courtship process. Ask if there are questions they wish they had asked and hurdles they had to overcome early in their relationship. Even the greatest cofounder teams have war stories to tell about stressful situations in their relationships and what they learned from these experiences.

- **Write a cofounder job description (JD)** based on insights from the listening tour. Include experience, expertise, and your ideal values and character traits for this person. If you already have someone in mind, try to stay objective and not write this JD to ensure they can fill the role (confirmation bias). Use this as your guide as you meet prospective cofounders and adjust as you go. Just like any hire for a new role at your startup, it's likely that the more prospects you meet, the more tweaks you'll make to that JD and find "the one."

  If there are two or more of you thinking about becoming cofounders, do the JD method as a diverge<>converge exercise. Discuss potential roles each may fill (CEO, CTO, etc.) and independently (diverge) write the optimal cofounder JD. Once each has done this exercise on their own, share these JDs with each other (converge) and discuss where you were each coming from for each role. Not only will this better define these roles, but it will allow you and your prospective cofounder(s) to expose perceptions and expectations of each other and of how the leadership of the business may play out.

  Note: While cofounders' titles are not terribly important early on and become more relevant once you start to hire people and/or raise capital, the conversation about who will be

CEO vs. other roles in the venture can be telling. Unless it's blatantly clear, such as one of you is an MBA (CEO) and the other has a technical background (CTO), this conversation can lend insight into what's important to each partner of the venture (e.g., control or ego instead of a title commensurate with experience/expertise). Avoiding the conversation can cause friction down the road. So, be clear about what each partner cares about when it comes to the role they will play at the venture and why a particular title makes the most sense. Also, I am not generally a fan of "co-CEOs" as it can create confusion for employees and investors when it comes to who is the ultimate decision maker. That said, I know of teams who have pulled this concept off without a lot of concerns. Just don't take that route because you're avoiding a hard conversation, because that conversation will happen at some point, and the longer it's put off, the harder it will be.

- **Try to meet at least a half-dozen people** who may solve for the gaps you are hoping to fill (expertise, experience) and to test your chemistry. Yes, this may mean you are "dating" more than one person at a time, but you'll be more confident about the right fit through this series of conversations.

  Finding a half-dozen candidates may not be easy. Tap into your network; ask prospective investors, former professors, etc., and tell them what you're looking for. Share the JD. Attend conferences, talks, or other industry events, post on social media, and be clear you are in the market for a cofounder. This is not the time to be shy. Put yourself out there!

- **Test the relationship in various situations:** Finding the right cofounder is akin to entering a long-term relationship, as the average lifespan of a startup is seven to ten years. It's therefore crucial to understand important factors such as emotional stability and how your prospective cofounder

94

responds to new situations and stress. Relationships are truly tested when the parties engage in experiences that allow them to see more dimensions of each other's personalities. Start by testing the relationship beyond coffee chats and dinners. Engage in activities that allow you to see how you make decisions together and handle competition or pressure from outside forces. For example, go on a road trip, try a new activity, play a game of mini golf, or cook a meal for a group of friends. These experiences can help you evaluate how you collaborate and whether your styles complement each other. If you are considering multiple prospects, repeat these activities to see how each handles different situations and whether their approach complements yours. You may find one prospect, for example, gets as stressed out as you do when you are running late for a meeting, while another is a calming force that offsets your stress. Which is right for you is completely subjective—do you want someone who balances you or someone who shares the stress?

Additionally, test the relationship with real-work situations. This includes building prototypes, interviewing customers, and pitching to prospective investors. It's one thing to know someone in a one-on-one setting and another to see how they perform in front of others and process experiences that lead to decisions for your venture. Dipish Rai knew he found his cofounder for Termgrid because his energy increased after each interaction and he'd be excited about their next activity. He noted, "Starting a company demands limitless energy to bring an idea to life, making it essential to choose cofounders who enhance your energy rather than drain it." It's important to know what criteria you are looking for beyond experience and expertise, and these criteria may not reveal themselves until you've had several interactions with different prospective cofounders. During this phase, don't get too caught up in equity, titles, and such. Startups evolve rapidly in the first year or so, and it's vital to know what it feels like to actually work with prospective cofounders. By engaging in both personal and professional activities, you can gain a comprehensive understanding of your prospective cofounder's personality and work style, as well as how well you collaborate under various circumstances. This holistic approach will help you determine whether the partnership is worth pursuing.

Note: If you are considering a first-time cofounder relationship with someone you've worked with at a company in the past, this does not give you a pass to skip this part of the process. Cofounding a business with a former coworker is like going from dating to living together. You are sharing responsibilities you likely did not have when you were colleagues at a company where someone else was accountable for the overall business and, likely, making more strategic decisions than you were. The stakes are much higher as cofounders.

- **Have vulnerable conversations.** One of the most popular sessions in my course at HBS is the discussion around one's relationship with money. Most adults have very different perspectives on money, and this is rooted in deep family or personal experiences, sometimes starting in early childhood. I'll cover more on this topic in Chapter 11, but when considering a cofounder, understanding how you each think about money will give you a lot of perspective when it comes time to raise capital, price your product, and pay yourselves and your employees. Similarly, it's important to talk about any peak (positive and/or negative) moments in past jobs or school that inform your attitudes about leadership, culture, and how products are designed/built. While these conversations may feel uncomfortable, it's a step toward a solid working foundation in what will be a roller coaster of a journey together. You will have context and a better understanding of your core values and where you are each coming from. Most importantly, these types of conversations don't stop once you agree to be cofounders; they must be ongoing throughout the life of your venture as each cofounder and the relationship matures.

- **Have the prenuptial (prenup) conversation** once you are feeling good and that things are looking positive as cofounders. This means talking about and crafting a cofounder agreement. So many cofounding teams dance around this because they don't want to mess things up and introduce stress into the relationship. However, this is one major difference between cofounder relationships and marriages— you *must* have a prenup to ensure there is no confusion about the stake you each have in the venture, and rules when it comes to key elements of the business, such as intellectual property, board seats, and exit scenarios. It is so hard to align on these things once the venture is in flight and, fortunately or unfortunately, it's this conversation that uncovers the true desires and character of a potential partner, as we learned about Sam and his cofounder in Chapter 1. Just like a couple considering a long-term commitment may discuss whether each party wants to have kids, cofounders should discuss desired outcomes and how they see their roles evolving as a business scales. During one prenup conversation, two cofounders I had been working with who had already aligned on CEO and CTO titles ended up bailing on the partnership because it turned out one wanted to exit fast for a quick return and the other wanted to build something that had IPO potential. They were not aligned on the long-term goals of the venture, and that was like trying to partner with someone who doesn't want kids, and you want six.

Note: Equity splits between cofounders can be tricky—especially if someone started the venture first and then brought someone in later to balance technical or management skills. There are many equity calculators online to help figure out what is best for you, but it can get personal, so consider the relationship first before just going with what an online calculator or your investors tell you to do.

- **Meet each other's partners/families/BFFs.** Not only does this further uncover the broader context of each individual's character, but it also helps these important people in your lives understand this new relationship you are building. So, when you are up until 2 a.m. messaging your cofounder about the upcoming pitch or how to deal with a customer issue, they know who that person is and understand how they are partnered with you.

  Note: For those considering cofounders who *are* your partner/family member/BFFs, I encourage you to enter with a mindset akin to taking a personal partnership from no kids to triplets in one leap. Partnering accelerates the relationship to a whole new level—fast. This type of partnership can be an incredibly rewarding experience for you, but it can also test a preexisting personal relationship to the max. While you probably trust each other more than strangers cofounding a business together, there is likely baggage that can create more emotion and triggers around certain issues than the average partnership. I have worked with endearing and high-performing cofounding teams made up of siblings, married couples, and BFFs, but I have also seen these teams erode due to irreparable events rooted in their personal history together. I guarantee you will not be able to put your personal stuff in a box outside your business, so do not take this choice lightly. Consider getting a coach early on who specializes in working with cofounders with preexisting personal relationships. Personal tensions will come up—either overtly or subtly—and having the support to work through them will be crucial to your long-term success. I'll offer more tips on how to balance these types of relationships in Chapter 17.

You cannot rush the cofounder courtship process. The most successful cofounder relationships I've seen inevitably end up being far more than simple coworker relationships. These founders are practically family, and while that means potentially more emotions are at stake, it's their mutual understanding and deep respect for each other that allows them to traverse this oft-treacherous journey. They have mutual trust and are committed to ensuring the success of their business, together.

FOR JOINERS CONSIDERING STARTUPS

If you are considering joining a startup, it's important to understand what you may be signing up for when it comes to the founder(s) you may be working with. Serial entrepreneurs will have a very different approach than someone who has limited real-world experience or only has executive-level experience from working at mature companies. And if there is more than one founder, it's important to try to get a sense of the relationship between founders. The stage of the startup will also impact a joiner's experience. Here are a few scenarios to look out for:

- **Serial entrepreneurs:** Working with serial entrepreneurs can often be the best-case scenario if you want to learn from those who have seen the movie before, but they may also try to overcorrect in areas where they made mistakes the first time, such as overanalyzing or delaying decisions, being too conservative on cash flow, or focusing too much on scalability too early in the product-development process. If you're interviewing with a serial entrepreneur, ask what lessons they learned in their last startup and how they're bringing those lessons into their new venture.

- **Industry veterans doing their first startup:** Founders coming from mature companies with no startup experience can have big-company confidence and be great at hiring and leading teams but, as suggested earlier, lack the scrappiness to work toward PMF. These types of cofounders may also be too used to taking risks with a big-company budget and relying on teams of people to do the dirty work. On the flip side, they often know how to implement best-in-class operational processes and have the network of people to hire to run them, so once the flywheel is moving and cash is in hand, they can get momentum quickly.

- **Early-stage founders with limited leadership experience:** Working with a skilled group of founders leading teams for the first time can be tons of fun. If you bring some experience to the table, as I did in three different startups, it can be gratifying to work not only from the ground up but also alongside these founders as they grow. However, it can be frustrating if you find yourself figuring things out on your own because there's no one in the company to mentor you or collaborate with. These situations can be rewarding if you're patient, and you can always get outside mentors and advisors if they're not available at this type of startup until it's operating at scale.

- **Hypergrowth startup with inexperienced leadership:** If they made it this far, they have either matured along with the business, or they are lucky, or both! More likely, though, they have surrounded themselves with strong, experienced leaders, investors, and/or advisors. You can learn a lot from joining a company like this, but they are rare! When companies scale too fast, they can also suffer from having people in roles that have outgrown their experience. It's important at this stage to ask whether the business plans to add layers where there's either growth opportunities for you or a chance to learn from someone more senior who may be brought in above you. I'll discuss this more in Chapter 8.

If you have experience at mature companies and this is your first startup, depending on the stage, you may have a hard time adjusting to the scrappy nature of the venture. You will be expected to be comfortable with ambiguity and a lot of shifts and pivots as the venture evolves. You may have to sacrifice a title and maybe some salary to get the equity, but those who sacrificed title and pay when they joined the startup can have an awesome payout if the company has a successful exit.

If this is your first foray into startup land as a joiner, remember that no two startups are the same. You may love or hate the first one, but it might be quite different at the next one. As you ponder whether you want to join a startup, here are some things to consider:

- **What tools do you want to add to your toolbox?** Will the role allow you to hone skills you already have and/or add new ones?
- **Who do you want to learn from, and how do you want to learn?** You can learn from experienced colleagues and mentors, but having bad role models can also teach you a lot about what not to do. Similarly, if you are an experienced hire coming into a company started by inexperienced founders, you may want to learn by mentoring or teaching these young leaders. Taking the skills you've developed over the course of your career and applying them to a new situation can be a very rewarding experience.
- **Who do you want to work with?** How important is the size and culture of the team you'll work with? Remember, you'll

probably spend more waking hours of the day with these people than anyone else in your life, and in startups this can be super intense and involve working longer hours than a "regular job."

- **What do you value?** At the end of the day, love what you do and decide what role will allow you to maintain the integrity of who you are and who you aspire to be—in other words, no matter the potential upside, don't join a startup that shows signs of illegal activities or with founders who are jerks. It's not worth it.

7.

ESTABLISHING A KICK-ASS ORGANIZATION FROM DAY ONE

A sentiment I hear often from founders is, "I know I could get so much more accomplished if I could hire two people with the cash I just raised, but I barely have the time to sell to and support our customers. How can I find time to write a job description, interview candidates, and negotiate compensation, let alone onboard a new hire?!" Indeed, it is a double-edged sword, but if you don't take the time to hire and, most importantly, hire well, then it will be near impossible to scale your business.

I'll get into the brass tacks of hiring and talent management in Chapter 8. But before we dig into that, let's talk about the two big elements that go into building a kick-ass organization that most startups miss. These are envisioning your company culture and creating your organizational strategy.

Each of these get you pondering the question: *What kind of organization do we want to be when we grow up?* Once you've answered that question, every step you take in growing your team will move you closer to becoming the company you've set out to create.

ENVISIONING YOUR COMPANY CULTURE

One of the coolest parts of creating a startup is that you can be super intentional about the company's core values and culture from the start instead of scrambling to fix issues once you're operating at scale. Many startups suffer from misaligned core values and cultural issues, including implementing diversity, equity, inclusion, and belonging (DEIB) best practices, after years of overlooking them. It can be a struggle to break old habits, and once you are at a team size of around ten people, it's super hard to shift the culture of an organization. You can avoid the need to address cultural issues in the future by being thoughtful about your culture and weaving DEIB practices into the company's DNA as it's being built.

It can be hard to know where to start since core values and culture encompass so many broad ideas. But they ultimately boil down to considering what you want your values and culture to look like in the day-to-day of your venture. Thinking about how you make your employees feel can help inspire concrete ideas. For example, as they drive home from work or log off their computer at the end of the day, what's making them feel great about what they're doing and who they work with and for? What are your employees telling their friends about your company? Are they eager to recruit others to work there too? Just like it is important to evoke a response from customers about your solution and how it solves their pain point, living by your core values and having a strong (positive and inclusive) culture should create a similar emotional response. A strong culture starts with establishing core values using a process like this:

1. **List the values important to you and what you believe the company stands for.** Cofounders and founding team members should diverge<>converge to get as many perspectives as possible.

2. **Identify themes in your collective list.** These themes often reflect the real, lived culture of the company and can form the basis of the core values.

3. **Narrow down the list to ideally no more than five core values.** Each value should be distinct and represent a fundamental aspect of the company's culture. Write these values as statements that make it clear what each means in the context of the company. Focus on specific behaviors and principles that each value represents. For example, some of DigitalOcean's core values are:

   o **Learning:** Embrace a growth mindset, value curiosity, and empower employees to learn, fail, and evolve

   o **Simple:** Prioritize simplicity and ease of use, and ensure tools don't block innovation

   o **Love:** Put people at the center of everything

   o **Community:** Keep the developer community at the core

Just having the discussion about these values with your team will foster shared accountability to maintain the company culture. The founders of Tidelift, an open-source supply chain management venture, crafted their core values before they hired their first employee. Cofounder Luis Villa notes: "There was some risk that it was too early, but we wanted to intentionally design a company we could be comfortable in and proud of, and building the values in from the beginning seemed like an important part of that process."[1] The four core values Tidelift created and built their culture around are *optimistic, practical, additive*, and *inclusive*. And Tidelift didn't just write their values down and put them on their website, they worked every day to uphold those values both inside the company and in their community.

The real work is to commit to living your values every day, and to *stick to them relentlessly*. The first half of my career I worked in mature organizations that consisted of huge teams of largely homogenous coworkers (read: privileged white men) and a noninclusive culture that tolerated discrimination, harassment, and other toxic behaviors. So, it was both a delight and a culture shock to join Akamai when it was still a tiny company. The startup's core values and sense of belonging were everywhere, in big ways and small. We had incredible representation across the organization, across multiple dimensions. Due to our founding CTO's Israeli roots, it was the first time I was working with many fellow Jews, and, while not very religious myself, I became more mindful about the Sabbath and kosher practices when it came to schedules and meetings. It was also the first time I learned how to create a supportive and adaptive environment for our neurodivergent and disabled employees, such as the programmer with limited use of his hands who coded using a very early rendition of a voice-to-text application (think 1999 version of Siri!). I was also well supported by HR when I started the "moms at Akamai" group to ensure there were well-equipped lactation rooms for pumping and better benefits for parents who wanted more family leave—a novel concept in the late 1990s when most companies only offered whatever was legally required. Akamai's ability to create a sense of belonging was consistent everywhere, including when one of our most beloved engineers underwent their gender transition with dignity and the support of the entire organization. And of course, the culture and our core values truly shined on 9/11 when we lost Danny and the whole company stepped up to support each other and our community.

It can be easy for you to get so caught up in building and selling your product that you neglect your responsibility to create a diverse and inclusive organization. You may think you are creating a culture that supports diversity by being thoughtful about balancing gender, race, and other markers of individuality as you build your team. However, even though there are gobs of data that make it clear that diverse teams perform better, without a focus on inclusion *and* belonging, these teams do not thrive. The aim of inclusion is to give equal access and opportunities and get rid of discrimination and intolerance so that there is a sense of belonging. But it's also about establishing a culture that ensures everyone within the business upholds these standards. If a startup's leadership team—regardless of whether they have cofounder titles—doesn't consider inclusive practices from day one, then any efforts to diversify may fail. Being thoughtful about diversity when hiring without factoring in inclusion and creating a sense of belonging could result in dissatisfied employees, poor performance, and high turnover. The four elements of inclusion as defined by organizational experts Frances Frei and Anne Morriss are:[2]

Safe: Feeling physically, emotionally, and psychologically safe in the workplace, regardless of who you are.

Welcome: Feeling welcome in the workplace throughout the entire HR life cycle, regardless of who you are; you can bring an authentic version of yourself to shared workspaces without penalty.

Celebrated: Feeling celebrated in the workplace because of who you are; being rewarded for contributing your unique information, ideas, and perspectives to advance the organization's goals.

Championed: Inclusion is seen as an ethical and competitive imperative for the organization, and there is consistency in the experience of belonging across individuals, teams, and functions.

Founders and first hires can set diversity and inclusion standards on day one. Not only can you agree on how you will ensure your team feels safe, welcome, celebrated, and championed, but also hold the line that activities that don't support these efforts will have consequences. There are entire books and training programs dedicated to this topic, but reading and training are only useful if the team commits to embody best practices. Every. Single. Day. This includes committing to serving as upstanders and allies and ensuring that the culture remains focused on diversity, inclusion, and belonging as the venture scales. This can be tricky at times, especially if you don't have someone on the team who can coach those not fully grokking best practices, or when you must let someone go because they made people feel unsafe. I once had to fire one of my best engineers because he was harassing his office mate. Letting this talented engineer go meant delaying a new product release, but the short-term impact was worth preserving our inclusive company culture, which had zero tolerance for harassment.

Harassment is an unfortunate and, thankfully, less common occurrence to consider these days than it was only a decade or so ago. More often today, it's microaggressions or making people feel unwelcome that can be the detriment to the business. One of the founders I work with was grappling with how to talk with an employee about his overt discomfort with using they/them pronouns. Whenever referring to a colleague who identified as nonbinary, the employee would use air quotes and emphasize the word "they" with an eye roll. I suggested that my client adopt Loretta J. Ross's concept of calling *in* versus the cancel culture of calling *out*.[3] So, the next time this founder noticed the employee air quoting his colleague's pronouns, instead of calling him out by saying something like, "Why do you have to air quote when you say our colleague's pronouns?," which could lead to shame or humiliation, I suggested the founder set aside time in a one-on-one meeting and say, "I noticed you may be adjusting to using nonbinary pronouns. How can I help you get more comfortable using these terms?" By using this approach, my client created a safe space and assumed positive intent. It turned out, although somewhat performative, the employee explained he was using air quotes to show support. He thought he was signaling to others to use his colleague's personal pronouns. This conversation gave the employee a chance to take a step back and rethink his actions going forward. But even more powerful, it brought the calling-in culture into the foreground and fostered a safe way to mitigate microaggressions and create a more inclusive workplace.

Maintaining an inclusive culture must span beyond the internal operations of your business. Whether one is interacting with job candidates, customers, at conferences, or even in board meetings, upholding the standards is tantamount to embedding this concept into your startup's culture. We can't "inclusion proof" everyone around us—like preventing an investor from routinely making sexually charged comments in board meetings or canceling a contract with the customer who aligns with a political candidate we disagree with—but when it comes to your startup, you can make inclusion a priority, and you and your venture will be better for it.

CULTURE CARRIERS

One of the reasons I believe Akamai was so successful in those early days, and why the company continues to thrive, is because of how seriously they took cultural best practices. They had a holistic approach to hiring that not only prioritized DEIB but also considered how each hire could thrive within the team. Our hiring practices set the tone for the business. My interview panel before I joined was carefully crafted to ensure I didn't just meet with only men or a much younger set of team members. It made me feel I would not be one of the few "older" women in leadership at the time (I was in my early thirties!). My candidate experience also turned me into a culture carrier. I saw how much everyone cared about my experience, and I wanted others to have the same feeling as we scaled.

Culture carriers tend to be your employees who are as passionate about the work experience and their coworkers as they are about the business. These employees actively embody and evangelize the company's values, influencing their colleagues to behave in alignment with those values. At Akamai, there were many culture carriers who fostered inclusivity and belonging. These team members held standards for how we talked with each other and our customers, and how we worked together. In my first few months, one of my favorite culture carriers, Joel Wein, noticed I was struggling to convince some of our senior engineers to adopt our new release process. He sympathetically pulled me aside and suggested I might benefit from asking them to demonstrate how a particular part of our technology worked. By doing so, I could be more empathetic regarding their concerns about the new procedures and likely turn them into allies. As a culture carrier, Joel not only helped me adapt to our culture of leaning in with curiosity but also enabled me to build better relationships with my colleagues. Akamai also had culture budgets for teams to do activities throughout the year that fostered community and personal connections among colleagues. One of my favorites was the annual beach bash I would cohost with the heads of the network and systems operations teams so that our three teams had a chance to bond with each other outside of work. Because the team members played beach volleyball and learned how to crack a lobster tail for the first time together, they were far more collegial in both the day-to-day work and in stressful times. Instead of pointing fingers at each department (*engineering broke this, network operations forgot to do that*) during a crisis, we worked together as a collective team.

At the VMware Cambridge office, our culture carriers organized an annual mini golf tournament. Carefully architected to foster connections, employees were encouraged to partner with colleagues they didn't work with every day to create a golf hole somewhere in the office. We were given the hole location, such as a conference room or the kitchen, a maximum budget, and a few other parameters to ensure safety and fun. On tournament day, everyone dropped what they were doing for a few hours to craft their holes and then play out the course. Not only was this tremendous fun, but the bonds that came from working together and playing each other's holes developed appreciation for everyone's creativity and good humor. Who knew that quiet engineer who coded all day was an incredible crafter with pipe cleaners or that our office manager was a wiz at rigging a circuit board to slide as a cover over a golf hole? What do these examples have to do with core values? One is that they fostered the "work hard, play hard" culture that both companies were committed to maintaining. The other is that the more often we had opportunities to take a moment to have fun and connect on nonwork activities, the better we performed. We loved working with each other, we had shared memories, laughs, and a deep appreciation of our coworkers beyond their actual work. Even when you are at the earliest stages of your startup, despite the piles of work to do and limited hours in the day, do not skip these opportunities. They will ensure everyone in your organization continues to carry the values and culture of the organization as you scale.

HOLD THE BAR

Not compromising on who you hire can be a struggle at a startup when you have limited funds, and top talent may be skeptical about joining your fledgling company. But making a bad hire can cost more in both cash and opportunity if you have to let someone go and start over again. When I was building VMware's new East Coast office in Cambridge, Massachusetts, from scratch, I wasn't just told to hire twenty people, I was told to hire the *best* twenty people I could get. Despite the pedigree of experienced applicants with degrees from MIT and Stanford, which was de rigueur for hiring practices at tech companies in the early 2000s, our founding CEO Diane Greene would not let me bring on new team members until I had hired a minimum of twenty seasoned industry veterans who were also not jerks; the latter being a very subjective and hard thing to test! At the time, it was frustrating to say "no" to so many candidates who looked good on paper, but I learned that our first amazing hires ensured our company's long-term success. This move was the epitome of hiring with a vision for the company that we wanted to be when we grew up. With their expertise, experience, and genuinely good natures, we not only attracted more great talent but also formed a group of leaders and individual contributors (ICs) who set the tone for the whole team. They knew how to mentor junior team members, how to make decisions, and, most importantly, they were great communicators, which is critical for any rapidly growing business. These early team members allowed us to move fast and execute well without lowering the quality bar. Super early startups can benefit from even just one of these team members, even if they are a contractor or advisor.

When I arrived on the scene at DigitalOcean in 2016, I found a culture somewhere between ultra-inclusive and Silicon Valley tech bro meets NYC. Over 50 percent of our workforce worked remotely, and there were many programs to ensure remote workers felt included when we did in-office activities. If we all went to see the new Star Trek film in New York City, we'd encourage remote workers who lived near each other in other cities to go see the film together and send us the bill. On March 14, Pi Day (a classic nerd event for the tech community), we catered a variety of pies into the New York headquarters and sent individual pies to all our remote employees. There was a solid onboarding process for new employees that covered everything from employee benefits to technical overviews of our products, regardless of what role they played in the business. Sammy the Shark was our company mascot, and twice yearly we flew all our remote employees to New York for an all-company Shark Week to bring teams together to learn and connect.

DigitalOcean had grown at light speed in four years. We had around 150 employees, and with a fresh $83 million of cash in the bank from our last fundraise, we were about to double in size. Most of our leadership team had never managed a business this size, and few had ever been team managers. We got some things right, such as our onboarding process and Shark Week, among others, but had to unwind a lot of negative cultural elements that caused strife, such as a wee bit too much partying after hours in the office and a lack of career development programs that resulted in unhealthy leadership practices. Part of the solution for the latter was hiring internal leadership coaches to help develop managers, but there was a lot of work to be done to shift our culture to create a high-performing team.

I oversaw all the engineering, product management, design, and marketing teams (yes, I had marketing too—that's a different topic). More than half of DigitalOcean's employees were in my organization, and more than half of *those* employees had less than five years of experience, with many never having worked in a startup. They were smart, ambitious, good humans that could figure out what to do, but without any prior points of reference, they lacked the necessary seasoning that I had seen at Akamai and VMware that allowed those two companies to move fast and scale. I loved having so many wonderful people on my team, but we just didn't have the time to get them all up to speed when we were desperately trying to break out of the growth plateau the business was facing. So, taking a cue from Diane's mandate to me when I first joined VMware, I decided that in this new wave of hiring we would not bring on anyone with less than eight years of experience, and, ideally, at least half of that experience had to be at a startup that had scaled. I was looking for muscle memory and context that my (albeit amazing) team lacked so we could just *go*.

This mandate was not received favorably by many of the employees on my team who felt I thought they were not good enough. They *were* good, but they just needed colleagues above or next to them that could raise the bar for everyone. I could have done a radical restructuring and rebuilt the team, but we had the runway that allowed us to weave in talent and add leaders, so we went for it. As new hires came on board, it became readily apparent that these talented engineers, product managers, designers, and marketers enhanced the team. I remember one engineering manager coming into my office a few months after the mandate and saying, "You know, I was offended when you told us about the new hiring rule, but now that I am working with these new people, I totally get it. I am learning so much and I am becoming a better leader just by having these role models." That manager has no idea about the huge sigh of relief I let out after he left my office. It was a big risk to take, but one that got us on track toward an organization that could scale beyond our scrappy early years. It was unfortunate that I had to make the team uncomfortable for a time to get back on the rails, and I hope you can avoid it by getting it right earlier on by setting and holding the bar.

YOUR ORGANIZATIONAL STRATEGY

Asking yourself, *What kind of organization do we want to be when we grow up?* helps you gain clarity on the culture you want to create. Once that foundation is set, keep asking the question, and this time, explore it through a hiring lens. Zoom out to imagine where your business will be a year from now. Think of it as the *how* and *who* behind the *what*. This will help you understand the kinds of functions, skills, and experiences you need to bring to the company so employees can help you grow into the organization you're hoping to become. When you hire with that foresight in mind, you're not just hiring the individuals you need right now, you're creating an organizational strategy that will help you build the team that will grow the company.

Let's return to Christina, the founder who was rapidly scaling her business, Cube, in 2022. Christina and I have done a lot of reflection around her team and hiring practices as she scaled her venture. We will use her story as a case example of how to navigate through the key areas of the *who* and *how* of your organization.

When Christina first started her venture with her technical cofounder, there was no real "organization" to speak of, as with most startups. It was the cofounders, a few contractors, and some advisors.

Within six or so months, the business began to get traction, and they went from a few pilot customers to several enterprise deals and raised a seed round of capital. Christina and her cofounder did what many startups do at this stage once their first round of funding comes in; they took a SWAG at what talent they needed (engineers, product managers, marketers), and the business grew organically from there. In their efforts to plow forward, they did not anticipate the magnitude of the challenges they would face when it came to how each of these individuals would work together to achieve company goals (the *what*). I call this the gestalt of an organization. Gestalt describes a configuration of elements (in this case, people) that is so unified that it cannot be described simply as the sum of its parts. When you're building a team, thinking about the gestalt of that team is as important as the individual talents and experiences of the people you hire. It's pausing to assess whether there will be the right chemistry, diversity of thought, and experiences to create a high-performing team. It's zooming out to consider not just the proverbial hammer for a nail ("we need to build software so let's hire some engineers") but also the functional needs of the organization ("how will we operate together to serve our customers and the business?").

Christina's first customers required a high degree of hands-on support to adopt early versions of the product. She and her cofounder were very involved early on to learn what worked and what didn't work for their first customers, but once they began to scale, they handed off most of the sales, support, and product management functions to their new hires. About a year in, Christina recognized that the talented team members brought in to work more closely with customers were struggling. Product managers were not talking to the sales or support teams (I'll cover this topic in depth in Chapter 14), the engineers were not aware of specific customer feedback on the product, and in essence, they were hammers hitting nails and not team members working together to accomplish company goals. Christina put a lot of work into coaching team members, instituting goal-setting processes, and replacing a few employees, but eventually she had to do a difficult restructuring and rebuild the team. An unfortunate, but necessary, do-over. While that was a painful process, her new hires were seasoned and prepared to scale the business, and she was more thoughtful about the gestalt and on how they worked together to achieve greater outcomes as a high-performing team.

It is nearly impossible to predict every type of hire you might need as your business grows, and even with your best efforts, restructuring can be a necessary evil because of strategic or market changes. However, you can minimize these costly and time-consuming activities by thinking about the functional capabilities of the organization. To accomplish this, I developed the white box exercise (WBE). This visioning exercise will allow you to assess your current team against your strategic plan so you can determine your future organization. When you are just starting to build teams, you should do this every few months and then less often as you scale. The WBE is a four-step process:

Step 1: Imagine the business six to twelve months out and outline the goals you hope to achieve and the assumptions behind them, such as a revenue goal that will determine what and how products are being sold, how many customers you may have, and what level of support they'll require.

Step 2: With the vision in mind, **sketch out a functional organizational chart**—without names of existing team members—to get clarity on what the business will need to look like not only to achieve those future goals but also to maintain and grow the business once you reach those goals. For example, today you and a product manager handle customer support, but if a goal in the next year is to double the number of customers as well as expand product offerings, then you may need to build a team of two to three people ready to serve those customers in a year. Or perhaps you are handling all the financial management for your startup today, but you are gearing up to run a time-consuming fundraising process in the next few months. You may have to hire an accountant now to get up to speed quickly so they can cover you when you do that fundraise. The key here is to focus on what functions the business will need in the future, regardless of who is doing it now. These are your white (or empty) boxes.

Step 3: Once you have a sketched out the white boxes, the next step is to **assess your current "bench" of team members and determine which boxes they'll be in down the road**. This is where these folks *will be* and not where they are today. From this step, you will have something like the following result:

- Employees who will be in the same box they're in now
- Employees with growth potential who will rise to a bigger role in six to twelve months (which may assume some amount of training and mentorship to get there)
- Employees stuck on the bench ("benchwarmers") because they are fine today, but their current performance suggests that they'll struggle to operate at even a slightly bigger scale; or perhaps you envision a major pivot where some skills— like a specific type of engineer or salesperson—will no longer be relevant
- Employees who may make lateral moves, such as a marketer who demonstrates strong product skills and takes on a product manager role
- Empty boxes for new roles that no one on your team will be able to perform or for new functions that don't exist today

Step 4: With this semicompleted organizational chart and some benchwarmers, the hardest next step is to *develop an action plan* by answering the following questions:

- **Which lateral movers or benchwarmers are you invested in keeping, even if they can't continue to grow, and where will they be in the organization in the next six to twelve months even if it means accepting that they might underperform?** These could be folks who are your culture carriers or add value through their network/credibility in your domain areas. You'll either leave them where they are for now or, for those moving laterally from one role to another, you may start to discuss with them the possibility of a transition and whether they are open to such a move.

- **For those with the potential to grow, what do you need to do to invest in their success?** Before preparing to promote anyone into one of those empty boxes, even when you see their potential, do not put employees in leadership positions who should not or don't want to be there! A great engineer often does not make a great engineering manager, nor does a great sales rep make a great head of sales—even if this is their career goal. It's critical to focus on what your venture needs and what you can support in terms of employee growth. This is not to say that you should not create space for growth in your organization, but rather to be thoughtful about that growth. If there is someone without management experience who wants to be a manager, and you or someone on your team (or an advisor) has time to mentor them, it may well be worth it to earmark that individual for a management role. However, you are doing a disservice to an employee if you anoint them into a leadership or more senior role in the spirit of offering growth opportunities or to retain talent and they are not able to perform that role with or without support. This can lead to the classic case of the system failing the person, not the person failing the system, which I'll go deeper on in Chapter 9.

Note: It is as important to design career ladders for individual contributors (ICs) as it is for leaders. Do this for *all* parts of the organization. A principal content marketer or even a principal accountant role allows someone to develop into a domain expert and mentor with the appropriate title and compensation without having to manage people.

How do you want to fill the empty boxes? Assuming you have the salary and equity budgets each role may require, consider the lead time necessary to fill these positions. Some of these functions may be better served by contractors until the company scales more and you have a better sense of what you'll really need before committing to a full-time hire. If it will be a full-time hire, assume you and/or your team will spend a lot of time finding the right people, interviewing, selling candidates on the opportunity, negotiating offers, and getting them on board. When deciding when to start the process for these hires, work backward from an ideal *readiness* date. For example, if you foresee you'll need a leader of a team in six months who is fully onboarded without your day-to-day involvement, and it will likely take two months to find the right candidate, another month to get them on board, and another two months before they are operating independently, then you have a few weeks before you need to start writing that job description!

- **Finally, what size do we want the organization, and each team, to be?** The size of a company can be wholly dependent on how much money you have, but you should also consider how much pain your organization can withstand as you grow. A team and how many direct reports a manager has (including the CEO and founders) can impact productivity in many ways. And teams that grow too fast or continuously add new people over long stretches of time can get stuck in the "storming" phase of team development, which I'll discuss more in Chapter 17.[4] Each team requires its own sizing approach depending on the type of team, manager, and employees.

Ask any first-time founder and they'll tell you culture building and hiring consume more of their time than they ever expected—especially if you aim to foster an inclusive culture and keep the bar high! Performing the white box exercise will not only provide a tactical plan toward growth in human capital, it can also foster alignment around strategic plans and operating KPIs. This alignment will only further improve your chances of reaching your goals for your venture.

8.

HIRING BEST PRACTICES

Once you have a good sense of the type of culture you want to build and your organizational strategy, it's time for tactical execution. This is the nitty-gritty of hiring: writing job descriptions, sourcing candidates, managing the candidate experience, negotiating offers, onboarding, and talent management. Hiring is one of the most important and time-consuming aspects of startup life. It can be especially difficult in the early stages of a startup when (A) you and your team may have never had the experience of hiring people and (B) you are not sure what you need for your venture—or both! The reality is that it usually takes a lot of reps before we develop strong hiring muscles. I've hired hundreds of employees throughout my career and definitely made my share of mistakes. From the perfectly qualified kernel engineer who was a luminary in the developer community but had no regard for authority and actually went MIA (we had to call his parents to see if he was still alive—he was, but just decided he didn't want to work "at the moment"), to the marketer who claimed to have deep

121

marketing expertise but could not develop a brand strategy if their life depended on it. After these experiences, I not only improved my instincts around assessing what I needed and who could do it, but also became more comfortable with firing—most people's least favorite, but important, skill to develop as a leader.

Talent management topics fill the pages of countless books, but there are particular aspects of these practices that can be most challenging in the early stages of a startup. In this chapter, I cover just the areas where I see founders and their teams struggle most often when it comes to hiring and talent development.

HIRING BASICS

Once you know what roles you want to fill and when, write a basic job description (JD) for each position. This gives you a tangible way to market the roles and also serves as a communication tool with your team to be clear on the expectations for the role, especially if they are new to hiring and helping with the interview process. Even if you are at the very start of the life of your company, this is also a good time to consider how you may hire at different levels—like a junior vs. senior engineer or manager vs. director roles—and the compensation you would offer for these different levels. Having an early sense of how the salary and equity would be for different roles will save you a lot of time when it comes to making an offer and prevent headaches later when you begin to scale. Startups who skip this thought process in the spirit of moving fast and getting talent on board as soon as possible often end up with major disparities across their teams, from wildly different compensation for the same roles to inflated titles that are not commensurate with experience or responsibilities. The recalibration exercise to fix these disparities later is time-consuming and can impact your company culture, so do your best to stay ahead of this.

AI tools can give you a good first draft of a JD, but making the JD unique to your startup will attract the best candidates. Remember, some joiners are skeptical about early-stage startups, so they will be extra sensitive to a poorly written or less compelling JD. Here are some basic tips on writing a good JD when it comes to startups:

- **Be clear about the stage of your venture and what's not figured out yet.** Saying you need someone who can develop your first content strategy will garner a different candidate than one who is looking to run with a content strategy already in place.
- **Be clear if you are looking for self-starters who are comfortable with ambiguity.** For example, "Self-starter open to taking risks but comfortable asking for help when needed" suggests you want someone who can work independently but who has humility and isn't afraid to say "I don't know."
- **Don't be overly prescriptive** about the way a role should be done, which can scare away experienced hires. If they are talented in their areas of expertise, they know how to execute. For example, instead of "Use XYZ tool to create a work plan for our marketing and sales teams," say, "Set up our marketing and sales team for success in achieving our revenue goals."
- **Highlight the potential and traction to date of the venture.** Create excitement about helping the business get off the ground and the equity value that comes with it. This is especially important if you are trying to attract more experienced hires who want to be sure your venture is worth taking the risk (and likely a lower salary) to join.

SOURCING CANDIDATES

Sourcing candidates goes well beyond just posting the JD on your website, but you should make sure you have a "jobs" or "careers" page and make it *great*. Candidates who go to that page should get excited about what you are doing and feel, "I want to work with those people!" Consider the best way to present your team that truly represents your company values and culture; it's important to emphasize that a candidate will be *additive* to your culture and not just a fit. Beyond your company website, post on other sites that are related to your industry. Consider industry associations, affinity or user group sites that have jobs channels. Alumni networks, certification programs, and accelerators may also have job posting platforms.

Posting the JD everywhere is table stakes when it comes to recruiting, but the best hires will likely come from people you know, and this includes your current employees, advisors, and your investors if you have them. Remind everyone at your company that they are on the hook to always be looking for talent, and be sure everyone on the team knows what roles you are hoping to fill. You never know where or when you might meet someone who could be a good fit for a role.

Because most startups have limited funds early on, you may question whether you should use outsourced or in-house recruiters or headhunters. If you think you're going to have a regular cadence of hires over the next one to two years or more, hire a permanent recruiter who can manage the entire lifecycle—from helping with job descriptions to sourcing, managing the interview process, and onboarding your new hire. Someone who's in-house will understand your product, your culture, and the kinds of people you hire. They will save you lots of time and energy when it comes to finding and hiring the best candidates. When David Cancel and Elias Torres started Drift, even without a product built yet, one of their first three hires was a full-time recruiter. As serial entrepreneurs with fresh capital, that was a no-brainer for them, but their underlying reason for prioritizing a recruiter was that they'd wasted years of time and effort by not having this valuable resource early in the lives of their prior ventures.

Outsourced recruiters or headhunters are great for targeted, high-ranking positions like a head of sales or a vice president of engineering, or in competitive times when you have a critical hire you just can't delay bringing on board. Don't waste your precious time combing your network for these people unless you find someone right away. That's what headhunters are good at. Have them work on a fee-for-placement (or "contingency") contract versus a retainer up front. The best headhunters will be happy to work this way. Whether in-house or outsourced—seasoned recruiters are great at finding and converting passive candidates. These are candidates who are not currently looking for their next role but may be convinced to leave for the right opportunity.

Finally, just like the adage "always be selling," every successful founder will tell you "always be recruiting!" even when you are not technically trying to fill a role. My rule of thumb is to be on the lookout for talent that I might need as far out as six months. I once got an email at DigitalOcean from an engineering leader who had worked for me at VMware about a candidate, Patrick Nguyen, that he couldn't hire because of budget constraints at his new company. He had worked with Patrick before and raved about his technical and leadership skills. I didn't have an immediate position open for Patrick, but when you get a referral like this, you must ask yourself, "Will I regret not having this person on my team in the next six months?" If the answer is yes, and you have the budget to make it work, do it. They may be underutilized a bit in the first few months, but it'll be worth it when your startup gets to a point where you already have them on board and you're not spending time hiring and getting someone new up to speed. I hired Patrick as a "jack-of-all-trades" to do a bunch of random things for me around developer tools and quality assurance (QA). He eventually became a VP and general manager of an entire business unit and is now the founder of his own startup. One of the best hires I ever made!

BEFORE THE INTERVIEW

Regardless of how you get their information, here is what to look for when evaluating candidates for startups. If you are an aspiring joiner, this will help you put your best foot forward as well.

- A **summary paragraph** either in the form of their cover letter or email introduction should help you understand a candidate's brand and what they are looking for in their next role at a startup.

- A **track record** in startups is important, but it's not unusual to see someone one to two years in one place and then another. Look out for "jumpers" who have worked less than one year in a few places. This suggests they either can't fit in or they have made a lot of bad judgment calls on the start-ups they've joined. One or two jumps among longer stints are okay though. Especially if it's someone who had a long track record somewhere else and is now trying to find their next long-term home.

- Look for **what someone has accomplished** to help a startup scale and succeed rather than their responsibilities—ideally with metrics. Examples could be building a startup's first engineering team and releasing an MVP in six months or creating a startup's first sales playbook and increasing monthly recurring revenue (MRR) by X percent.

- **Seeing education at the top of a resume can be a flag.** What someone has actually done is more important than where they've been educated or their GPA. Anyone with no work experience is suspect for a startup. Even summers as a camp counselor (I am a big fan of those folks—camp people are fun, extremely hard workers, and know how to GSD!) or waiting tables can demonstrate they can handle the startup life. Education at the end of the resume is a nice "cherry on top." They are experienced *and* educated.

- Finally, **googling a candidate for anything "suspect" never hurts.** If you have the budget, hire a service to do back-ground checks. But, a good check can be just looking to see if you can find arrest records or other behaviors that may not gel with your company culture. However, not every bad find on a web search is a flag not to hire. Some people who drank too much in college have gone on to have wonderfully successful professional lives. 😊

THE CANDIDATE EXPERIENCE

Keeping the candidate's experience in mind is especially important when you are still figuring out what you are looking for in a new role. You can have an idea of the perfect first product manager for your startup, but it may not be until you meet a few different candidates that the definition of "perfect" becomes clear and may even require you to rewrite the JD. Candidates can usually sense this uncertainty, and it can be off-putting if not clarified up front. So, setting expectations when starting the process is key. "Tell the first couple candidates that you are excited that they are at the start of your search and that it will probably be a few weeks before all candidates complete the interview process," says my dear friend and longtime startup talent leader, Loren Boyce. "They might be fine with that time frame, but it will also let you know where you stand with them if they can't wait too long because they are weighing your opportunity with others." But even if they are weighing other options and seem too good to be true, don't rush the process. Fear of missing out on a good candidate can drive you to push through without a proper vetting process. This could result in a mis-hire, and the process to remove them and start over can be a huge waste of time. Very few job candidates are unicorns, so as much as it might pain you up front to possibly miss out, stick to a process.

Being clear that you are early in the process can also be exciting and an invitation to candidates to help you figure out the role. Helping to define my role was one of the things that attracted me to Akamai when I interviewed for a project-managerish position (that's how it was described to me) that led to me becoming their first release manager. This was similar to when I hired my jack-of-all-trades, Patrick, at DigitalOcean. The transparency and collaboration led to a better outcome for all involved!

There are many good resources available for best practices for interviews, so with the above in mind, here are specific pointers when following customary processes for interviews at a startup:

- An AI tool can help formulate basic interview questions, but be sure to add some that are unique to your business or industry.
- Be organized! It can be hard to run an organized process if you don't have an in-house recruiter and your startup is moving a zillion miles an hour. Do your best to line up the right people to interview the candidate and be clear to each of the interviewers on what their role is for the interview. All interviewers should see the JD and candidate resumes at least a day before the interview.
- It is not uncommon at startups to have less-experienced interviewers. So, make sure anyone talking with candidates knows the basics around what they can and can't share about your company strategy, financials, etc., and make sure they are clear that if they don't know the answer to a prospect's question, that they or someone else will get back to them. Don't make stuff up that could trip you up later, and make sure everyone who interviews candidates knows what's illegal to ask, such as personal questions about their families, lifestyle, etc.
- If you are operating in stealth and/or are worried about protecting your intellectual property, have candidates sign an NDA before interviews start so you can share more with them about the role and what you're building.
- Only the recruiter and/or hiring manager should inquire about compensation requirements, including equity.

BEYOND THE INTERVIEW

While you can't prevent occasional mis-hires, you can try to minimize the possibility by including a project phase in your hiring process or even considering a project as a paid consulting engagement ("try before you buy") for both you and the candidate. This allows the candidate to demonstrate what they are capable of and what it might be like to work with them—and them with you—once they are on board full time. Projects can give you a higher degree of confidence that this is "the one," which can be super hard in the early stages of your startup when you are not sure what "the one" even is. If this is not a try-before-you-buy situation, I recommend that projects are performed just before you are ready to do reference checks and make an offer. This can be an especially helpful step if you are down to two finalists you really like so you can compare how each one approaches a project.

Unless you plan to do a trial engagement with them, try not to choose a project that takes more than one to two hours to do unless you pay them for the work. A startup I've worked with offers to pay for the time taken to do a project, and if the candidate declines payment, the startup makes a donation to a charity of the candidate's choice as compensation for their time.

Below are some projects that can be effective at startups. Keep in mind that these projects test the candidate's approach more than whether they do the work perfectly. Build alignment with your team on what good looks like for each project and plan to debrief once the assignment is complete and/or presented. Here are a few examples of what good might look like.

"The First 90 Days"

This is a good general test for any new hire, especially an executive, but also for a people manager or technical leader. Have the candidate explain what their first ninety days on the job will look like. Either leave it wide open or offer a few prompts like, "Who will you spend time with?" or "How will you get to know the business?" or "What accomplishments do you hope to make by the end of the first ninety days?"

Engineering and Design Projects

While there are some nifty tools out there that can test coding skills for engineers, I am a strong advocate for testing the softer skills. Those who design and/or build your product should be able to demonstrate their work beyond coding or portfolio samples. The best type of project here is a brief scenario about building a new feature or capability for your product that will allow the candidate to demonstrate not just depth of syntax knowledge or design best practices, but also how they will work on a problem with your team. These projects can be done as "homework," although it's nice if it can be done in person or as part of a video interview. Present a scenario and ask the candidate how they will approach it. You could give them some alone time to think about it and then ask them to talk through it. Ask them to cite how they thought about it and to explain the direction they took and why. Prepare to have another approach or idea for the scenario when they walk through their work. This can help gauge how the candidate handles feedback and if they are willing to collaborate on ideas.

Scenarios for Non-Engineering Teams
(Marketing, Sales, Product)

I prefer scenario tests over presentations of a non-engineering candidate's past work because such tests will show you how they use their experience to approach something new. Scenarios you may ask them to work through can be actual challenges you are facing, or they can be hypothetical. Here are some quick examples of scenario tests for a few functional areas:

- **Product:** Our CTO just came back from a "listening tour" with some of our customers and wants to explore a new set of features to expand our product offerings. These offerings are not on the product roadmap. What steps would you take to understand these new features and how would you approach the prioritization process?

- **Marketing:** We're about to launch a new product for our customers. What steps would you take to plan for this product launch and how will you measure its success?
- **Sales:** We are building a product to attract new customers in a new segment. What information do you need to prepare your team to sell this new product and how will you set sales goals for the team?

You could imagine similar scenarios for finance, customer support, or other functional roles. Remember, these candidates don't know how your business functions day-to-day, so this isn't about whether they have a perfect plan but more about how they approach the problem.

With all the interviews and projects, you still may not get it right every time. Again, hiring is *hard*. That's why the try-before-you-buy approach is often the best way to go for both the candidate and your startup. One way to ease that process, if a trial candidate can work full time before converting to a permanent employee, is to offer them equity in your startup that will be granted when they convert, but with a backdated vesting schedule to when they started their trial.

If you're hiring for a role for the first time and no one on your team has experience with that role—so no one knows what good looks like—ask an experienced advisor, investor, or friend with experience to be part of the interview process. They should be able to interview the candidate and help you formulate the projects you may assign.

TO HIRE OR NOT TO HIRE

You can be desperate to bring someone on board, but terrified that you're making a bad decision when you are in the early stages of building your startup. It can feel like choosing a nanny for your first-born or a caretaker for your puppy. And if you've already made a few hiring mistakes, you may be paralyzed with fear about repeating those mistakes. One founder I worked with had been burned so many times by bad hiring decisions that he'd come up with the most bizarre reasons *not* to hire someone, like he didn't like the color shirt they wore or that they didn't use Oxford commas in the thank-you note he received. Ultimately, though, you are never going to scale your startup if you put off hiring to aim for perfection, so how do you decide when it's time to make an offer or pass?

For very small startups, you may decide to build consensus with your team before making a call. The first twenty or so hires will work closely with everyone, so there can be a tendency toward consensus building to respect the team and set up a new hire for success. If you go the consensus route, be careful about giving team members too much room to be neutral on candidates—which can leave you guessing on whether a candidate is a fit. For her first fifteen or so hires, Christie Horvath, the founder and CEO of Wagmo, a pet insurance company, used the "I will quit" bar to decide on candidates. Each early team member said they will quit if someone *is* or *is not* hired. That's it, no maybes, even if it took longer than desired to get a great candidate. This was a very effective way for Christy to make the best early hires for her team.

Ultimately though, any hire is the manager's call. At Digital-Ocean, I was hiring a new head of product. My six product managers (PMs)—who were temporarily reporting to me—had struggled with prior leaders and rejected every candidate I brought in. Most of them had no experience working with a great product leader, but I did, so I found a candidate I just had to hire. Empathetic to the team, I asked this candidate to spend a day with them as his interview project. I asked each PM to bring an issue to the candidate as though they were bringing it to their actual boss. By the end of the day, most of the

PMs figured out this candidate was great. While I didn't just force this leader on them, I also didn't try to build a consensus either and accepted that a couple of the PMs were still not 100 percent on board with my choice. I made a call I knew was good for them and the venture, we brought the candidate on board, and they thrived as a team.

For a great candidate experience—whether you decide to hire them or not—a fast turnaround is important! Do not leave a candidate hanging, and inform any candidates you're passing on as soon as you can. If you're passing, just say they are not a match for the role and move on. If an offer is coming, ask for references and be specific on when they should expect to see an offer. Also, don't be shy about getting a few backdoor references in addition to the references your candidate provides; the latter will likely have good things to say no matter what. Try to find someone in your network who knows the candidate or who can introduce you to someone who does so you can get a more objective perspective on the candidate.

MAKING THE OFFER AND CLOSING THE DEAL

Making the right offer for a startup hire can be tricky. Most startups offer compensation that includes salaries and equity and often provide the option to go lower on one in exchange for higher on the other. If a candidate is new to startup land, they may need some educating on how equity and vesting schedules work. Some candidates will care more about salary because they have a mortgage or college tuitions to pay for and even if they value equity, must ask for less in exchange for a bigger paycheck. No two candidates are the same, so before you dig into each candidate's needs, decide what kind of company you will be in terms of compensation. As noted in Hiring Basics on page 122, there is no right or wrong way to do this; what's important is ensuring there is alignment about compensation among the founding team and/or early investors. Considerations should include:

- Is equity something you want your employees to value more than salary? How much equity will you put aside to refresh grants/hire future team members?
- Are you willing/able to pay market rates for a couple of key hires? If you can't, can you set expectations that you will adjust salaries upon future fundraising rounds and/or revenue growth?
- What will the vesting schedule look like (usually, four years with a one-year cliff before they start vesting monthly) and what will your options exercise window be?
- Will it be a take-it-or-leave-it offer, or will you build in some room to negotiate salary/equity depending on the candidate's needs?
- Will you offer benefits like health care, 401(k), or maybe pay for remote-office equipment? Not all startups can afford these perks, but if you can, it may make a difference for some candidates considering your offer.

Finally, the earlier the startup, the more some candidates try to negotiate title as part of their deal. Practically speaking, this behavior will give you further insight into what makes this potential employee tick. A good negotiator can be a great salesperson! But it also can be a tell if a candidate seems to care more about title than salary and equity. Or, they try to negotiate title to get themselves more salary and equity. It can be tempting to say yes to these types of negotiations, especially if it's an experienced hire who you really like. A founder of a small software startup came to me for advice about an excellent candidate she extended an offer to who was pushing back hard on the title. "She's been a VP for nine years and this is a director title. I honestly don't care except we don't have any VPs here now. Our head of sales was also a VP at his last job, but happily took the director title." She was debating both whether this candidate was VP level at *her* company and how bringing her in at that level would impact her head of sales. In the end, she gave this hire a VP title because it was an optics issue for the customers she would be working with. Lucky for the founder, the head of sales was fine with this and saw it as a growth opportunity for him to earn a VP title.

I've also seen bad endings though, such as when a head of sales at one startup insisted that he would only leave his current position to join a new startup if he was given a COO title. The founder, desperate to get a strong head of sales in, caved and ended up with an overtitled employee with far too much equity who never grew into the COO role as the venture scaled. It is much easier to promote someone and give them more equity than it is to demote someone and claw it back or fire them. When you run into title negotiations, the best approach is to focus on equity value and the possibility of growth into a more esteemed title (with additional responsibilities) if the startup does well. I left Akamai as the VP of all of engineering but joined VMware as a senior director of one engineering division because the senior director–level employees had experience and responsibilities equal to mine. Regardless, I cared more about who I'd be working with and the opportunity to build a whole new engineering site from scratch. I also believed in the value of my equity (it ended up paying for all three of my girls' college tuitions and then some!) more than my title. And I was promoted to a VP level a few years later.

Negotiating compensation and titles should not drag on forever—especially if you know the candidate has other offers on the table—as this can be a way for them to negotiate other deals, wasting your time when you could be going after another candidate. Set a timer for the offer process with a clear expiration date. A week is more than enough time to decide. If they can't decide within that time frame, they may not be that excited about the job and you may have dodged a mis-hire!

ONBOARDING

Your candidate has accepted the offer! Hurray! Do the standard new-hire stuff like getting their benefits, email, and other tools the company uses squared away. After all the basics are out of the way, co-create a 30-60-90 day plan with your new hire to ensure they have time to get up to speed on the venture. The first thirty days may be focused on getting up to speed on the business and the team; by sixty days, they are starting to make contributions; and within ninety days a new hire should be fully on board and accountable for their required role. Remember, startups are moving so fast through the chaos that a new hire may get lost in the shuffle without this type of structure early on. So, have a great onboarding process for your joiners!

You may spend as much time learning how to get hiring right as you do executing on the rest of the business. Just learning how to run a startup itself can be hard enough without adding a bunch of strangers into the mix to figure out how to do it with you. That said, when you get hiring right, it can mean the difference between a massive success and an all-out failure. Because, at the end of the day, great people are the foundation of any great company.

9.

SEPARATION

As thoughtful and diligent as you may be during the hiring process, the reality is, many first hires do not work out. Whether it's because of poor performance, a bad fit, or just because the startup has outgrown someone, letting someone go can be painful—especially if it's your first time doing it. This chapter walks you through best practices for separation to help everyone part ways with their dignity intact. But the first, most important step is to make sure you're clear about *why* the hire didn't work out. Without this understanding, you're likely to repeat some fixable mistakes—and you'll wonder, again and again, why you can't seem to assemble a team that just *gets it*. Beyond the general challenges of learning how to manage people for the first time, the biggest, and often overlooked, reasons early hires don't work out in a startup are:

Inexperienced hiring teams: Many founders, and often early joiners, are first-time managers who don't have the network and instincts to find and bring on the best talent. They also haven't developed the pattern-matching skills that come

from lots of hiring and firing to distinguish a great candidate from an average one or to quickly catch flags that
may not seem obvious to a new manager. It took dozens
of hires and fires for me before I could properly assess a
candidate. Hiring is a muscle that needs lots of repetition
before you are strong at this skill. Weakness in this area can
result in poor hires for reasons ranging from incompetence
to role or cultural mismatches. A common role mismatch
can be an engineer who claims they can code but hasn't
coded in years and never jumps into the "player coach" role
(both coding and managing engineers) that you hoped they
would play before you scaled enough for them to be purely
a manager. Cultural mismatches are usually when someone
struggles to adjust to startup life, such as lacking flexibility
when business priorities change or not being able to handle ambiguity. Tapping into advisors, investors, and friends
with more hiring experience can help you vet candidates to
mitigate these hiring mistakes, but you still may not get it
right until you've had a few more times at bat.

Not knowing what you need: There's a difference between
knowing you need engineers or marketing help and knowing *what kind* of engineering or marketing help. A great
coder may not be able to work independently without a lot
of oversight. A marketer may be great at planning a social
media campaign, but not know how to write excellent content. Sometimes, it takes bringing someone on board and
then experimenting to identify the talent/skills you really
need and what their strengths are. A best practice here is
to set this expectation up front with first hires. I am talking
about actually saying, "I think your skills and experience are
what we need, but honestly, until we start to work together
and as the business evolves, that could change." Scary as that
may sound, it is a healthy way to manage what could be a

tricky situation if you realize you've made a bad hire—not because they are bad or incompetent people, but because you just didn't know until you knew! This is another good reason to take a try-before-you-buy approach if it's possible.

Scaling challenges: Even when you get the right candidate and it's a good match early on, sometimes people just can't scale with the business. This isn't always years later. For some ventures, a great hire at a four-person company can last a good six to twelve months, but even with a little growth they can become a bad fit. One of my client's first engineers was once so threatened by the two new engineers they had hired in their second year that the engineer started to control the whole code base. No one could check anything in unless that engineer had approved each line of code. This not only bottlenecked the whole product process, but it created a toxic culture, and the newly hired engineers were ready to quit within weeks of their start dates. As much as the founders loved this first hire and valued their work, they did not anticipate this challenge and knew they were not going to be able to scale with this situation at hand. Fortunately, through a hard conversation, my clients were able to get the first engineer to be more of a team player, but it doesn't always work out that way.

Every startup will run into at least one of these scenarios. It's just part of growing as a company and learning how to manage people. However, it is not uncommon for first-time founders to either ignore (denial) the mess or just keep churning through employees without stopping to examine whether there's a bigger issue at play. There will always be reasons to let people go, but if that's happening a lot, it's important to pause and take a broader view of the situation so you can overcome your blind spots. Chronic performance issues that are unaddressed can cause morale and cultural issues that can be hard to unwind, and chronic firing of team members can create a lot of psychological safety issues, which inevitably *causes* performance issues! I'll touch more on psychological safety in Chapter 15. Meanwhile, let's delve into how to handle performance issues and separations.

IS THE PERSON FAILING THE SYSTEM, OR IS THE SYSTEM FAILING THE PERSON?

Ahead of giving someone performance feedback that may lead to letting them go, there is usually a suspicion building in your head that they are not working out. You may also be hearing grumblings from other team members, customers, or investors, and signs are pointing toward a need for separation. Before you decide to separate, and doing so carefully to avoid legal issues, I advise you first do a gut check to ensure the person is indeed failing versus the system failing the person. Questions to ask yourself and/or their manager:

- **Did you set this person up for success?** Did they have the right information, tools, and connections to team members and customers to meet expectations? For example, if you hired someone to launch a new marketing campaign, but you have not had time to sit with the new marketing person to walk them through your vision for the business, is it any wonder that they are struggling to get the messaging right? There's also a classic example of an unproductive engineer who is waiting for a new product manager to come on board to specify what needs to be built. They are doing the best they can to guess priorities, but are they actually failing? My executive coach when I was at DigitalOcean was Jerry Colonna. One of his famous quotes is: "How am I complicit in creating the conditions I say I don't want?" This question urges us to take a step back to be sure we are not creating the conditions, in this case, that may be causing an employee's poor performance. Before giving feedback to a team member, putting an individual on a performance improvement plan, or firing someone, ask yourself if you are either partially or completely complicit in creating the problem (this works in our personal lives too!). A 30-60-90 day plan as discussed in Chapter 8 can help mitigate this type of situation for a new hire, but systems can fail a person later in their journey, which I'll cover more in Part IV.

- **Are you being clear about what "done" looks like?** World-renowned author, speaker, and professor Brené Brown's term "painting done"[1] means to be completely clear about the "expectations of what the completed task will look like, including when it will be done, what you'll do with the information, how it will be used, the context, the consequences of not doing it, the costs—everything you can think of to paint a shared picture of the expectations." If we do not paint done, it's likely people won't meet our expectations. Recall Christina's situation in Chapter 6 when her teams started to struggle as the venture scaled. One of the symptoms that arose during this time was a mismatch of product features being released with what Christina believed her customers needed. As she dug into a particularly hairy issue that was going to cause a complete overhaul of a feature, she realized that she, as a domain expert and someone who spoke with customers all the time, was unclear about an aspect of the feature. She hadn't painted done. This is extremely common with founders who are moving so fast that they forget that no one knows exactly what they are thinking. This causes impatience and frustration on their part when employees are just doing the best they can with the information they are given. And sometimes, even if you think you are the nicest and most approachable founder ever, employees can be intimidated by the founder/CEO hat you wear.

They may fear embarrassment (or worse) if they ask clarifying questions. If you think you're not being clear or may be unintentionally intimidating your team, adopt the painting done concept and invite them to ask questions and get clarity. A simple "Do you have any clarifying questions?" at the end of a discussion will not only make you more approachable but will also create a more inclusive culture where the team can be curious and feel safer and more grounded when they need to ask for help. If the founder/CEO paints done and is open to clarifying questions, this approach will likely permeate across the organization.

LOVE MY BABY

I've witnessed a lot of frustrated employees quit or be fired because they didn't love the startup baby enough. In other words, founders felt that their employees didn't show the same level of passion or dedication to their startup as they did. You may expect a strong work ethic and atypical, sometimes extreme, hours to get a new product out the door or to close an important sales deal. It's not just about work ethic, though. It's about a feeling that your team has truly bought in and is as passionate as you are about the company and what you are building. Not every employee will exude this passion in the same way as you. There can be lots of hand-wringing when an employee doesn't respond fast enough to a message or isn't willing to defer a vacation to meet a deadline—things many founders will do (I know several who put off their weddings, honeymoons, and starting families for years until their businesses were stable enough or failed). When you don't see this level of dedication you may decide these employees are not a fit for your startup. Be careful about making this a reason to let someone go. There's a difference between employees putting in more than the standard forty-hour week at your startup, but still taking a break on weekends, and truly not caring about the business. Be sure you are measuring their actual performance, such as meeting deadlines, achieving KPIs, and delivering great results. Because it's likely, even with the most hardworking, dedicated people on the team, no one will love your baby as much as you!

BETTER THAN NOTHING

Founders struggling with poor performers often say things like, "I'd rather have an employee who's good enough for now than go through the hassle of performance management or firing them and taking the time to find their replacement and get someone new up to speed." And this may in fact be okay. What's important in these cases is to have a plan that will mitigate this issue in the longer term.

It could be that a poor performer is a single point of failure (SPOF) who has the only knowledge of a particular part of the business (such as your code base or customer support tool). Your plan could be to keep them until you can hire one or two new people after a fundraise process who will assume this employee's role. Once these new hires are on board and up to speed, you can let the poor-performing SPOF go. Or, perhaps you have someone who is a culture carrier and adds value to the business in other ways, such that their mediocre performance is okay for the sake of the team's morale. Unless you are running out of working capital, an employee or two like this will not drag down the whole business in the near term, and maybe, as you scale, more experienced hires will come on board who can manage them and improve their performance. Just be honest with yourself if this is the situation, and commit to a plan that you feel you can accomplish. As with any poor performer, you'll likely have to deal with it at some point, so don't put it off forever.

WHEN THE WRITING'S ON THE WALL

There are some employees who just need to be fired for cause (legal, ethical, or other serious issues). If so, do it and get it over with. No time to waste, and while it can be painful, it's part of the job. More commonly, though, startups let go of people because of the reasons noted at the start of this chapter. Then, there are those who, no matter how much you want to improve your leadership skills and the systems to support them, you may have to give up on because you just don't have that time. I have had several employees who, had we had the time to invest in their growth, probably would have thrived in our company, but alas, we had to let them go. I've also had my share of "regrettable resignations"—employees who, had we taken a beat and realized we were not serving them well, we may not have lost to another company. There is no perfect solution here other than to work at it when you can and cut your losses when you can't.

My good friend Kim Scott is a leading expert in performance feedback, bestselling author, and cofounder and CEO of Radical Candor, LLC, a company that promotes uncompromising honesty in the workplace to improve communication. She suggests that when firing an employee, it's crucial to be direct and provide clear, specific feedback about their performance issues, even if it's difficult, rather than avoiding confrontation or being overly nice. This approach aligns with her philosophy of balancing caring personally with challenging people directly and avoids what she terms "ruinous empathy": not giving necessary feedback for fear of hurting people's feelings, which can ultimately be detrimental to the individual's career development.

Regardless of whether you're cutting your losses or you just have a classic firing-for-cause situation, have a standard approach to letting people go and seek counsel from an HR person and a lawyer to be sure you follow legal guidelines when it comes to offering severance and how you want to handle equity and vesting schedules for the people you let go. Employees who have been with you for under a year will likely not be vested in stock options. This is always negotiable, but you are not obligated to give them any equity.

Companies big and small may ask departing employees to sign separation agreements waiving rights and claims and to protect the venture's intellectual property and other matters. Severance may be offered in exchange for signing these agreements, even if an employee leaves amicably. However, in February 2023, the National Labor Relations Board (NLRB) ruled that employers cannot offer severance agreements in exchange for employees signing these agreements because these provisions violate employees' whistleblower rights. You can't demand silence for severance. However, the decision does not apply to agreements for people in supervisory roles.

Letting people go at a startup can create bigger waves among remaining staff than it might at a mature company. Not only will your employees be concerned about potential added workload, but they may worry about whether the company is okay or if this is the start of more people being let go. You should never share the details of why someone was let go; that is between you and the employee, and it preserves their reputation by treating them with dignity and respect. You should let your team know if someone is no longer with the startup and, if applicable, how their work will be distributed. If employees ask why someone was let go, you can simply say, "They know why they are no longer here" and leave it at that. It is appropriate to check in with your team to see how they are doing after someone has been fired. You may be surprised how much the team will appreciate this. After letting a poor performer go, a founder told me, "I was so worried the team would think I was too harsh on that employee, but instead they said that they really respected me for making such a hard decision and that they knew I cared about keeping the bar high." He later reported that this event raised the bar for everyone on the team. "They worked harder than ever, both because we all cared so much about what we were doing and because they knew I wasn't afraid to make a hard call."

PART II

PEOPLE TOOLBOX

The Cofounder Courtship

- Apply these three lenses when evaluating whether you need a cofounder: partnership, expertise, and experience.
- If you decide to court a cofounder, don't rush. Follow a cofounder courtship process.

Establishing a Kick-Ass Organization from Day One

- A strong company culture starts with establishing core values.
- Don't just write your core values, live them.
- Hire and nurture culture carriers—employees who are as passionate about the work experience and their coworkers as they are about the business.
- Hold the bar high on talent—when the bar is high, the culture is strong and performance will be high.
- Create your organizational strategy by following the white box exercise (WBE) to assess your current team against your strategic plan.

Hiring Best Practices

- Once you know what roles you want to fill and when, write a basic job description for each position.
- The best hires will likely come from people you know. Remind everyone at your company that they should always be looking for talent.
- Always be recruiting, even when you are not immediately trying to fill a role.
- Consider "try before you buy" before committing to hiring/joining a startup.

- When putting together a job offer, consider how you want factors like equity, salary, title, vesting schedule, room for negotiation, and benefits to fit within the big picture.
- When onboarding, co-create a 30-60-90 day plan with your new hire.

Separation
- Before letting someone go, consider:
  - o why they didn't work out so you don't repeat mistakes. Reasons often include inexperienced hiring teams, not knowing what you need, and scaling challenges.
  - o whether the person is failing the system, or the system is failing the person.
- If you do need to let someone go, be sure to have a standard approach in place and seek counsel from an HR person and a lawyer.

Part III

OPERATIONS

You can have the best idea that solves a problem many people have and perfect market timing, but without the right team and administrative processes, your business may be doomed to fail. The explosion of AI-enabled applications for administrative use cases is certainly helping startups and offering some relief to overhead costs. "With AI, I am doing the work of twenty people with a team of five," said a serial entrepreneur I work with. But, even though AI shows the promise of handling many operational tasks, it's going to be a long time before humans will be completely replaced as operators. And, as history has taught us, innovative breakthroughs happen, markets change, people change, and world events disrupt even the best of plans. So, while you can certainly optimize operations with AI, your startup will be better served if you master the operational elements of the business.

Some of the mundane but important operational activities that consume a lot of founders' time include basic things, like setting up company email, to the critical legal, financial, marketing, sales, and communication matters that come up. Mai Vu is the founder of an organic wine company focused on sustainability, Mai Vino. She was ready to launch her first product, a white wine, but before she could sell the product direct-to-consumer (DTC), she spent more time than she had expected figuring out how to set up the website, deciding how to process payments legally, setting up bank accounts, and having the proper bookkeeping systems in place for tax purposes. In addition to everything she had to do to produce, package, and ship the wine, there were a lot of operational to-dos just to get that first product ready to sell!

Mai's example may sound extreme because of the complexities that come with selling alcoholic beverages, but even founders of the most straightforward software startups often struggle because they underestimate the importance of operational activities and the time necessary to do them well.

When I first started working at Akamai, we were the classic early-stage startup with little structure in place for basic operational functions. We did not have standard practices for things like meetings and email. We had no company-wide budget or product-prioritization processes; cross-team interactions, such as ensuring there was a feedback loop between sales, support, and product, were practically nonexistent; and while we had a dependable twice-weekly food delivery service (ice cream sandwiches aplenty in the freezer!), we totally flew by the seat of our pants when it came to many fundamental operational processes. All of these challenges were totally normal for our stage of business, yet they made us dangerously vulnerable. Remember the story from the beginning of this book where a single engineer effectively took the internet down? This was largely due to our lack of focus on business operations.

In this part of the book, I will break down the most common operational areas that you should be aware of and how to approach them. In Chapter 10, I'll dive into the less sexy, but critical, elements of startup land: legal matters, which can seriously trip up, slow down, and be expensive for a startup. In Chapter 11, I will start with an exercise to get you in touch with your relationship to money—because your emotional connection to money drives just about every financial decision you'll make throughout the life of your venture. Then, I will provide an overview of financial basics like budgets and other financial elements of running your startup.

Chapter 12 will cover the brass tacks of fundraising—not just what to expect if you fundraise but how to think about the implications of taking outside capital, or even if you can, and how to work with investors after receiving their money.

After covering the legal and financial matters, Chapter 13 will give you an overview of what goes into the go-to-market strategy of a startup—from establishing your brand and creating a marketing function to product pricing and launches. In Chapter 14, I'll focus on adopting best practices to operate the sales, product, and support functions together, and in Chapter 15, I'll provide an overview of key stakeholders in your business and how to handle some of the most common communication challenges I see in and outside of startups. This part of the book provides the necessary operational tools you'll need to ensure your startup's success. You may find these chapters very timely if your business is just getting off the ground, or you may be grateful to know these are things you will need to prepare for and refer back to as needed.

10.

LEGAL MATTERS

If you're at the beginning of your startup journey, the thought of lawyering up and signing all sorts of agreements may sound daunting and unnecessary. "Why sign a cofounder agreement when we don't even know if this is a real business yet?" said two cofounders of a generative AI business when they were only a few months into their discovery efforts. As discussed in Chapter 6, I've seen too many situations where that "prenup" agreement was put off because founders are so heads down and everything "seems fine," and then as soon as there is a disagreement on direction, there's nothing to fall back on when it comes to decision-making. You can be so eager to get your first customer or hire your first employee that you miss critical legal issues that cause great angst down the road. The customer who refuses to pay for the design partnership because you won't do a custom feature for them can result in lost revenue if there was no signed contract in place. Then there's the contractor you hired to build your MVP who takes too long and delivers less than what you asked for, but there was never a signed statement of work so you are stuck with what you've got (and it's late!). There are so many gotchas for early-stage companies that can be mitigated by taking simple legal precautions, and while I can't cover every single legal thing that can happen with a venture, I can give you a heads-up on some of the more common challenges and how to handle them. However, I am not an attorney and recommend that any legal actions should always be verified with your counsel.

LAWYERING UP

When you move to a new city or town, finding a new dentist or primary care physician is usually on your short list of to-dos. I recommend a similar mindset when it comes to finding counsel for your startup. And just like you might look for a primary care physician who is bilingual or a dentist who takes your insurance, it is critical that you get counsel who understands startups. I can't emphasize this enough: lawyers who don't know the language, the nuances around financing and equity agreements, and who can't be patient as you come up to speed on startup-ese can result in wasting thousands of dollars and in lost opportunities. When discussing the employment agreement for a designer who would receive a salary and equity as a first hire, a founder reassured me that his uncle was reviewing this employee's contract pro bono before it was sent to be signed. When I asked about his uncle's experience negotiating the terms and conditions of equity grants, I found out that his uncle was a real estate attorney and had no experience with startups. While some of the legal terms were straightforward enough, this experienced lawyer did not appreciate the impact this agreement had on the startup or the prospective employee. Not only did this founder almost give away way too much equity for a first hire, but the contract had no details about the vesting schedule of their equity grant, and this designer's personal intellectual property was not protected. Bottom line, the boilerplate items that would be included in a startup's employee agreement were not considered at all.

It's critical to engage startup-savvy counsel early on so they are at the ready if something comes up. The attorney you select should have experience and be comfortable with the basics about the following areas:

- Cofounder and employee agreements
- Preferred-stock investor term sheets, bank loans, or other types of financing
- Private company board governance
- Corporate filings and tax laws—see the "83(b) and QSBS" box
- Trademarks, patents, and copyrights
- Commercial contracts for customers, suppliers, and other collaborators
- Common litigation areas such as IP infringement law

In addition to the common startup-specific areas of expertise, if your business is in a regulated domain (like health care, food and beverage, import/export, government contracts, etc.), you should find a firm that has experience in these areas or that is connected to a network of additional attorneys for these specific areas.

Startup-friendly law firms will often defer fees until you raise capital or meet a revenue milestone and you can pay them their full rates. This can be a great relief if you don't have the capital on hand to pay legal fees. However, be careful not to let these fees unexpectedly mount up. If you arrange for deferred fees, set a cap for general services and/or ask for an estimate for each engagement. And watch out for lawyers who take advantage of inexperienced founders. A founder I worked with had a lawyer invite a few of his associates on several calls related to her startup's modest series A financing and then sent a bill for $100,000 for everyone's time on these calls. Another founder had a lawyer forget to send him a bill until a year later after reconciling their books. This was after the founder had closed a recent financing round and had not disclosed this liability on his P&L statement (because he did not know about it). In each case, these founders refused to pay these sketchy lawyers. And that's the last point here; you can push back! Unless you signed something that says you will absolutely pay for a service, don't get swindled. Unfortunately, there are a lot of bad apples out there who prey on inexperienced founders.

Finally, there are tools available that can handle legalities without having to pay lawyers. For example, if you are setting up an LLC (see more about these in the next section), there are websites that can do some of the basic work for very little cost. So, before paying legal fees, check with experienced founder friends or advisors to see if there are inexpensive tools that may be good enough for your startup's needs.

WHAT TYPE OF LEGAL ENTITY SHOULD WE BE?

It is usually when money is about to exchange hands that founders consider forming a legal entity. Creating a legal entity is important, because if you were operating the business as an individual (also known as a "sole proprietorship") you would be personally liable for all of the business's debts and obligations and there would be no legal distinction between your personal and business assets. So, if your business were to be sued for some reason, you would be putting your personal assets at risk. There are several types of business entities, each with its own characteristics, advantages, and disadvantages. Choosing which one depends on factors such as the type of business, liability considerations, tax implications, and operational flexibility. Here are three of the most common types of startup entities and reasons why you might choose one over the other:

- **Limited liability company (LLC):** Owners of an LLC are not personally liable for the business's debts and obligations. LLCs benefit from pass-through taxation, meaning that profits and losses are reported on the individual tax returns of the owners and not on the returns of the LLC. Some startups start as LLCs if they are still unsure whether their business will have legs and don't want to get into the additional requirements of a full C corporation or a PBC (below). You can convert an LLC to a C corporation, but it's usually best to go right to a C corporation or a PBC if you are starting to earn revenue and/or plan to raise venture capital.

- **C corporation (C corp):** A C corp provides limited liability protection to shareholders and is subject to double taxation, meaning that profits are taxed at the corporate level, and then again when those profits are distributed to shareholders as dividends. C corps offer greater access to capital markets and have potential tax benefits for certain types of businesses. This is the most common entity designation for most ventures.

- **S corporation (S corp):** S corp owners receive limited liability protection like a C corp but avoid double taxation. Forming an S corp legally separates the business and its owners. As a result, shareholders aren't personally responsible for business debts or liabilities. However, there are several restrictions and limitations with S corps, especially if you are raising capital, so not all startups will qualify for this distinction.

- **Public benefit corporation (PBC):** A PBC shares many administrative similarities to a C corp, but the key difference is their purpose. A PBC is a for-profit company intended to produce a public benefit and to operate in a responsible and sustainable manner, which may align with your company's true north and can be a positive signal to employees and customers.

When deciding which type of entity to choose, consider factors such as liability protection, taxation, operational flexibility, regulatory requirements, and your long-term business goals. You should consult with legal and tax professionals so you can make an informed decision based on your startup's specific circumstances.

ETHICS AND POLICIES

Many in and outside of the startup world are aware of the infamous downfalls of founders like Theranos creator Elizabeth Holmes, who was sentenced to eleven years in prison for wire fraud and conspiracy, and FTX founder Sam Bankman-Fried (SBF), who was sentenced to twenty-five years for securities fraud. These founders were so determined to "win" in startup land that they lost sight of their ethical (and moral) responsibilities when it came to operating their businesses. The pressure on Holmes as a young, woman founder may have led her to act in extraordinary ways and break the law. For SBF, perhaps it was pure arrogance. Regardless, both ventures' boards of directors neglected an important element of their fiduciary duties—the duty of oversight with respect to each company's compliance and controls—which not only affected people's lives but lost investors millions.

What pushes founders like these to fly so close to the sun? And how do you ensure that with all the passion you may have for your startup, for solving a problem, and/or for making lots of money (often what drives bad behavior), that you are ethical, put proper controls in place, and don't break the law? Here are a few things to consider:

- On day one, **set up an accountability system and find your person.** You don't need a board of directors right away, but you should at least have someone who is experienced and/or has the appropriate network of people to hold you accountable, like a lawyer, business advisor, family member, coach, or even a professor you trust and who knows what they are doing. This should be someone who can give you some straight talk if you think you are about to do something a little bananas. Someone who understands that startups require risk-taking, but not lawbreaking, and can serve as a mirror to ensure your moral compass is pointing in the right direction.

- **Seek counsel on what to document** and keep all documentation safe on company (not personal) systems to ensure it can easily be retrieved if audited. That said, with few exceptions, *everything* documented is discoverable. A team of founders told me once how humiliated they were when deposed over a patent dispute with a huge tech company and they had to awkwardly listen to lawyers discuss old company emails that included details of dates they went on and other personal matters.
- While early-stage ventures do not require an official board, it is healthy to get in the habit of **establishing best practices for governance**. Have quarterly meetings to review business matters with cofounders and/or advisors. Some investors will ask for these meetings even if they don't have an official board seat. It's a great way to build this muscle and get business in order while things are simple rather than waiting until you scale and things get more complex.
- Even with just one hire, it does not hurt to **create a simple employee handbook** to avoid any issues with employees. These usually cover topics that range from behavioral expectations and work schedules to how performance reviews and terminations are handled. Founders often share these types of materials with each other, or you can find examples of these policies online or use AI to help you get started.

TAX LAWS

While taxes are considered a financial matter, abiding by tax laws can be a matter of life and death for a startup—especially in the United States. Just like finding a startup-savvy attorney is ideal, the same is true for an accountant. The ROI on a good accountant is usually high in the long run, from avoiding unnecessary tax penalties to optimizing liabilities with potential deductions and various tax credits. The following are common areas where accountants can be helpful for startups, but you may require other expert help if you operate all or part of your venture outside of the United States:

- Figuring out your federal, state, and local taxes based on the **type of entity structures** (LLC, C corp, PBC) you choose. This is both what you may have to pay and what you can do to qualify for **tax credits and incentives**. A startup-savvy accountant should be aware of what credits would work well for your venture.
- Determining tax **withholding and remitting payroll taxes**.
- If your startup is selling a consumer product, accountants can tell you whether you will be subject to **collecting, reporting, and remitting sales tax** to the appropriate taxing authorities.

Mismanaging taxes can be not only a legal risk but a financial one. The virtual-assistant venture Zirtual[1] had to temporarily shut down its operations in 2015 due to financial difficulties, leaving many clients and virtual assistants in limbo. Zirtual's temporary closure was primarily attributed to converting their hundreds of independent contractors to employees of the company—something they were feeling pressure to do as they saw other gig-economy ventures scrutinized for similar tactics. Having virtual assistants as contractors offered tax exemptions that contributed to huge margins for Zirtual. However, once these employees were on the payroll, there was a 20–30 percent added cost per employee, including taxes and other overhead that exploded their burn rate to the point that they could not operate their business. Uber has and continues to face similar challenges in the various countries in which they engage drivers who also operate as independent contractors. These disputes have raised questions about the company's tax liabilities, employment practices, and compliance with local tax regulations. While Zirtual eventually resumed operations (and was subsequently acquired by a private equity firm) and Uber has denied any wrongdoing, these examples highlight the complexities and challenges that startups may face in navigating tax issues. And remember, all of these complexities will not only be costly when it comes to legal and accounting fees, but they also can be a huge time suck and distraction away from other important aspects of running your business.

FORM 83(b) AND QUALIFIED SMALL BUSINESS STOCK (QSBS)

You should be aware of the US tax benefits associated with 83(b) elections and QSBS.

Form 83(b) refers to a specific IRS tax election form that applies to the taxation of restricted stock awards or other types of equity compensation for employees and advisors. The upside of a Form 83(b) is the potential to save stockholders a boatload in taxes if your startup has a net positive exit. The biggest risk of filing Form 83(b) is that if the stock ultimately becomes worthless or is forfeited it before it vests, stockholders won't be able to recover the taxes you paid. Therefore, make sure you consider the potential risks and benefits before making the election.

QSBS is a tax provision in the United States that allows certain investors in qualifying small businesses to potentially exclude a portion of their gains from capital gains tax. To qualify, the stock must meet specific criteria outlined by the IRS. If the stock meets these criteria and is held for a certain period (five years at the time of this writing), you and your investors may be eligible for a significant tax exclusion on a portion of financial gains when selling the stock.

Consult with a lawyer, tax professional, or financial advisor about QSBS qualifications and before making the 83(b) election. They can help you assess your specific situation, understand the tax implications, and determine what the right decision is for you. Regardless of what you choose, keep detailed records of your holdings and/ or investments, including documentation of the purchase of the stock, the holding period, and any other relevant information. These records will be important in demonstrating eligibility for QSBS treatment in the event of an IRS audit or inquiry.

Finally, remember that tax laws and regulations can change over time. Stay informed about any updates or changes to QSBS or 83(b) provisions to ensure ongoing compliance and to take advantage of any new opportunities or requirements.

CONTRACTS AND AGREEMENTS

All operating businesses have contracts and agreements they need to create or sign. You can find templates for most of what you'll need on the internet or your attorney will have them on hand. However, just be sure you're not under- or overdoing it. Also, when doing business with third parties, such as contractors, customers, partners, or suppliers, you may have to decide whether you will ask them to sign your paper or agree to sign their paper ("paper" is a common term for who wrote the contract). If doing business with larger organizations, it's more likely that they will want you to sign their paper, but this could be a lot to navigate and expensive if you engage an attorney to redline their contract. When Cristina, the CEO and cofounder of a SaaS integration platform company, signed on a multinational customer based in Denmark, the customer insisted on using their paper for the customer agreement. It turned out that their paper referred to a lot of Danish-specific laws that were hard to understand to determine potential risks to Cristina's business. "They seem like a great company to work with, but I was worried there was some clause that if we mess up their data, they own our company!"

In 2007, renowned investor Marc Andreessen wrote a blog post[2] about how a startup going after a large-enterprise customer is like Captain Ahab going after the elusive white whale, Moby Dick. "When Captain Ahab went in search of the great white whale Moby Dick, he had absolutely no idea whether he would find Moby Dick, whether Moby Dick would allow himself to be found, whether Moby Dick would try to immediately capsize the ship or instead play cat and mouse, or whether Moby Dick was off mating with his giant whale girlfriend. What happened was entirely up to Moby Dick." Large enterprises are similar to Moby Dick in that they have complex operating systems, a lot of bureaucracy, and can be unpredictable when doing deals because of so many different constituents that need to be involved. Often the sponsors inside these large organizations who want to use your product are not the ones authorized or with the budgets to buy your product. As much as a big logo would be great for both financial and marketing purposes, closing a deal with such a company can take a lot of time, and if you happen to get close to landing a deal it can be scary to push back on contract terms or pricing for fear of losing that potential customer. José faced this challenge when he was about to close a deal with a huge technology company based in the Pacific Northwest. This customer's legal department returned the contract with changes to the terms that he had originally agreed to with his point of contact at the company. He feared pushing back on these changes would send the customer running, and this was a logo he was eager to secure to position his business well for his next round of fundraising.

For Cristina and for José, there were easy solutions. Cristina got resourceful and was able to talk with other US-based businesses that had contracted with this same customer to get a sense of how the papers were handled for them. She found out that the company was fine with using others' paper so she asked and was able to do the same. José reached out to his contact at the customer to get their take on whether they could push back on their company's lawyers, and the sponsor reassured them that they would ask their lawyers to fix the contract in favor of their original agreement.

Just like it can be daunting to push back on terms or whose paper to use when working with a big company, it can be equally daunting when you are signing a term sheet with an investor—especially if you need fresh capital to keep your venture alive. When Sarah, the founder of a B2B digital health venture, was concerned about her first big institutional investor insisting that they use their paper to ink their deal, it took her counsel and the support of her peer network to assure her that as long as their contract terms were boilerplate for startups, she could use their paper. The good news was that the investor was using the National Venture Capital Association (NVCA) template for investments, which is an industry standard. Using NVCA's template meant they were not really using either party's "paper." This established a middle ground that each party was able to agree to without much negotiation once the material legal and financial terms had been decided.

Third-party contracts are the most onerous to deal with for any venture, but all contracts will require attention and take time and legal fees to develop until you reach a scale point where you can hire inside counsel to manage these if needed. Some examples of other common contracts and agreements that you'll likely run into include:

- **Employment agreements**, which, as noted prior, may vary for founders, senior hires, and general employees. These are usually bundled with **options and equity grant agreements**.
- **Nondisclosure agreements (NDAs)** can often be included in employee, customer, and partner agreements, and in other circumstances like terminations and separations. However, they are usually frowned upon when talking with venture capitalists (VCs) who will insist their reputations depend on them maintaining confidentiality and, as such, won't sign NDAs.

- **Noncompete agreements** are put in place to prevent employees from leaving your company to either start or join a competitive company, usually within a certain time frame. As of the time of this book's publication, these agreements are pending an FTC ruling to be banned. Be sure to check the status of this ruling before instituting such agreements.
- **Terms and conditions** (T&Cs) are used for any customer-facing product or service and are typically standard across the industry. Most startup-savvy lawyers have templates for T&Cs that they can tweak to be specific for your company instead of having to create them from scratch.
- **Contractor agreements** can differ from one another if you are hiring freelancers or contracting firms like offshore developers, marketing firms, or even accountants.
- **Stakeholder contracts** for convertible notes like the Y Combinator (YC) simple and generally accepted SAFE agreements,[3] term sheets if you raise an equity round of financing, and advisor agreements for anyone receiving equity in exchange for supporting your venture in some meaningful way.
- **Letters of intent** (LOIs), which are not legally binding but can be great to have when engaging with potential customers to show investors you have tangible interest in what you are doing.

IP, TRADEMARKS, AND COPYRIGHTS, OH MY!

There used to be a time when protecting intellectual property (IP) was fundamental to the defensibility of a startup. These days, however, unless you are doing a new biotechnology, rocket science type of business, or have a novel technology that came out of a research lab as we did at both Akamai and VMware, IP is not as protective for a business as it once was. Certainly, filing patent applications can't hurt—Akamai and VMware each have thousands filed and granted—but at the end of the day, it's how you execute that will really determine the success of your venture more than how many patents you hold. Trademarks and copyrights are also good protective measures, but again won't necessarily ensure a venture's success. All that said, it is important to understand the nuances between each of these protective measures.

- **Patents:** These protect an inventor from having others make, use, or sell their inventions. Patents protect the invention from fourteen to twenty years depending on the type of patent and the invention's utility or design. Sometimes, you can be accused of infringing on another venture's patents even if you had no intention or idea you may have done so. There are ventures that solely exist to troll for these situations, which can be costly for a startup if they get stuck in the web of a troll; another good reason to have startup-savvy counsel to mitigate and handle these types of situations. If you think you have IP worth protecting, provisional patent applications will act as a temporary placeholder for your invention and enable you to lock in an early filing date. This may be important if you think there are other inventors working on similar IP. Provisionals last twelve months and give you the time necessary to completely file a patent application.

- **Trademarks:** These are names (like "Nike") or logos (like the Nike "swoosh") that represent your venture and are generally used to protect against consumer confusion about the brand. Once filed, they are protected forever as long as they are renewed.

- **Copyrights:** Books, movies, marketing content, and some other types of creative content can benefit from copyright protection. Copyrights are supposed to protect an author's ability to express their ideas (not the idea itself) and protect the work for the life of the author, plus seventy years.

However, digital content can be hard to protect. At least once a month I hear from a frustrated founder who just had their entire website copied by a competitor. While "imitation is the sincerest form of flattery," it can be infuriating to find that a fresh new look or great content on your product pages—that perhaps you paid an outside firm to create for you—was ripped off by another party. I refer to these companies as "bottom feeders" whose only way to survive is to follow others' lead. It is important to keep your focus on your bigger vision than worry about these annoyances. So, while it may be important to register your work for copyright protection and keep your filings up to date, it's not worth spending too much time or money litigating on these matters. Just go build a great business!

You may not avoid every single legal thing that can happen with a business, but you will have the support to handle the most common challenges by taking simple legal precautions and retaining startup-savvy counsel. Depending on the type of business you build, you may eventually have a team of lawyers or even hire a general counsel (legal executive) to oversee all the legal details. But until then, be sure to stay on top of legal matters and don't break the law!

11.

FINANCIAL MATTERS

Frequently intertwined with legal matters are financial matters, which include topics such as profit and loss statements, cash flow forecasts, and banking considerations. If you are new to running a business, as most founders are, I suggest you go deep on this topic by taking a course or reading the many great books out there to learn the financial management basics, some of which are included in the Resources section. Even if you get to a point where you can hire a bookkeeper or a director of finance, knowing how the money works is a vital skill, and the topic of money itself tends to be emotional. These are common things I hear from founders when it comes to money:

- "All of the money we've raised is still in the bank, but I am afraid to spend it."
- "I've got two weeks to raise more capital or I can't make payroll next month."
- "I need to pay myself more than my employees because I am the founder."
- "I need to pay myself next to nothing because I am the founder."

Statistics show that financial issues are the cause of approximately 40 percent of divorces, and 80 percent of business failures can be attributed to poor financial management and having unexpected expenses. In marriages, financial issues are usually due to different mindsets around income and expenses. Just like marriages, if you and your team (and even your investors!) are unable to reconcile your perspectives around money, you may be destined to be part of that 80 percent. So, while I will offer some basics on financial management at the end of this chapter, it is important to first cover the emotional stuff.

RELATIONSHIPS TO MONEY

All situations, personal or business, that concern finances are influenced by one's emotional connections to money, many of which started when we were children. These emotional connections drive certain behaviors around operational activities. Domingo García-Huidobro grew up in a multigenerational household with eight siblings, two sets of grandparents, and his parents all under one roof in Santiago, Chile. After several years as a business-development professional at a large corporation, he cofounded Ruuf (pronounced "roof"), a leading provider of climate and sustainability solutions in Latin America. As a CEO, he had different views from his cofounders when it came to the business's financial matters. Domingo grew up in a household where every penny had to be managed carefully, and he was extremely frugal with Ruuf's cash. His cofounders had different relationships with money, were less cautious, and took more risks spending money on business needs and initiatives without much concern. This created tension between the cofounders and slowed the venture down. With time, they came to realize that this dichotomy is a particularly great complement between cofounders. Leveraging these differences has also helped them to create a balance between building fast and cheap MVPs versus more robust and expensive products and features.

Meanwhile, Olivia had a well-paying corporate job and was accustomed to living a lavish lifestyle that included wearing designer clothes, driving a fancy car, and going on jet-set vacations. When she left her job to start her company, she had not anticipated the compromises she would have to make living on a founder's salary (typically well below market standards). So, she raised a lot of capital to fund both (!). Not only did she put the capital she raised into her venture, but she also chose to pay herself the same salary she was making as a corporate executive. "I am the CEO, so I deserve a CEO salary," was her response to investors when they questioned her salary on the startup's financial reports. Had her venture been growing exponentially, this may have been tolerated, but because it was pre-revenue and struggling to gain traction in the market, it raised a lot of concerns about her fiduciary responsibilities as CEO and created a lot of tension between Olivia and her board.

Founders bring very different relationships to money into their venture journeys. For some, it's a forcing function to scale fast and raise lots of capital, and for others it's reserving cash to the extent that they are starving the business. And sometimes, their relationship with money causes irreparable damage between cofounders, employees, and/or investors. If your business is already underway, this concept may resonate deeply with you, but if you haven't started it yet, it will come up one way or another. What's most important either way is to take some time to consider what your relationship to money is, how it got that way, and then translate that into how you and others in your business will operate knowing this information.

When I first joined VMware, I learned that our founding CEO, Diane Greene, was tenacious about our financials and had a rigorous budget process informed by her past startup experiences. Diane explained, "We made three plans: optimistic, likely, and worst case.

The CFO and I were constantly checking on how we were tracking, and he let me know if it looked like there was a change one way or another. We could be more generous on head count where it was needed if we were achieving on the optimistic plan and could slow things down if it were the worst case (which miraculously never happened!)." Diane instilled a culture of fiscal responsibility across the organization. "My attitude about building a company was simply that you wanted to be able to always handle a worst-case scenario but not stifle growth by being overly conservative. Whenever we could calculate the return on an investment with high confidence, we invested appropriately." When the United States experienced a financial crisis in 2008 and other companies were laying people off or shutting down, VMware just took basic measures like freezing salaries and limiting large capital expense. Our fiscally responsible culture allowed us to continue to thrive during that time.

I am not suggesting you operate your startup with a tightly held budget, but rather to understand that we handled our finances the way we did because of our founder's relationships with money. And it's not just founders who bring personal baggage around money into their ventures; everyone who is connected to your venture has their own unique relationship with money. Your investors took a bet on you and are relying on you for a return. Your employees may be anxious about the venture's financial stability and whether they'll still have jobs in a year. And don't forget partners in your personal life, if you have them, who may have their own fears about money and how the success or failure of your venture might impact your homelife. So, when someone is hounding you about budgets or acting skittish about spending, take a step back and question what may lie underneath this concern. This is a vital conversation to have with your personal partner, if you have one, cofounders, and key stakeholders before you start a new venture or as soon as possible if you've already started. Things to discuss should include:

- **Personal stories about relationships to money:** How you each grew up and when you first became "money aware," the first time managing money for yourself or a business or perhaps even a club or sports team. Peak moments when you feared you would lose housing or let family or partners down or perhaps when you had a financial windfall and what that felt like.
- **How you think about cash management, debt, and prioritizing spending:** Share the tools you use to track your budgets (or not) and how much debt you're in, if any.
- **Your backup plans if money gets tight** like asking parents for help or turning your startup into a side hustle if you need to get a "real job."
- For investors, you may ask **how your venture is viewed by the fund** and whether your venture is critical to the fund's return versus one of many similar-sized bets.

The more you understand your own and others' relationships with money, the more you will be able to manage the finances of your startup and the feelings that may arise as you ride this crazy roller coaster.

FINANCIAL BASICS

Getting a handle on your relationship with money is important, and knowing what to expect in basic financial management of a startup is equally important. Below is a short breakdown of the more common financial-management areas that you should be aware of as you get started.

- **Banking:** Once you establish a business entity, you will need at least one bank account to hold your cash and pay bills. Most startups have more than one bank account, with one usually in a big national bank instead of just a founder-friendly bank. This mitigates the risk against bank failures—like when startup-focused Silicon Valley Bank failed in 2023. Bank accounts usually come with a credit card for operating expenses like monthly subscriptions to software tools and other low-expense items.

Having a line of credit (LOC) is pretty standard for startups as a contingency plan and easier to get if business is going well (like after a recent fundraise or closing a big deal). LOCs are usually tied to forecasted growth and income and/or can have covenants like requiring a drawdown of cash by a certain date. LOCs are great to have, but they should not be relied upon as a long-term strategy for keeping your business afloat.

- **Budget accounting and bookkeeping:** You must have a budget and stay close to the money personally until you reach a level of scale where you can hand off financial management to a person or team of experts. Having a budget and understanding how money comes in and goes out will help you manage everything from hiring decisions to how you will price your product and manage your inventory if you have physical products. As soon as you can afford it, bring on a part-time bookkeeper to track expenses and prepare for tax season, but do not use this as an excuse to stray away from financial matters. One founder I work with handed off her finances to a bookkeeper only to find out months later that the company had been defrauded over $300,000. The bookkeeper was great at tracking expenses, but was not regularly checking the bank account balances. They were able to get the money back from their bank, but it was a huge scare, and a big distraction from running her business.

- A **balance sheet** that tracks the company's assets and liabilities, including cash, accounts receivable, inventory, fixed assets, accounts payable, debt, and owner's equity.
- A **profit and loss (P&L) statement** (or income statement) is a summary of a company's revenues, expenses, profits, and losses over a specific period, typically monthly, quarterly, and annually. It is a full picture of the company's financial performance and is crucial for assessing the profitability of a business, understanding its financial health, and making informed decisions about operations and strategy. You should update P&Ls monthly and look back twelve to eighteen months depending on the life of your venture.
- A **financial forecast** projects how you expect your financials to look in the future, usually for a specific period, such as the next quarter or year. Financial forecasts are used for planning purposes, such as the financial impact of certain strategic decisions or preparing for potential changes in the business like a new product direction or expanding (or contracting) the team. Investors or lenders will often ask for both P&Ls and financial forecasts as part of their diligence process. But remember, it's just a model and does not guarantee outcomes given the number of factors that can impact a business—from people, to markets, etc.
- **Financial KPIs**, as discussed in Chapter 5, are metrics you will need to track to determine the health of the business. Common financial KPIs include bookings, annual recurring revenue, cost of acquired customers, customer lifetime value (LTV), gross margin, days sales outstanding (DSO) for receivables, and months of cash on hand.

Staying close to all financial aspects of the business for at least the first few years will better inform you about expenses and what roles you will need to fill at scale. I ran into a former employee of mine, Ben

Schaechter, in downtown SoHo one Saturday morning with arm-loads of laptops and peripherals. Ben is the CEO and cofounder of Vantage, a VC-backed cloud analytics business. "Our first new hires start Monday!" he said gleefully. "But I'm still responsible for getting all their hardware. I hadn't considered that they'd all need new hardware even if they are all working from home. We only have one corporate credit card, so it was my job to go to the Apple store today to get what they'll need before Monday." At the time, Ben was not just the CEO but also the financial and operations manager for their venture. By being this close to the daily operations, he was learning about what types of expenses came with hiring new team members. Two years later, Vantage was thriving and Ben hired both business-operations and finance-operations leaders to take over these duties. Expenditures you may have to account for include but are not limited to:

- **Employee salaries and benefits**
- **Office supplies and rent**
- **Cloud computing** and related expenses
- **Back-office software** like applicant tracking, payroll, email, websites, and other productivity tools. Startups often suffer from SaaS "sprawl" and end up with dozens of apps they've paid for and never use. This can cost a venture tens of thousands of dollars if you are not paying attention.
- **Legal fees**
- **Insurance**, which is often bundled for small businesses and includes things like workman's compensation, general liability, commercial property, and business interruption insurance
- **Travel and entertainment** (T&E)
- **Training and development** programs and services for you and your employees
- **Marketing expenses** including your website, search engine marketing (SEM), conference fees, and others

- **Membership fees** for trade associations or other organizations that either lend credibility to your venture or gain you access to customers or partners
- **Inventory**, for businesses that sell physical products
- **Outside services** such as contract designers, marketing agencies, legal and accounting services
- **Capital expenditures** such as real estate for brick-and-mortar businesses, office furniture, and materials for consumer products

Whether you are starting a bootstrapped venture, a venture-backed business, or even a nonprofit, money is necessary and obtaining it and managing it are critical. Be sure you have a handle on your relationship to money and decide where it will come from. There's no perfect answer to whether or how one should gain access to funds. One founder's visions of unicorn status and an IPO or major exit could be another founder's worst nightmare. One founder's desire to swing for the fences and raise a ton of cash could put the fear of God into another. If you hope the money will come from outside investors, you should understand what that entails, and this is what I will cover in the next chapter.

12.

FUNDRAISING

I have a lot of feels about the topic of fundraising. First and fore-most, not every venture needs to, should, or even can take investor capital, and if they do, they should understand that once they are on the fundraising hamster wheel, it's super hard to get off! I am not anti-fundraising. Heck, I'm an angel investor myself and serve on the boards of venture-backed startups, but remember that fundraising is like getting fuel for your speedboat to reach a destination. It is not the boat or the destination itself. I once worked with a founder who loooooved fundraising. This is the antithesis of how most founders feel about the process. Most founders loathe the idea of being pulled away from running their business to do fundraising. And as much as they love to promote the awesomeness of what they are building, most founders hate asking for money unless it's to pay for their product or service (and some don't even like that!). This founder was different. They knew how to schmooze and sell ideas to investors and had no problem raising millions of dollars for their venture. However, despite lots of capital raised, their business model was unclear and they had not closed any revenue-generating deals in the more than six years the startup was in business. It was an unfortunate moment when the eventual exit of this venture was a sale for less than the amount of capital they had raised. This demise does not imply it was all due to the founder's lack of execution (they worked extremely hard!). There were also misalignments between investors and the company leaders, and the business was in a complicated market targeting huge, slow-moving corporations. Even though this founder was great at raising capital, they learned the hard way that fundraising is not the end-all be-all. You may decide not to raise capital at all, but if you do opt to take this route, it is an operational activity unto itself and complementary to managing your finances and other key elements of running a business.

Admittedly, when I joined Akamai I knew almost nothing about the venture world, how equity worked, or even what it meant to have low-priced, pre-IPO stock options as an early startup joiner. We were operating during an exceptional time in the late 1990s when raising $120 million and going public in less than two years with only $4 million in revenue was unprecedented until the dot-com bubble era. We were scrambling to become a more professionally run organization that was going to be flush with cash if the IPO went as well as expected. We IPOd at $26 a share and Akamai's market capitalization surged to about $13 billion with the stock closing that day at $145 per share. At its peak, the stock hit $327 per share before the bubble burst, and it bottomed out at close to 70¢. Yikes! In those early years, there were many upsides to being flush with cash, and I began to learn what it meant to have major pressure on our business not just from our investors but also from our shareholders.

By the time I got to DigitalOcean in 2016, I not only knew a lot more about venture-backed startups, but the investor market had changed drastically from a few large raises and swift IPOs to many large raises over multiple years with eventual exits that usually took the form of mergers and acquisitions (M&A) deals with a smattering of IPOs. Shortly before I joined the company, DigitalOcean had closed their B-round and had a fresh infusion of over $83 million in cash to add to the $40 million they had previously raised in earlier rounds. Most of our sales and marketing materials touted our $123 million in capital raised as a metric of success. Meanwhile, at only four years old, DigitalOcean's annual recurring revenue (ARR) was well into nine figures with exponential forecasted growth. With a board made up of seasoned investors from large firms to smaller boutique firms—who, together, put significant venture capital into the company—there were a lot of expectations about the business. I had landed in the thick of it and experienced firsthand the stress and heartache that can happen in a venture-backed business—all of which I'll get into below.

SURVIVE OR THRIVE

There are plenty of ways to get a venture off the ground, scale it, and have a healthy exit without raising capital. Eric Paley of Founder Collective did some research back in 2016 that suggested raising a ton of capital doesn't have a correlation with success.[1] Of the twenty most successful publicly traded startups in the prior five years that he examined (measured by current market cap), fourteen raised in the neighborhood of $100 million or less. Six raised less than $50 million, and one raised no capital at all. And this trend is growing as more founders opt to build businesses with alternative capital that allows them to work with more freedom and without diluting their equity stake in their own ventures or the proverbial monkey on their backs.

Knowing that there are alternatives and fundraising is a hamster wheel that's hard to get off of, why fundraise at all? For some ventures, especially in tech, the advancement of AI and endless available productivity tools let you build a lot with very little. You no longer need teams of engineers to stand up a basic back-end system or front-end application to put something in front of customers (another case for why you should spend more time doing discovery work). But for companies getting traction with their MVP and ready to scale or for those who are building a brick-and-mortar or physical-product business, diluting your equity (issuing ownership to others reduces your stake in the business) and raising capital may be necessary.

While you may decide fundraising is necessary, before you start the process, you must first determine if your business is venture backable. Investors will expect your startup to meet the following criteria at a minimum:

- Measurable evidence that there is a problem to solve and now is the time to solve it
- Proven traction and a unique value proposition for your product or service
- Clarity about how your startup will differentiate in the market and your competitive "moat" (what keeps other companies from putting you out of business)
- You have a team with relevant industry expertise and/or a proven track record
- A fleshed-out business model, financial forecasts, and a well-defined path to profitability

If you believe you can meet the criteria above and are able to tell a good story through a pitch deck and a software demo or physical product sample if you have one, you can then start to think about raising capital. There are different types of capital that are available to most startups:

- **Venture capital (VC)** is, despite the growing trend away from it, the most traditional form of capital raised. VC funds are usually backed by limited partners (LPs) who invest in these funds. LPs do not engage in the day-to-day operations of the funds they invest in; however, VCs have a fiduciary responsibility to report fund performance to their LPs. VCs are also referred to as institutional investors.

- **Family offices** are private wealth-management firms that manage the assets of high-net-worth individuals and are also referred to as institutional investors. Unlike VCs, who often seek quick exits for short-term gains, family offices prioritize long-term growth and can offer strategic guidance, access to extensive networks, and the ability to tailor investments to a startup's specific needs.

- **Angel investors** are high-net-worth, accredited individuals who provide capital in exchange for equity or convertible debt. Angels who are also domain experts often serve as advisors to the startups they invest in and can make valuable business introductions.

- **A special purpose vehicle (SPV)** can streamline a venture's cap table by consolidating angel investors under one legally distinct entity, which protects confidentiality, reduces legal risks, and makes communication and governance more efficient. What's especially nice is that the SPV is one line on your cap table (the list of who has how much equity). This is good because if you are to raise more capital later, VCs can get a little spooked by a messy cap table that could involve getting approvals from a lot of people during the transaction.

- **Government and foundation grants or competitions** that may be aligned with your venture's impact model, such as climate or affordable housing, or that have a special interest in certain affinity groups, such as underrepresented founders or certain ethnic groups, may be another source of capital. These can often be nondilutive investments where they don't get an equity stake in your startup, they just give you cash.

- **Crowdfunding** platforms like Kickstarter or Indiegogo allow startups to raise small amounts of money from a large number of people, typically in exchange for early access to products and rewards instead of equity. These platforms are more common for consumer products and require some expertise to use them, so find someone who knows how to navigate each platform and can advise if it makes sense to use this method to raise money. A lot of interest in your product on a crowdfunding platform can be a great signal for investors in a future fundraising round.

- **Friends and family investors** as an option for capital requires clear communication and formal agreements to avoid potential conflicts. Do not take money from anyone who doesn't understand that they may never see their cash again or who expects to be overly involved in your venture (unless it's helpful in some way). Some friends and family translate their investment as a front-row seat in a TV show like *Silicon Valley*, and while they could find participating fun and entertaining, it's not the best way to ensure their capital is worth something someday unless they can truly be helpful.

- **Incubators and accelerators** can be a great way to get funding, mentorship, and resources in exchange for equity. Y Combinator and Techstars are two of the best known in the United States, but there are scores of these organizations worldwide. They are all different and each is dependent on who is running the program, their experience, the program's track record, and how much exposure they have to other investors and experts who may help your venture. Most participants of the more successful programs will say the network and the community were the most valuable part of the experience, but also that these programs can be a big distraction from actually running their ventures. So, if you take the time and effort to apply to one of these programs, do so only when you have talked to a few program alumni to ensure it's a good use of your time.

- **Strategic partnerships** formed with established companies that have venture funds can not only provide resources and/ or market access in exchange for equity or revenue-sharing agreements, but they can also be a great exit opportunity down the road.

There are also ways to get cash without diluting your stake in your venture. These include:

- **Financing companies** that offer debt funding in exchange for a percentage of future revenues until the loan is repaid and **peer-to-peer lending** platforms that connect startups with individual lenders willing to provide loans.
- **Small business and microloans** offered by banks, nonprofit organizations, or community lenders. Some banks also specialize in debt vehicles, which are usually only for when you are at a certain level of revenue.
- **Bootstrapping** and using your personal savings, reinvesting profits, and keeping operating costs low to fund the business without external financing is always an option. Some founders even borrow against their homes or use personal credit cards to fund their business; but going back to the points made about your relationship with money, I don't recommend this unless you and/or your partners can handle the emotions that come with that level of risk.

Just like deciding whether it's the right time in your life to buy a house and get a mortgage, raising capital is a major decision and one that should not be made lightly, because raising capital for your venture is like taking on a big-ass mortgage. And because your investors expect you to earn them an order of magnitude more than what they gave you, it can feel like an even greater form of debt than a typical home mortgage. Technically you don't have to pay investors back like you would a mortgage with a bank (if your startup fails, they take it as a loss), but you must in good faith try to earn investors a return. Most investors want a 10x or more multiple on their investments, but the average multiple a startup exit may earn an investor is 4–5x. Only around 20 percent of the money investors put into startups actually bear fruit, which is why they tend to put a lot of pressure on the ventures they fund. So, before you gear up to fundraise, take a step back and decide whether it's for you and how you might want to go about it.

FUNDING ROUNDS

I've mentioned funding rounds a few times, but let's add a little more context to what these mean before we unpack the process of raising capital. Funding rounds are usually based on the stage of the venture. The most common stages of funding are:

- **Bootstrapping** (self-funding the business), usually at a very early stage when you are still ideating and need cash for experiments and discovery work that you cover with your own personal funds. Some businesses commit to bootstrapping forever.
- **Pre-seed** rounds, sometimes called **friends and family** rounds, are common when the business is starting to show some traction, maybe with a beta product in market or the promise of a breakthrough technology you've been working on, like an AI engine or a prototype of a consumer product. Pre-seed rounds are commonly funded by noninstitutional investors, although some VCs are known as "first check" investors and aim to get in as early as possible on a startup when the price is low, even before there is a product to sell.
- **Seed** rounds sometimes skip right past pre-seeds if the company is getting traction very early and the value of the business shows promise. Otherwise, this is the next logical step in the stage of a startup and may be when you begin

introducing VCs into your cap table. Both pre-seed and seed rounds are usually done as a convertible note (the industry standard is a SAFE) that will convert these early investors to priced shareholders.

- A **priced round** usually follows a seed round and is when the valuation of the startup is explicitly set by a lead investor (the one who puts in the most money). There are typically several priced rounds (usually lettered A, B, C, etc.) as ventures evolve. Investors in these rounds, in addition to negotiating a share price, may also negotiate for additional rights, such as liquidation preferences, board seats, antidilution preferences, and voting rights. Priced rounds can be complex and require a lot of legal work to finalize terms. Too many of these rounds can also leave you extremely diluted with very little ownership of your venture. In fact, because of so much dilution, many of the big exits we see in the headlines where ventures were sold for hundreds of millions or even billions of dollars resulted in very little cash in those founders' pockets.
- **Down rounds** are when a startup does a priced round at a valuation lower than its valuation in previous rounds and new investors pay a lower price for the company's shares compared to what earlier investors paid. These are either because the previous round was overvalued, or there was a market correction.
- A **bridge round** is a type of funding that provides a VC-backed company with capital until it can secure a larger, more substantial funding round; to wait for more favorable market conditions; or to achieve a specific milestone that will make the company more attractive to investors in the next round. Bridge rounds can be viewed as a signal that the venture isn't doing well if it can't secure more substantial

funding. But, they can be a great solution if you just need to buy time and pay the bills until the timing is better.

- The final stage is some sort of outcome event, which can range from an **acquisition** to an **initial public offering** to, for 99 percent of startups, **failure.** I'll explain this stage in more detail in Chapter 18.

There are no official rules around sizes of rounds, when to raise each round, or even when to exit. Every startup has different needs and risk tolerances so it's more important to focus on what you need and who you want to get it from. And before you start the process, seek advice from experienced founders, lawyers, and advisors to devise your plan.

THE GOTCHAS OF THE FUNDRAISING PROCESS

If you decide you can and want to raise venture capital, and you're new to this game, here's a heads-up on common things that can trip up first-time founders:

1. **Most founders dislike the fundraising process.** It is time-consuming, distracts them from running their venture, and it usually means hearing *no* a lot. So you're not alone if you don't enjoy it.
2. **The process for first-time founders requires an average of one hundred meetings and pitches.** Yes, *one hundred.*
3. **Investors are looking for both founder-market fit and market potential.** The former questions whether you (and your cofounders) have the expertise, passion, conviction, and strong emotional intelligence (EQ) necessary to run the business. The latter, market potential, will be determined both by your and their research. In other words, do your homework, because they will too.

4. **Warm introductions to investors are always best.** Cold outreach is a long shot. Tap your network to get intros whenever possible.

5. **Try *not* to send a pitch deck in advance.** Decks save investors time but make it too easy to pass before getting to know you. If investors insist that you send a deck, see the next point.

6. **You will need at least two pitch decks:**
   ○ A **readable** to whet the appetite for an investor to be interested in setting up a meeting. You don't want the deck to be the end of the story. This takes time to perfect, so send this deck to a few investors you are less excited about to test a few iterations out before going for the ones you really want to raise capital from. Less than ten slides should cover the opportunity, the team, and traction so far. Never send the readable as an attachment that can be easily forwarded. Always use an online tool that forces anyone who looks at your deck to enter their email address so you know who is looking at your information.
   ○ A **narratable** is what you use in the meeting with the investors. This should also be around ten slides with few words to read and more images and numbers because what you really want is a conversation. You can ask the investor in advance if there are particular details they want to hear about and have a huge appendix of slides to quickly reference anything they want, but the goal again is for them to get to know *you* (and your team if applicable). This is also an appropriate format to link to a demonstration of your product.

7. **The process can drag on forever if you let it.** Timebox your fundraising process for six to eight weeks to ensure you don't spend too much time on fundraising. Easier said than done, of course. In certain market climates, it can take months, or rounds can be done in phases where you close some amount

of the round and then leave it open for a few more months for new investors to join the round.

8. **Investors talk to each other and do backdoor references.** Some investors are borderline unethical and will share deal information with other investors and even competitors. Make sure you have your decks protected for this as noted above, and, if they ask for customer names, tell them you are happy to get preapproved references and make introductions for them. You need to respect your customers' time and control that narrative. This won't prevent investors from getting backdoor references (just as one might do with a job candidate)— especially if you have customer names on your pitch deck or website—but at least try to manage it up front.

9. You will need to **set up a data room** when you have serious interest from investors. This is a secure online space that allows you to share confidential documents with potential investors and other authorized parties like your lawyer.

10. **Until there's cash in the bank, there's no deal.** No matter how great the pitch went, or the number of visitors to your data room or partner or investment committee meetings you attend, there are all sorts of reasons why investors will pass. Most of them are bad about giving feedback about why they are passing on a deal because of the reputational risk. So even though the interest can be exciting, and even if you get a term sheet, it's not a deal until the cash is in the bank.

11. **Raising venture capital is like marrying someone you cannot divorce.** So, as good as a term sheet may look, know who you are taking money from. You could end up with a great investor who supports you and is helpful or wind up with someone that may micromanage you or, sadly, even cause harm to the business. Before you take their money, do reference checks with other founders who have worked with these investors—

including any who exited their companies to hear how the investor supported their transition (even if it was a shutdown). Otherwise, the juice may not be worth the squeeze.

12. Sadly, **bias and discrimination is still a prevailing issue for women and founders of color raising capital**. In a research study done in 2018, investors asked male founders "promotion" questions (*How big can this get?*). However, women founders were asked "prevention" questions (*How will you protect against competition?*).[2] As a result, women tend to defend their businesses in pitches rather than discussing upside potential, contributing to lower funding outcomes for them.

Founders of color face significant hurdles in raising capital due to limited access to investor networks ("The Warm Intro Problem"), pattern-matching bias, and the racial wealth gap, making it harder to secure early funding. They also encounter stricter investment terms.

Diverse investor networks, alternative funding sources, and strong financial narratives can help bridge the gap for women and founders of color, but there is still a lot of work to be done in our industry.

These are just the highlights, but again, there's a lot more to fundraising, including how to read and negotiate a term sheet, which I suggest you have an advisor, mentor, and/or lawyer help you do if it's your first time at bat. The final point I'll make here about the process is that when you are in the middle of it, you may feel like *I just need to get through this and then things will settle down*. However, after the raise, you're expected to use that money to scale your business. So while closing a round means you can get back to operating your startup, the real work is about to start. With this in mind, let's talk about how your investors can be helpful after you get their money.

INVESTORS—BEYOND THEIR FUNDS

Many entrepreneurs say they'd like to get help from their investors but worry that asking for help signals weakness. Conversely, I've heard investors say they wish the founders they invested in would be more transparent about challenges they are facing and ask for help. As one investor said to me, "They already sold me on the business and have our money. It's now my job to help them succeed." Not all investors have that mindset, but many of them do, so how can you make sure that you lean into this? In a social media poll I conducted, 56 percent of founders said their most common ask of their investors is for hiring help, 31 percent ask for introductions to potential partners or customers, and a small percentage (13 percent) tap their investors for financial management advice. Most often, unless your investor is a former operator, the advice will come from what they have seen at other portfolio companies instead of firsthand experience, which can still be quite valuable!

Some of the bigger venture firms have full-time experts and part-time entrepreneurs in residence (EIRs) who can help with hiring, marketing, and other operational needs when your startup is still building its own operations team. Whether they have these experts in-house or not, once you've received their money, here's a list of things investors can help with:

Hiring and People Stuff
- Making referrals and warm introductions, posting job links on their websites
- Selling the potential for the business to prospective senior candidates
- Getting backdoor references on potential hires
- Offering you feedback on employees they are interacting with. Just remember, they don't make hiring or firing decisions. That's the CEO's job.

- Giving leadership advice—especially if you are a first-time CEO or other member of the C-suite

Marketing, Sales, and Partnerships
- Introducing you to potential customers and/or partners
- Leveraging their social media presence for sharing news and events
- Sharing their perspectives on not just current market trends, but historical context and how they've seen markets shift over time
- Providing insights on industry trends and connecting you with domain experts
- Developing your company and product story

Product
- If they can, they better be using your product and talking about it!
- Offering thoughts on how your product can improve

Finance
- Helping you think through financial forecasts and prepare data for future financing
- Giving you compensation data and advice when you are trying to figure out salary and equity packages—especially for senior hires
- Supporting a subsequent funding round by helping you perfect your pitch, making introductions, and serving as a reference for new prospective investors

For any of the above, if your investors can't help you directly, they probably know someone who can. Good investors won't expect you, especially if you are a first-time founder, to figure it out all by yourself.

I always appreciate the humility that comes from anyone who knows what they don't know and asks for help. It is impossible for anyone to know everything. And your investors are no different. Most genuinely want to be helpful and appreciate when you ask!

TOXIC INVESTORS

I have had the unfortunate experience of having to work directly with toxic investors both as fellow board members and as an executive. Let me tell you, it sucks. Bad behaviors I've experienced firsthand include racist comments in board meetings, investors bullying CEOs, and undermining founders by back-channeling with their direct reports or colluding with other investors to drive the narrative of a business. Often, these behaviors are due to their insecurities, fears, and/or potential mental health issues that have not been properly addressed. Sadly, there are more of those bad actors out there than we'd like to admit, and it's important to be aware of this because once you take capital from an investor, you are in a permanent relationship. Even angel investors and advisors can be prone to crossing boundaries, bullying, and creating a lot of distractions and heartache for founders.

The CEO of a startup I work with was raising her series A and had several top-tier investors preparing to give her term sheets. This round would result in adding the lead investor to their board. I had known this founder and her cofounder since the early days of their startup and had advised them on many operational and strategic challenges as their venture scaled. Therefore, I was happy to oblige when the CEO asked if I would be a reference for her fundraising process.

One reference call was with an investor from a reputable firm. We went over the standard questions about how I knew the founders and what I saw as opportunities and challenges for the business. Then, this investor threw me for a loop. He said, "You've known the CEO for a while, what can you tell me about her personal life?" After

I scraped my chin off the desk, aghast at what I just heard, I answered, "I'm sorry, how is that relevant?" Without blinking, the investor went on. "You know . . . she's young. Like if she's in a serious relationship is there a likelihood she's going to get married and want to have kids, yadda yadda." If there was a cartoon bubble over my head at that time it would have read, "He knows it's 2022, right??" I did my best to finesse an answer without outright shaming the guy while in my head I was still processing, *My God, would he have asked me about this if a young guy was the CEO?*

I gave a vote of confidence that this CEO was a kick-ass leader and wouldn't allow anything in her personal life to impact the success of the business (you know, like a *guy*). Then, as soon as I got off the call with this investor, I called the CEO and said, "Unless you have no choice and he offers the best terms imaginable, I am not a fan of this guy becoming your boss on your board." Fortunately, she got better terms from a different, wonderful investor and passed on this investor. I still face-palm when I think about it, though.

There are many sad stories of women founders being hit on, harassed, or bullied by investors, but it's not just women who run into challenges with investors. I worked with a CEO whose lead investor was so furious about the CEO's decision to part ways with a team member, who the investor had a personal relationship with, that the investor stormed into the startup's office and planted himself in the middle of the open floor plan to "keep an eye on the business." The CEO was mortified, and his employees were wondering why a board director was sitting, arms crossed with a pissed-off look on his face, just glaring at them all while they worked. I coached the CEO to gently ask the investor to leave the office as it was both uncomfortable and undermining his leadership for him to behave in such a manner. The investor acquiesced, left in a huff, and the working relationship between him and the CEO was irreparable (the CEO was removed from the business less than a year later). You can't make this shit up!

The moral of these stories is to be clear about what you are signing up for beyond the capital and valuations you are getting from your investors. Do backdoor checks on your investors just like you would with anyone you hire. But even if all checks out, remember that they are worried about the performance of their portfolio companies and, like you, trying to keep stakeholders happy. So sometimes the ugly stuff doesn't show itself unless things go south. If they are on your board, they are doing their best to straddle the line between being fiduciaries of your business as well as their own. Most investors are not as bad as the ones I described here, and you can often address these issues by adopting some of the techniques around managing conflict that I'll touch on in Chapter 15.

STARTUP ADVISORS

Advisors can be amazingly helpful to your venture. They bring experience, expertise, and support that can augment your team until you are able to hire more talent. However, some advisors do not understand the boundaries of their roles, so here are a few final things to consider when it comes to managing advisors:

- **Formal advisors should be added with care.** These are usually industry leaders or domain experts and tend to be most helpful in the first few years of a startup's life. I've seen three types of advisors:
  - **The domain expert** who just wants to be helpful, takes a call here and there, is included on your pitch deck for credibility purposes, and/or serves as a mentor to you when you need a kind and experienced ear.
  - **The consultant** who may make key business introductions or can help with a particular part of your business for a discrete period of time. If an advisor is putting twenty-plus hours per month into your venture, you may consider

paying them a small consulting fee in addition to equity. Just be sure to write a statement of work to make it clear what those hours and consulting fees are for and over what time period.

- o **The control freak** (especially common for advisors who are also angel investors). I worked with a founder who had two advisors with strong connections in her target market. Not only did they hold their connections hostage in exchange for the founder agreeing to their advice (!), but they also colluded behind her back to manipulate the way the company operated and undermined her leadership with her employees. After many wasted, and stressful, hours managing their bad behaviors, she had to ask both of them to step out of their advisor roles.

The first two types of advisors are terrific and are usually contractually compensated with stock options in your venture commensurate with the amount of time they'll be giving you. The Founder Institute created the FAST (Founder/Advisor Standard Template), which is an industry standard and has a simple format for determining how much equity you should give an advisor depending on the stage of your business and their level of involvement. Advisors are usually brought on in two-year intervals and their equity vests monthly with no cliff. To avoid the less desirable third type of advisor, if you haven't brought them on already, set expectations up front with a clear agreement about their scope of involvement. If they are already working with you, you may need to have a hard conversation and/or fire them if they are creating more work or more harm than good.

Finally, a quick note on boards of directors versus advisory boards. Your official board of directors will usually start when you do either a seed or your first priced round and will include the founders and investors. Part of the negotiation process when raising capital will be how many independent director seats you can add to the board. Independent directors are not investors in the business and are typically selected by you and approved by the board of directors. Independent directors at startups are usually compensated with equity and serve as objective fiduciaries of the venture. They serve the venture best when they bring expertise to the board. As an independent director myself, I usually fill in the product leadership and general management expertise that the founding team lacks. Other independent directors bring marketing, sales, or industry expertise. Together, the board of directors operates at a strategic level and must act in accordance with the company bylaws and maintain fiduciary responsibilities. Ultimately, the board of directors' primary job is to manage the CEO and not get involved with the daily operations of the venture.

Advisory boards can be super helpful to both foster collaboration and innovation as well as to build discipline around board governance before you have a real board of directors one day. However, they are not necessary and can create more work than help. It's nice to introduce advisors to each other (I've met some great humans because we were all advising the same company!), but don't feel obligated to set up an advisory board unless you really think it will be valuable to get this group together on a regular cadence.

If you take anything away from this chapter, I hope it is to enter into the fundraising world carefully. Do your homework, seek counsel from not just founder-friendly lawyers but from other founders and friends who have experience fundraising. And remember, fundraising can be a great way to fuel your startup, but it's not the only way to get a cash infusion. So, consider all your options before jumping on that hamster wheel!

13.

GO-TO-MARKET STRATEGIES

The term go-to-market (GTM) is a catchall for many different things from pricing and selling your product to branding and packaging, social media, public relations, and sales collateral. GTM is complicated, multifaceted, and some would argue an art much more than a science that can cost a company a lot of cash if not done right. GTM strategies are highly dependent on not just what product you are selling, but who you are selling it to and how you sell it. While I am not a sales and marketing expert, I have a lot of experience managing and working with marketing teams and know when a good GTM strategy is working. A poor execution of a GTM strategy can cause your venture to flounder once your product is out in the wild.

You and/or your cofounder(s) are usually the first salespeople for your startup. Spinning up a sales function is complex and highly dependent on the type of business you are building and where you are building it. So, I won't get into a lot of details here about building a sales strategy or operations function in this chapter, but I have included some readings for those who want to get deeper on the topic in the Resources section of this book. So, let's focus here on GTM. A good first step for most startups is to use early funding to hire a "full stack marketer" to do some basic activities like get your website in order and improve brand awareness by doing search engine optimization (SEO) or by building up your social media presence. This role is best filled by a contractor because you are likely not sure what your GTM strategy will be for your venture, yet. But once your venture starts to get traction and you are close to or have reached PMF, it will require a diverse set of skills to do GTM well. In this chapter I'll offer the basic aspects of a GTM strategy, highlight the blind spots of marketing brands and products, and suggest how to think about pricing your products.

BRANDING AND BRAND AWARENESS

Branding and brand awareness are related concepts but serve different purposes in the world of marketing and business strategy. It is important to define each because whether you are doing the work yourself as a founder or joiner, or you are going to hire a consultant or full-time person to do this work, you need to know the difference!

- **Branding:** Patrick Campbell, branding and pricing expert and founder of ProfitWell (and regular guest in my classroom), says, "Brand is the likelihood someone does something (and the magnitude to which they do it) when you ask them to do it." Building a brand is the process of creating and managing the brand's identity and positioning it uniquely in the market. This typically involves defining the core values, mission, vision, and personality of the brand, and expressing these through elements like taglines, logos, website or packaging design, colors, images, and messaging.

Branding shapes the perception of the brand in the minds of customers, differentiating it from competitors and building a strong, recognizable identity.

- **Brand awareness:** This refers to ensuring that your target market is familiar with and recognizes your brand. It determines how well the target audience can identify the brand under different conditions and is often considered the first step in the customer journey. A brand that has high awareness is a brand that is easily recognizable and memorable to a target market, which can lead to increased trust and preference.

Effective branding lays the foundation for building strong brand awareness, and high brand awareness can reinforce and amplify the efforts of branding. The two are deeply intertwined. Your efforts in both areas focus on filling the "funnel" of potential buyers, and when done well, will move these buyers from consideration to purchase. Lauren Davis, a fractional CMO and founder of the firm Alkali Marketing, has worked with dozens of startups. She says, "It's important to know which part of your funnel (or sales pipeline) needs care and feeding. Do you need more top-of-funnel activity (awareness campaigns) or mid-funnel (nurture campaigns) or bottom-funnel (account-based marketing) to make your business successful?"

At VMware, which was founded in 1998 when using Reddit, Twitter, or TikTok to market a product was not yet a thing, we were selling to developers, and our target audience didn't much care about how pretty our logo was or even what our name represented—but we needed a brand that would resonate with our top of funnel. The first logo was a basic VM in a square with a "ware" next to it to offer a visual representation of what we offer, virtual machines (also known as "VMs"—a term we learned we needed to market unto itself because most of our audience didn't understand what virtualization even was or why it was important). The logo eventually evolved to overlapping squares to signify multiple VMs, which was a quite literal brand approach. At Akamai, however, we hired an outside firm to test out name ideas that resonated with the way our founders wanted the brand to be perceived, more than what we did (content delivery networks or CDNs—again, a concept we discovered needed its own marketing). The word "akamai" means smart or clever in Hawaiian. Playing on the Hawaiian theme and to evoke the idea of speed and riding on a new emerging technology, our logo included a wavelike symbol that has evolved over the decades, but it's still a wave that most in the industry recognize as Akamai Technology's logo.

While both companies' logos have evolved over time, neither VMware nor Akamai ever changed their names, and their brands are ubiquitous in the platform and infrastructure industry. But you don't have to select a name, logo, or even a web domain that has to stay with the venture for life. Many companies, like the familiar cap table software company Carta, which was once known as eShares, change their brands over time either because they are addressing a new audience due to a pivot or because they run into other hurdles like trademark issues or public relations challenges. In the case of trademark issues, SAYSO, which we met in Chapter 3, was originally named Steep't to represent the method by which customers used their cocktail tea bag product. While the original brand name was a great representation of their product, they ran into an issue when they filed their trademark application and another company called Steeped contested their use of the name. At that point they hadn't invested much in the brand, so it was easier to change the name than incur legal fees. Further, because the name "Steep't" was also a literal representation of how their first product was used, they determined it was limiting when planning for product expansion beyond the tea sachets. As to why they went with SAYSO, one of the cofounders, Chloe Bergson, explains, "We were in a 9 a.m. session with our formulator tasting new cocktails. We taste everything with alcohol and just with water to make sure they are good as both cocktails and mocktails. We were several cocktails in and still working through what our formulator had prepared for us. Alison looked at me and said, 'Do you want another?' I said, 'If you say so,' and that was that!"

When and how to build awareness of a brand is not the same as marketing a new product, but sometimes they can overlap. VMware built early brand awareness at the same time they were gearing up to release their first product, VMware Workstation. They took a bottom-up (or "land and expand") approach and built brand awareness among programmers by attending conferences and joining chat groups of programmers talking about how to optimize their workflows. The goal was to get these programmers to start using the product at work (land) and then convince their peers and eventually bosses to adopt the product across the organization (expand). VMware Workstation was announced in 1999 at a conference where emerging technologies and new products are showcased. The intent was to build excitement for the beta release due out a month later by showing off how the product would improve developer productivity. I wasn't at the company at this time, but the founders love to share stories about how on the day of the beta launch we had so many customers try to order the product (it was shrink-wrapped software back then) that our order system crashed! We had clearly found a pain point for our customers, and as we scaled we took on more mainstream brand awareness techniques like newspaper and television ads, which were expensive but necessary at that time to ensure we continued to be a known quantity in our industry.

VMware began to market Workstation just before the product was ready to release, but some startups create the brand and build awareness well before a product is born. This can build an audience ready to buy. Building a brand early can be for the company itself or it can start with the founder, who can then lead their followers to a company brand. Emily Weiss did the latter with her renowned Into the Gloss website. This website offered Emily's beauty tips and product recommendations and allowed her to build a massive following before she even had a product. Her audience loved her perspective on beauty, and she was relatable to a younger generation of consumers at the time. As a result, when her venture, Glossier, announced their first products, their buyers were ready to buy. By first building Emily's and then Glossier's brand and audience pre-product, Glossier didn't have to rely on advertising so their customer acquisition costs were lower, and they also didn't need to give retailers a cut of their profits. This meant Glossier could continue to sell their products directly to customers at lower prices, which was part of the brand's appeal.

DigitalOcean's massive early growth was largely due to a brand strategy developed by Mitch Wainer, a cofounder who knew almost nothing about IT infrastructure. Because he was empathetic to customers who knew very little about cloud computing, he was able to develop a GTM strategy with a customer-first mindset. His strategy was to write content on the company's website that covered cloud technology basics in layperson's terms. He intentionally avoided pushing our product in this content to position DigitalOcean as approachable experts in cloud computing. The result was a trusting audience that chose our product over the bigger, more complicated, and expensive brands up-market.

KEY MARKETING FUNCTIONS

Brand and brand awareness are the two most important areas of GTM that most early-stage companies focus on. But there are several other key elements of your GTM strategy that will give your startup more light and may require different types of employees, consultants, or agencies to execute on each. Let's walk through the most common elements and how they come together to form your GTM strategy.

- **Public Relations and Communications (PR/Comms):** It's not always easy to tell your story such that the *what, why,* and *how*[1] of your venture/product is clear. Comms and/or PR specialists are great at coming up with memorable tag-lines, clear copy, and imagery on your website's landing page, and content that articulates your core values, products, and story. They can also be well connected to influencers and with various media channels that will ensure these mes-sages get out there, such as news outlets, industry analysts, conferences, and podcasts. It can be money well spent to hire an expert to do this instead of trying to figure it out yourself.

- **Social Media and Content Strategy:** Every business these days has a social media presence of some kind. Your choices around which platforms to use and how you'll use them go beyond your founder brand (see the "Founder Brand" box). The first step is to know where your audience is, which can often come out of your early discovery work. Once you decide where to have a presence, you'll also need a content strategy—including what you'll do organically or pay for like ads on social media, newsletter placements, etc.—for each platform that maps out details such as what topics you'll cover in blog posts, newsletters, or podcasts; who will write/speak on them; what images will be needed; whether you will create original content, repost others', or use stock photos, etc. It helps to develop a social media and content strategy calendar so it's clear what's coming and what con-tent you'll need, and align this strategy with other company activities like conferences and events, product launches, and perhaps deals or partnership announcements.

- **Product Marketing:** This is a strategic function within a company that focuses on bringing a product to market and

ensuring its success throughout its life cycle. It is a role that
sits at the intersection of product development, sales, and
marketing and serves to position the product effectively.
Product marketers can be part of a marketing team, but
sometimes they are within the product management or even
sales teams. It's less important where this function lives than
how it is used, which can range from market research to
sales enablement and everything in between. Most startups
don't bring on a product marketer until they have the basic
marketing and sales functions in place. Then, a product marketer can amp efforts around messaging and training, and
leverage many other tools they have to foster adoption and
scale the use of your product.

- **Conferences and Podcasts:** Part of VMware's early marketing strategy was to not only attend conferences, but also
launch our own an annual conference, VMworld. VMworld
served as a way to educate our target audience on virtualization as well as introduce our customers to the growing
ecosystem of virtualization startups building complementary products. VMworld was renamed VMware Explore in
2022 and continues to attract tens of thousands of attendees
from around the world. Podcasts are also a common and less
expensive way to build an audience with fewer logistical challenges than creating or attending a conference. In the height
of the pandemic when attending in-person conferences was
completely off the table, Chris Savage, cofounder of Wistia
whom we met in Chapter 6, spun up a podcast series called
Talking Too Loud (because he talks loud when he's excited
about things) not only to promote the company's brand as
a thought leader in marketing, but with Wistia's new pod-
casting product in the market, it was also to "eat their own
dogfood"[2]—a term referring to when a company proves the
quality of their product by using it themselves.

Setting up your own conference or podcast series may not be an option early on. Both are time-consuming and can cost money to set up and promote, and, these days, there are so many podcasts that it can be hard to differentiate your platform. However, you can promote your business by attending conferences or being a guest on others' podcasts. Just do your homework before you take these on to be sure it's worth the effort. A poorly attended conference or a relatively unknown podcast with few followers is not a good use of time or resources.

- **Messaging:** Ultimately, everyone and everything related to your business is marketing. This means it's critical that there is alignment across all aspects of your business when it comes to messaging. Davis emphasizes, "Your messaging should be clear, compelling, and consistent. This creates 'stickiness,' which is important when you are trying to make your marketing dollars go farther. People often need to see a message several times before really digesting it. So if your marketing materials are not all speaking the same language, you aren't just confusing people, you're also not making your way toward 'several times.'"

In addition to the key elements above, remember, how you behave in and outside of work, and how you are perceived as an employer to your community and to the broader ecosystem and industry, all impact your brand. When my team launched a "girl geek dinner" series at VMware, we were seen as not only an innovative technology organization in the tech industry, but one that supported diversity and inclusion. Events like these supported our employer brand and our efforts to increase the number of resumes we got from women and other underrepresented candidates. So, as you are developing your GTM strategy and each operational effort, it is important to have a common message that flows throughout.

FOUNDER BRAND

Building a founder brand can be an incredible way to build a business.[3] But not every founder is keen on self-promotion, and for some, it can be not only challenging but potentially destructive. For women, this has been an ongoing struggle as we attempt to break the glass ceiling. There is a double standard to get out there and promote yourself and your venture, but not do so in a way that is off-putting to "nonfemales." If you are a woman of color, it's even more challenging. Black women risk being perceived as angry instead of strong, or sassy instead of confident, and if you come from a culture that values modesty, promoting oneself is considered taboo. Stella—founder of Dowa, a maternal mental health platform—was raised to be successful, quietly. "I was to smile, hide my emotions, and not bring controversial attention. Privacy meant security. When I'm told I need to be the face of the company and get personal on social media, it's not just uncomfortable, it feels dangerous." Because of this cultural expectation, Stella can't just jump onto TikTok or Instagram to promote her business without considering the emotional impact it could have on her and her family.

Your startup can become so strongly tied to your identity that it impacts the company brand in the eyes of customers and business partners. This was the case with Emily and Glossier, and it worked to the company's benefit in the early growth years. However, it can have negative implications if a brand is associated with a founder like Adam Neumann of WeWork, whose deep flaws in leadership, governance, and financial management impacted investor confidence and public perception of the WeWork brand. The WeWork saga[4] serves as a stark reminder of how your actions could profoundly influence the trajectory and reputation of a business.

Founder branding may not be for everyone. However, if you choose to go that route, then storytelling is the best way to start building a memorable and engaging brand. It's important to focus on your story and know where your audience is so you can get the best results. Karen Young, a founder of the beauty brand OUI the People (OTP), was grappling with putting herself out there on TikTok, a commonly used platform for promoting beauty products. As a Black female founder and self-proclaimed introvert, it was hard enough for Karen to be willing to be a voice on a podcast let alone a "personality" on TikTok. After much hemming and hawing, she leaned in to her Guyanese roots and made a TikTok video about how her uncles never had ingrown hairs and how that inspired her to create OTP's first product, a single-blade razor made for women. She demonstrated the razor while swaying to Caribbean music in her first viral video, which received tens of thousands of shares and likes from those who could relate to her story. That experience unlocked Karen's confidence to continue to build her founder brand. While not everyone who buys her products has a personal connection to her story, the video made Karen authentic and approachable, and she continued integrating more founder stories into her marketing strategy.

Having a story and knowing where your audience is gets you two-thirds of the way there when it comes to your founder brand approach. The final piece of the puzzle is to know what metrics to measure to determine if your founder brand has impact. Emily at Glossier's early metrics were likely the number of followers and newsletter subscribers because these were the future consumers of her products. Karen, with OTP already in the market, measured impressions (views) and new and repeat purchases through links on her social media accounts.

Are you ready to take the plunge and start leveraging your founder brand? If so, take some time to think about *your* story. What makes you unique as a founder? What is relatable to your audience regardless of your background or cultural differences or *because* of those differences? And finally, where is your audience and how will you measure the impact of your efforts to be sure these efforts are time well spent?

PRODUCT-LED GROWTH

Companies may choose to adopt a product-led growth (PLG) strategy, which means they leverage their product(s) as their primary driver of customer acquisition, expansion, and retention. In a PLG strategy, the product plays a central role in attracting, engaging, and converting users into loyal customers. The eyewear venture Warby Parker's PLG strategy is to allow consumers to try on frames at home before they make a purchase, whereas the communication platform Slack's PLG strategy is to offer a free version of its software with essential features, making it easy for teams to start using the product without any up-front cost. In both of these examples, the goal is to hook the customer with as little friction as possible as a primary marketing strategy. The generally accepted core tenets of PLG are:

- **User experience:** Make it exceptional to deliver value to customers quickly and effectively. At DigitalOcean we did this by ensuring that even the most inexperienced cloud user could adopt our product fast and cheap.
- **Referrals:** Encourage customers to share and recommend the product to others (word of mouth or WOM) through social media, email campaigns, and other promotional activities like conferences and events.
- **Self-service:** The product is easy to discover and use without requiring extensive support or sales intervention. Users can sign up, onboard, and begin using the product on their own, like Slack or Dropbox.
- **Try before you buy:** Offer free trials and freemium versions to whet a customer's appetite and entice them to upgrade to a paid version. Slack also does this well by offering a fairly robust free version for small teams and businesses, but if you want to start adding a lot more users or use their cool AI tools, you have to upgrade to a paid plan.

- **Customer feedback:** Allow customers a way to share their ideas and issues into the product development cycle, ensuring that the product evolves to meet user needs and preferences. Notion, a workspace for note-taking, project management, and collaboration, has a feedback system where users can submit suggestions and report bugs directly within the app. The company also actively engages with its user community through forums, social media, and public roadmaps, where users can see upcoming features, vote on what they want to see next, and directly interact with the Notion team. No wonder it's one of the most popular collaboration tools used by startups!

- **Fear of missing out (FOMO):** For PLG, this is often done by restricting access in a closed beta or invitation-only release. When Gmail first came out, it was by invitation only and was considered a badge of honor if you were able to get your first name @gmail.com. But the FOMO approach can also backfire. The real-time, audio-based social network Clubhouse had an exclusive closed beta release impeccably timed in April 2020 at the start of the pandemic lockdown when people were craving connection. Clubhouse became popular among celebrities, influencers, and industry leaders, fueling its viral growth and driving more invitations and WOM sharing. It was a great way to kick-start this new app; however, the founders and their investors (who put millions in when it was barely a product) made many vulnerable assumptions about the amount of time people would spend on the platform once users were no longer on lockdown or how many users they'd need to onboard before more established platforms like Twitter, which had millions of users, could create a competing solution. The company continues to evolve, but it's no longer the darling it once was in 2020.

PLG focuses on making the product so valuable and easy to use that it essentially sells itself. By centering the growth strategy around the product, companies can create a more sustainable and scalable business model, leveraging user satisfaction and organic growth to drive success. But, as with the other elements of operating a startup, PLG alone will not drive any venture's long-term success.

PRODUCT PRICING

In the early stages of a venture, pricing intersects with sales and marketing as you figure out what customers are willing to pay (WTP) for your product and how the brand and value proposition resonate with customers. As discussed in Chapter 3, testing WTP is not a great way to do discovery work when you are still trying to suss out who your target persona is and what product you are actually going to sell. But if you've done proper discovery work, by the time you're developing your marketing strategy you should be at a point where you know you have enough interested buyers. That's when you can start to experiment with pricing. Sean Grundy, cofounder of Bevi, a smart water cooler for offices, did a lot of trial and error in the early 2010s to figure out what his customers would pay for a Bevi machine in their offices. They did a number of early trials first to ensure they built a machine that was useful and met their customers' needs as well as to learn their maintenance requirements, flavor preferences, and a host of other considerations. When charging for the first few machines, Sean created prices based on what he knew these customers were spending on single-use bottles of water and cans of seltzer. Sean explains, "We noticed that they always gave us their spend using monthly numbers (e.g., $500 per month) rather than on a per-drink basis (e.g., 50¢ per can), so we presented our pricing in the same way." He essentially performed a MaxDiff analysis as we discussed in Chapter 3 and priced on the high side for some customers and offered lower prices to others. It was easy to learn when he was charging too much, but it took a few iterations to discover the price point that was too low for his customers to take him seriously. "We ended up offering a flat price per month that was lower than what companies were spending on bottles and cans," Sean said. This worked for his ICP and maintained the margins he needed to achieve the unit economics necessary for a healthy venture.

Pricing can be done in a multitude of ways, but the following are the most common approaches:

- **Cost-plus or markup pricing** is simply figuring out the cost of making the product and then determining your desired profit margin. This approach does not consider market research or the value that your product gives your customers. For example, it may cost you $100 to make a widget and you want to make 50 percent margin so you will charge $150 for that widget. Or, you may be creating a marketplace business like Etsy, which takes a commission fee as a percentage of each sale made on the platform.

- **Competitor-based pricing** is as it sounds and bases your price on what your competitors are charging. This approach can be effective if it ensures that your product price is comparable, but if your competitors aren't conducting proper market research, then their pricing may be way off or not aligned with the value proposition. I am not a fan of using competitor analysis for pricing or for product development for this reason. It's good to know what the competition is up to, but that should never drive important business decisions.

- **Value-based pricing** is the strategy I strongly recommend and is based on how much target consumers believe the product or service is worth. Using the widget example, although it costs only $100 to make the widget, what if your customer can save $500 by adopting this widget? Should you only charge $150 to capture a 50 percent profit margin or could you charge even more, perhaps $250, because in the end, the customer is still going to save $250 for every widget they buy? Value-based pricing focuses more on your customers' pain points, and by helping them resolve that pain, they are likely to be more inclined to buy your product no matter what you charge. This strategy can take a lot of time and resources, so if time is limited, one of the prior options can be a better way to get started.

- **Dynamic or demand-based pricing** factors in things such as consumer demand, market conditions, and competitor prices, to optimize pricing in real time or over specific periods. For example, airline tickets and hotel rooms fluctuate based on demand, seasons, and booking times. Or ridesharing services fluctuate prices during surge times like rush hour or bad weather.

There are all sorts of ways to think about experimenting with pricing, from free to premium pricing for certain features, tiered pricing based on usage, by number of users or "seats," customer size (which could be annual revenue, number of employees, or even number of customers they have if they are a B2B venture), or even variable pricing, which is done on a case-by-case basis (usually for large-enterprise sales). Figuring out the right pricing approach for your startup serves as another marketing lever in the arsenal of ways to grow your brand awareness. Whether you take a trial-and-error approach like Sean did at Bevi, or hire a pricing specialist, know that your price will likely not be "just right" in the early stages and you should expect to change your product's price as often as every few months in the first year or so of your venture's life.

PUBLIC LAUNCHES

A public launch event for a startup is an effective way to promote your product and the venture itself. It usually involves a comprehensive plan to coordinate marketing, sales, product development, and customer support (which may be just a handful of people in an early-stage business) to bring awareness to your product and your company—all the elements of a great GTM strategy that I've covered in this chapter. A public launch speaks to your customer's pain points and makes it immediately clear how your product's value proposition and features address those pain points. It also incorporates brand identity and key messages for the brand, the product, and sometimes even the founder and often includes a call to action (CTA) to spark buyers to make a purchase. A notable example is when Hims & Hers, a direct-to-consumer telehealth startup that offers a range of wellness products and services, launched in 2017 with a high-profile marketing campaign that addressed stigmatized issues like sexual and mental health and leveraged social media and influencer marketing to create buzz. In 2014, the dating app Bumble had a launch that focused on female empowerment and challenging traditional dating norms. Bumble's founder, Whitney Wolfe Herd, used strategic partnerships and endorsements to promote Bumble and organized events that highlighted its brand values and attracted media attention that drew users to the app. Both of these startups had wildly successful IPOs in 2021. If you are considering a public launch to promote your first product and bring attention to your venture, you should plan for these essential phases:

- **Prelaunch:** This phase involves generating buzz and anticipation through teasers, sneak peeks, and marketing campaigns. It could also involve collaborations with influencers and thought leaders to build credibility and build a broader audience and, especially for software products, could include some beta testing with a select group of users to gather feedback, improve your product, and garner some early-adopter testimonials or case studies for the public launch.
- **Soft-launch:** Sometimes in parallel with a prelaunch, companies will do a soft launch to start to build excitement for

what's to come. Robinhood, a commission-free trading platform for consumers, soft-launched in 2013 by offering early access through a waiting list. The soft launch allowed Robinhood to test their software, build anticipation, and ensure that everything worked smoothly before doing a public launch in 2014.

- **Launch:** The launch itself starts early, even before prelaunch, with your first step being to develop a detailed timeline that includes key milestones and deadlines. Early planning also involves identifying the most effective channels for reaching your target audience, such as advertising, social media, building relationships with influencers, email marketing, PR, and live events. Create a content schedule that includes a cadence of blog posts, videos, press releases, and other materials to support the launch. Also, integrate your sales and support strategy into your launch plan so, if you have team members in these functions, they are equipped with the necessary training, materials, and incentives to effectively sell and support the product. Finally, include details in your launch plan that ensure the product is available through the appropriate distribution channels, whether online, in stores, or through partners. On launch day, make sure the team is prepared and knows their places, such as who will be answering the phones or monitoring support tickets, and what the "crash plan" is if something goes awry (remember when VMware's website crashed because of too many customers on our launch day?). You should also have clear service level agreements (SLAs), which I will discuss more in the next chapter.

- **Postlaunch:** Activities include tracking the launch's performance through metrics such as sales, customer engagement, and customer feedback. Have a process in place to ensure collected data will be used effectively to make necessary adjustments and improvements to the product, marketing, sales and/or strategies. Postlaunch plans should also include continuous marketing efforts to maintain momentum and drive long-term success. While launch day itself is a big one, momentum is critical!

You're more likely to have a successful public launch if you carefully plan and execute each of these phases, but keep in mind that launches are rarely perfect. Some are bittersweet, like the VMware launch, but sometimes, they turn into duds. At DigitalOcean we planned a big launch with press, media, and a massive website overhaul when we were introducing our new load balancer product, only to result in crickets on launch day. Why? Because we had not done the right customer research. All our customers had said having a load balancer was critical for them to use more of our service. However, because we didn't have this capability for some time, they had found alternative solutions. So, instead of our current customers jumping at the chance to use our shiny new product on launch day, we had to wait weeks for new customer adoption.

What should be clear from the breadth of topics in this chapter is that early GTM strategies are complex and involve a lot of variables to get a new product and/or venture to market. Don't underestimate the time and expertise needed to get this right. Tap into advisors, investors, and your network to take each aspect on instead of trying to figure it out yourself. Time is better spent focusing on the core development of your product and services, where you are truly differentiating and adding value to customers.

14.

A TALE OF
TWO STOOLS:
HOW INNOVATION
AND DELIVERY CAN
SIT TOGETHER

In the earliest stages of a startup, you are usually juggling the interplay between sales, support, and product development—the latter of which includes product management, engineering, and design functions—and early on, you may be doing most of these functions yourself or with a cofounder(s). Staying close to all of these activities is critical as you develop an understanding of what to build and how to price, pitch, close, and support customers. Over time, you will hire people to handle these functions, so it's good to begin to build a process for ensuring all of them work well individually and are aligned in what I like to call the "three-legged stools." There are two types of three-legged stools:

- **Engineering, product, and design (EPD)** is the more common three-legged stool in product development, and the three functions must play well together to build great products. More common in tech businesses, but also in other industries, these functions decide what to build, when and how to build it, and the aesthetics of the product itself.
- **Product, sales, and support (PSS)** is the other, and often forgotten, three-legged stool that ensures there is a solid feedback loop between all the people who interact with your customers. Without this, you run the risk of unhappy customers, leading to churn, reputational, and revenue challenges.

I am not going to tell you how to structure your product organization (that's a whole other book), build a sales playbook, or the best way to build a customer support team. But, what I will do in this chapter is break down how to think about each of these functions in a startup and how they can work well together.

ENGINEERING, PRODUCT, AND DESIGN

The EPD team members define and build the solutions your customers buy and use. Let's break down each in more detail:

Engineering

Depending on what you are building, these are the software and/or hardware developers who build things. At a startup, these team members should be adept at understanding customer pain points and business objectives. Engineers can be contractors early on until you can afford to hire full-time employees, and that's usually best anyway since you are likely still trying to figure out what to build and how you want to build it!

Product Management (PM)

Product management does customer research, specifies requirements, and partners with designers and engineers to build and release products. They are often the first voice of the customer, and sales and support become the second and third voices once your product is ready to be out in the market. PM usually drives and manages the product roadmap, partners with marketing for launches, and often does market and pricing analysis for new features and products. The best PMs partner well with all key stakeholders in the venture and deeply understand business goals and objectives. While they tend to be great project managers, their strengths are their ability to translate pain points into prioritized solutions and bring new concepts to life.

Design

These are the people who craft the UX of the company's product, and user interface (UI) if that product is software. They are deeply involved in the entire development process by conducting user research (with PMs), creating wireframes and prototypes, testing designs, and collaborating closely with engineers and PMs to bring products to life. They may also partner with the GTM function to design the brand, website, and other collateral.

PRODUCT, SALES, AND SUPPORT

The PSS team members are the customer-facing team members who ensure you are building and selling the right things and that your customers are happy. In this stool, Product represents PM, as described above. So, let's break down sales and support each in more detail.

Sales

Every startup will have a different approach to their sales process depending on the type of product they are building, problems they are solving, and market segments they are going after. Direct-to-consumer approaches will rely heavily on product-led growth and organic growth with no sales team at all, as we did the first four years at DigitalOcean. Some will have an inside sales function with reps doing outbound calls to generate and qualify leads that an outside sales rep or account executive can close. For ventures that do enterprise sales, they may have to develop a whole sales playbook to understand how to go from user to buyer, meet regulatory requirements, and pass other hurdles to close a deal with a long sales cycle. You may also have to develop different playbooks for different kinds of accounts. For example, selling to government agencies will require a different tack than selling to a large tech company, including having to hire sales reps with security clearance.

Even if you have figured out your sales playbook, handing over the keys for a sales leader to drive can be scary. You may worry the salesperson won't be as passionate or credible about the product as you are and fear they will lose touch with their customers if you let go of sales. You may never let go of sales completely and continue to manage the biggest VIP deals yourself. This is perfectly fine, especially if the deals are high stakes. If you are still part of the sales process, be sure you set up the sales function for success—including being thoughtful about how they will work with your product and support teams. The very first sales rep may need up to ninety days at a startup to get to know the product and your ICPs before they are actually closing deals.

Customer Success

Customer success (CS) is the more common name for the support function in startups. This function ensures that customers achieve their goals when they use your product and have a positive experience. This team usually focuses on driving customer satisfaction, retention, and growth. Most startups build a CS function once they are starting to see signals of product-market fit and the founders and early joiners are less engaged in daily troubleshooting activities. That said, stepping too far away from this important "front line" of interaction with your customers can be dangerous. These teams are vital for identifying early indicators of bigger problems, and well-run CS teams can forge relationships with customers that open lines of communication in a unique way that you can learn from.

The first job I had out of college was essentially a CS role for a tiny nonprofit trade association in Wellesley, Massachusetts, that had created software for their members who managed warehouses and sold wholesale electrical products to retailers like lighting stores and electrical contractors. The trade association, National Electrical Manufacturers Representatives Association (NEMRA), was basically a startup, but in 1989, that term "'startup" had yet to enter the mainstream lexicon. My primary job there was a CS-type role to debug software issues and report user problems to our contract-development team. Our users were early adopters of technology in the late 1980s and were eager to give me feedback on our product. Once, one of our product managers came into the office to demo a fancy new sales-analysis product he was working on for our users. I knew our users would be delighted with this new capability, but I also knew from my interactions with them that this product would fall flat when our customers had real challenges with some of our most basic functionality. "You know, Wayne, that's super cool and I am sure they're going to love it, but the product-description field in the inventory product is only twenty-five characters long and their product descriptions can be up to sixty characters long. This makes data entry for these products impossible so they just don't put them in. This means this tool you're building will be missing a lot of important data and tell a false story." In my CS role, I had insights our product manager would have never known about! Thankfully, Wayne got it, and our users got not only a fancy new sales-analysis tool but also a useful product-description field along with it.

Being close to customers on the front lines allows CS teams to resolve issues and identify trends. These team members are often the best people to build relationships with customers and can make the difference between customer retention or churn. Before establishing a CS function in your startup, consider the types of roles they may play and how best to leverage your existing team in the near term to cover these roles until you are ready to build a CS team. These roles may include:

- **Onboarding customers** to train and guide them through the initial setup of the product, ensuring new customers understand its features and how to use them effectively.

- **Writing documentation** to help customers get started and maximize the value of the product.

- **Creating work-arounds** as stopgaps to address bugs that will require more development time to fix—especially if you have a complex product where fixing one bug can easily create another.

- **Establishing and monitoring service level agreements (SLAs)** that include performance metrics, response times, and responsibilities and will ensure accountability and clear expectations between your venture and your customers.

- **Maintaining customer engagement** through regular contact with customers to gather feedback, monitor their progress, address any issues, and offer support until you have account managers or sales reps on board. In this capacity, they can also be responsible for upselling new features or moving a customer to a higher pricing plan.

- **Monitoring growth metrics** such as a net promoter score (NPS), conversion rates, and customer acquisition cost (CAC) can offer a valuable perspective on how effective your marketing efforts are at fostering customer loyalty and word-of-mouth referrals.

- **Tracking customer retention metrics** can identify at-risk customers and provide proactive support before customers churn (stop using and paying for your product). They should also track net revenue retention (NRR), which takes into account expansion revenue (upgrades, cross-sells, or upsells).

A startup's CS team usually consists of a customer-success manager (CSM) who will be responsible for managing customer relationships and ensuring their success, customer support representatives (CSRs), and/or technical account managers, depending on the type of venture you are building. Some consumer product companies have CS teams who work with their manufacturing and distribution partners, separately from their direct customers, and some startups have a professional-services organization either as part of the CS team or working in parallel with them (as a fourth leg of the stool) when a product requires additional services that can be monetized.

THE THREE-LEGGED STOOLS IN ACTION

As you start to bring in talent for your product organization, the EPD stool will likely be facilitated by an engineering or product leader. These team members will have a high level of engagement with each other, every day. They may have daily thirty- or sixty-minute standups to review what's going well, not well, and to discuss any blockers that are preventing the team from delivering on product-related deadlines. Many startups use a sprint process, which involves chunking out the work to be done into a two- or three-week cadence. PMs are typically responsible for helping EPD teams do sprint planning, but sometimes an engineering leader or technical project manager (TPM) facilitates that process. The important thing here is that these three legs of the stool work collaboratively to avoid silos and foster the gestalt of the team (as discussed in Chapter 7) to drive innovation.

For the other three-legged stool, PSS, be mindful that balancing resources and maintaining a great sales process and high-quality support can be challenging, especially if the product is still evolving and your startup is trying to gain traction. As soon as you start to establish roles and teams like CS, sales, and product management, make sure they meet at least weekly to share insights from interactions with customers and are part of the product-prioritization process. Adopt a software tool or even a spreadsheet to share insights and track resolutions where you can look for trends such as many customers starting to request a similar feature (like the load balancer at DigitalOcean) or complaining about the same issue. These trends should be discussed at the routine meeting. One of my favorite activities throughout my startup journey as a product leader was when I met with members of our sales and support teams together. It was *so* helpful for me to hear what our customers were struggling with or what was keeping sales from closing a deal. I also found that sharing my product roadmap with them helped them appreciate all that we were doing and set expectations on the level of importance for certain requests.

The best PSS teams I have worked with were those that emphasized empathy and had a deep understanding of customer needs and goals. They were motivated to delight their customers and learn from them in order to improve their product instead of offering little-to-no support or blaming them for "not getting it." We have all experienced the difference between getting on a call with a service rep who says, "No problem, we are happy to issue a refund or send you a replacement product," no questions asked, and the unreasonable rep who tells you it's against company policy to make you happy. Don't be that second company. Even if your product is still fragile and prone to issues, keeping customers happy ensures they stay with you and tell their friends about you. Unhappy customers churn and are not afraid to make sure others churn too, through word of mouth and social media channels.

So, even when you are ready to hand over some of the day-to-day tasks of these functions in your business, be sure to foster a great relationship between all the legs of these two important stools. Depending on their skills and interest (technical/strategy), most founders still participate in the EPD and PSS discussions as their ventures scale. What's important here is to empower these teams to work well together even when you are not there so they can innovate and deliver the very best experience for your customers.

15.

COMMUNICATION STRATEGIES

This chapter could fit in any of the parts of this book, but because communications (what, how, why, and with whom we communicate) is core to almost every element of founding and scaling a startup, I put it in this section. From sharing plans with team members to articulating challenges, how you say it is as important as what you say. Not everyone communicates the same way, and ambiguity can create a lot of fear, uncertainty, and doubt (FUD) in a business.

In my course at HBS, I address this topic by workshopping a series of role-plays of common scenarios I've seen founders grapple with, and I'll share some of these scenarios in this chapter. In these role-plays, we do not focus on what the founder should do, but rather *how* they will communicate in each scenario. Becoming a strong communicator takes time and practice. The goal in my class and in this chapter is to bring awareness to this necessary skill for anyone involved in running a business and offer some tactics for specific situations depending on the stakeholders involved.

There are many key stakeholders in any venture and each commands a slightly different communication approach. This requires a lot of adapting and context switching no matter what role you play within the startup. This is not unique to startups, per se, but there are some types of communication challenges that can be much harder when you are in an early-stage venture.

COMMUNICATION HIERARCHIES

When you are just a few people in an early startup, communication can be pretty simple. There is usually a lot of asynchronous communication through an internal messaging tool, regular video meetings, or, if you happen to be in the same geography, you can have regular in-person interactions in a shared space. Information flows constantly in these early days and you all feel in sync about what you are doing and why. Even in this early stage, there still can be communication challenges when there's a difference in opinion, but these are usually much easier to resolve than when new stakeholders start to come on board. With more people, even if it's just going from two of you to a six-person team, communication quickly gets more complicated, and you may feel like you are spending more time communicating back and forth than doing your actual work. From setting milestones and directives to coaching new team members and keeping your stakeholders informed, it's a lot of cognitive load.

And as the team expands, there are different types of communication of the same issue, depending on the audience. Consider when you have to let an employee go. The firing itself will be a hard conversation, but then there's explaining to the team why an employee suddenly departed the business without sharing any details, and perhaps telling your board you had to let someone go. You may have to navigate a hard conversation with a customer who wants to change the terms of an agreement without losing the deal, and then explain to your lawyers why you are changing the terms of the deal. The point of these examples is that once a decision is made, you then have to figure out how to communicate that decision, sometimes to multiple stakeholders who need to hear things differently.

Before diving deeper into the best practices for handling common communication scenarios at startups, I've outlined the most common stakeholders you'll communicate with, within and outside of any startup, and what types of communication you may do with them:

- **Board of directors:** Communication with your board is usually done quarterly as a group and regularly with each director one-on-one. These conversations are strategically focused and most information is highly confidential and not shared with other internal and external stakeholders.
- **Angel investors:** These investors have a small stake in the venture and should receive basic information about the company's performance, but not as much as your board.
- **Advisors (or mentors):** These domain or skills experts will engage with you to offer their guidance on specific areas where they can be helpful. As such, you may communicate specific operational details of your startup but not all the operating or strategic details.
- **Former founders:** Once a founder, always a founder, so if you had one or more that are no longer with the venture, they may still have a board seat and/or be a significant shareholder, thus will expect updates on the health of the venture. Otherwise, they are in the know as much as an advisor or as the operating founder(s) feel comfortable (not all cofounders leave a venture on good terms, unfortunately).
- **Internal leaders:** As a venture scales, there will be a distinct management team or teams and there can be some growing pains in terms of what can and can't be shared with this group. Some company leaders may start to partake in board meetings and as such be more privy to strategic details and,

unless they are seasoned startup leaders, they may need some guidance on what is okay and not okay to share both with board directors and with their own teams. It's better to clarify these expectations with these leaders than hope they use good judgment because many honest mistakes can happen, like the first-time leader who accidentally tells their team about an upcoming layoff they heard about at a board meeting. Oops.

- **All company:** Somewhere around ten people in a startup is a good point to start having regularly scheduled communication from the founders to the whole company and a routine all-company meeting. A lot of startups do these weekly, and then as the venture scales, these meetings may taper back to biweekly or monthly. An all-company meeting agenda should be thoughtful and not only share updates like important milestones for the venture or announce key hires, but also be an opportunity to educate and celebrate. Consider having a different team present something about their work, or do a demo of a work in progress. Including time for shout-outs for teammates who did something exceptional is also a great touch, and all-company meetings are a great forum for Q&A with founders and key leaders or even with customers, advisors, or board members.

  Because not everyone processes information the same way, send a follow-up email after an all-company meeting that shares any details you want to be sure everyone understands. So if you explained a change in how a team will be structured, or announced at the meeting that there's a new vacation policy, send those details in an email too. This is especially important if there is a big announcement like a major change in company direction, which, once it's stated at the meeting, can cause some team members to "check out" and stop listening in the meeting as they think about how that big change will impact them.

Note: The heuristic for communicating with the whole company (live or online) is to share only what you would be comfortable seeing in a social media post. You hope you can trust everyone and ensure confidential information doesn't leave the company, but in today's world, there is always a risk of leaks. Manage it carefully.

- **Customers and partners:** In addition to standard product announcements, strategic partnerships, etc., startups often need to do a lot of support-related communication as you work through the kinks of a smooth operation. This can range from direct communication with specific customers and partners to broader communication with your customers on various media outlets.

For any communication strategy, be sure it aligns with your company values. This includes whether or not you decide your venture will take a public position on political, social, or environmental issues. Finally, anything you communicate should feel like it's coming from your company—not from an outside agency or a well-meaning but inexperienced employee unable to properly represent the ethos of the business and what you stand for.

BEST PRACTICES FOR BOARD MEETINGS

The outside directors on your board (nonfounders/employees) are fiduciaries of the business. Their first priority is to manage the CEO, but these individuals should also be helpful to the business. The best board meetings I have attended are those where the CEO is adept at setting expectations and leveraging their board for the greater good of the startup rather than using the meeting just to report on business performance, which we can learn about through regular one-on-one meetings and email updates. Preparing for board meetings should not consume all your time either. Your time is more valuable running the business than preparing for these meetings. This is what a healthy board meeting process should look like:

1. **Set expectations up front about meeting cadence and content as soon as the board forms.** Unless there is something urgent happening (like an exit), most startup boards meet as a group no more than once a quarter. Your board members may share what they like and don't like to have happen at board meetings, but that should not dictate what you do. And you will likely revisit the structure and content of these meetings as the venture evolves—especially if you do new funding rounds that result in bringing on new board members. After one such event, the CEO of a startup for which I was an independent director took that opportunity to change who came to the meetings, adding his head of product and head of marketing for a more fulsome conversation in both areas. He also changed how he shared company performance metrics with the board. He let us know ahead of the meeting that he was making these changes so there were no surprises.

2. **Send a detailed board package a few days ahead of the meeting.** The board package usually includes a slide deck for the upcoming meeting and PDFs of important documents such as spreadsheets with financial performance information, past meeting minutes and/or stock options to be approved, and other board business such as proposed changes to bylaws, 409A valuations, audit results, etc. The package should also have a summary memo that provides an overview on company performance by functional area, challenges, and a specific list of topics you would like to discuss at the meeting.

3. **The meeting should *not* be a recap of the board package.** Assume your board has read everything and will come prepared to the meeting to focus on the proposed agenda. Unfortunately, some board members do not do their homework, and this may require some managing-up to reinforce this expectation. Most startups do not have inside legal counsel, so you will want to engage your outside counsel to prepare motions and attend the meeting to take minutes and advise on legal matters if needed.

4. **The agenda** for a three-hour (max!) board meeting should be:
   - **CEO/founders with their leadership team, the directors, and counsel:** Discuss tactical challenges, ask for input/help, such as connections for sales deals or partnerships or how to handle a market challenge.
   - **CEO/founders with just the directors and counsel:** This is when motions are voted on (like new bylaws or option grants) and deeper topics are discussed that the whole leadership team may not be aware of, such as budget cuts.
   - **Just the directors:** (CEO/founders and counsel leave the meeting.) Directors discuss their thoughts about how the startup is doing and the CEO's performance. Remember, ultimately, that is the board's primary job—ensuring the CEO is performing. In this session, one director should synthesize the feedback from the others to present back to the CEO.
   - **Just the CEO rejoins the meeting and feedback is delivered:** Common feedback could be around performance in a particular function of the business, observations of their leadership of their team, or how they are handling a fundraising process. Feedback can also be about professional-development areas, like encouraging them to be more of an external voice of the company or

giving tough feedback like when we had to tell one CEO whose board I was on that they had to stop putting off replacing a poor performer. Getting this group feedback ensures it's timely and avoids the miscommunication I've seen when each board member gives conflicting feedback to a CEO sometime after the board meeting.

Outside of the board meetings, it's good hygiene for founders to have one-one-one meetings with each outside director on a monthly cadence to follow up on any action items from the last meeting, to get advice, and to keep them informed on important topics you know they'll be asking about at the next board meeting.

Having a productive and healthy board culture is a process that takes time to develop, just like getting a healthy team culture as discussed in Chapter 7. And as discussed in Chapter 12, when well managed and leveraged for what they can offer beyond their funds, investors and independent board members can be an incredible superpower for founders.

MANAGING CONFLICT

One of the toughest communication challenges is handling conflict, and it's especially hard when you are a first-time leader of your own business. When you have to fire someone for the first time or tell your cofounder you're not aligned on something, it can create a lot of anxiety. This is especially true if we have a history of trauma in our lives or bad experiences with conflict in past jobs or educational settings. Our amygdala response (fight-or-flight) can be triggered in these situations. How one manages conflict at work often has to do with how psychologically safe they feel in a particular scenario. My colleague at Harvard Business School, Dr. Amy Edmondson, bestselling author and organizational behavior expert, codified the concept of psychological safety as the belief that one will not be punished or humiliated for speaking up with ideas, questions, concerns, or mistakes, and the team is safe for interpersonal risk-taking. When we set up psychologically safe cultures within our organization, healthy conflict can result in amazing things!

I experienced a culture of healthy conflict at both Akamai and VMware where our founders encouraged debates and productive discourse. This ensured we saw all aspects of a challenge so we could create solutions without confirmation bias or hierarchical pressure. In the architecture boards I ran at both companies, I intentionally included our biggest contrarians to ensure we had a healthy debate on tough architectural decisions. In most cases, this resulted in far better outcomes than had we stuck to a group of engineers who tended to always agree on everything. We all felt safe and encouraged to explore all points of view on a problem, and we celebrated when a perspective we hadn't considered took us to a new and improved solution. However, in many startups, an unsafe culture and the psychological baggage that various players bring into the business can prevent healthy discourse and wreak havoc, causing a conflict trap. A conflict trap is when there is discourse without resolution because the parties involved do not feel safe or do not know how to shift discourse toward positive outcome.

No matter how much you may try to set up a psychologically safe culture that supports healthy discourse, you will undoubtedly find yourself in a conflict situation at some point along the startup journey. In these situations, it's important to consider that there may be more going on than you realize, and, by taking a compassionate perspective, you can often get to the root cause of conflict. An angry investor could be flipping out at a board meeting because his firm is struggling to raise their next fund, or perhaps he's dealing with a personal issue that has him misdirecting his frustration at you. Or perhaps your cofounder is lashing out at your team about closing a deal because the business is running out of cash. She may not just be worried about the impact on the business if you lose the deal, but she may also be worried about her personal finances if the startup were to fail. So, before armoring up for a battle with a colleague, first ask yourself, and if you are comfortable ask them directly, "Is there something else going on here that is causing this tension?"

Just asking what's going on opens a door for a psychologically safe conversation. In the examples above, for your investor, you might ask a direct question: "John, I noticed you seemed upset in the board meeting. Is there something else going on that I can be helpful with?" For your cofounder, before bringing up the tension with her, you might first ask yourself, *What can I do as her cofounder to support her?* Then, just tell her you've noticed she's been showing frustration with the team and ask what you can do to help. Odds are, she may not even realize how she's been behaving. By simply acknowledging the situation to yourself or others, you have begun to shift the conversation from conflict to resolution.

Sometimes, we are the root cause of the conflict. Remember in Chapter 9 when my executive coach Jerry Colonna suggested asking yourself, *How am I complicit in creating the conditions I say I don't want?* When in conflict, it's important to ask yourself about whether you may be contributing to the problem. The founder of a startup I work with was having daily arguments with his product manager about design decisions. When I asked him how he might be complicit in this situation, he stepped back and considered that he'd spent almost no time with her discussing design principles and his expectations for new product features. Recall Brené Brown's term "painting done," mentioned in Chapter 9. Had this founder been clearer about his expectations, he may have avoided all this strife.

Brené also has a fabulous quote about clarity and truth: "Clear is kind, unclear is unkind." She explained at a live speaking engagement I attended that when a situation is ambiguous, our fight-or-flight response kicks in, and, whether we like it or not, our brain creates stories to calm us down. So, when someone doesn't respond to a text right away or ambiguously changes their behavior (even if with good intentions), you will likely invent stories in your mind about what's really going on. When you are being ambiguous, you are stimulating this same response in others. Say you send an email to an employee to schedule a one-on-one meeting without context. This ambiguity could result in the employee thinking they are about to get fired. So, whether you are in a conflict situation or simply communicating with your team, it's important to ask yourself, *What stories am I (or they) telling myself (themselves)?* before addressing the issue or making the change.

"Painting done" and "clear is kind" are powerful tools to get ahead of conflict before it even begins to simmer. As much as we are racing against the clock, especially in early-stage startups when every second counts, when we slow down just a bit, are clear about our expectations and paint done, we will likely save tons of time and cognitive load and significantly reduce conflict situations.

Despite best efforts, there still will be times when conflict is necessary. We may end up with a poor performer who needs to be fired or an unreasonably angry customer who is threatening to post something negative about your business on social media if you don't comply with their demands. You and your cofounder are at an impasse on a critical product decision. These situations can be a huge distraction as you think about how to resolve them or hope they'll just go away—which rarely happens! As long as it won't break your bank account, make the angry customer happy even if they are wrong. Let the bad performer go by adopting the separation tactics covered in Chapter 9 and get a coach or mediator if you and your cofounder(s) are having issues. In other words, conflict is inevitable, so lean into it and get help when you need it. It's part of the job!

CRISIS MANAGEMENT

Every startup will have a crisis—hopefully not many—through the course of its lifetime, and not all these ventures will have seasoned leaders and the grit necessary to survive these crises. Many founders were unprepared when it came to managing the crisis surrounding the Silicon Valley Bank collapse in 2023. In addition to the operational learnings around banking and ensuring not all of their cash is in one vulnerable place, it was a big wake-up call for many founders in terms of how they do everything from keeping their cool with employees, investors, customers, and partners to how they communicate and manage tricky processes under pressure. You can't predict when a crisis will happen or how it may manifest, but you can create a simple crisis-management plan to prepare for the inevitable. This is a quick and dirty approach that I suggest a founding team put together as both an alignment exercise and to have something actionable to start with. This should be revisited as the venture evolves and scales:

1. **Define three levels of a situation** with measurable impacts that the team agrees would justify each level. Think of measuring the impact as "sizing the hole" in a leaky pipe. A small leak may just need a quick fix, but if it gets bigger, a lot more damage may ensue, requiring a bigger repair. I suggest color coding these levels like so:
   o **Code green:** It's annoying, but easy to address. This could be a technical bug that has a manual work-around until new code can be deployed or a typo on the website that is easy to edit.
   o **Code yellow:** Fixable, but may impact a business process and/or require additional customer communications, refunds, etc. This may be a delay in a shipment that prevents a customer pilot from starting on time, but the customer is flexible so it's not dire. Or, perhaps there is a billing mistake that causes customers to be overcharged. You can let customers know and offer refunds once fixed,

but it's extra work to get that done (and may be a little embarrassing/cause some customer churn).

o **Code red:** The business is at risk in a material way, such as major financial, reputational, or security issues that could impact customers or third parties. There must be alignment on the definition of "major" for something to be deemed a code red.

2. **Have an action plan and a directly responsible individual (DRI) for each code.** Depending on the type of business and the size of the team, the action plan may be situational. For example, it could be, for any code-green situation, the DRI will be whomever reported the issue, and they will develop and communicate the action plan. For a code yellow, the DRI will be the most appropriate team member (e.g., if it's a technical bug, it's the engineering lead, but if it's a pricing issue, it's the product manager). For a code red, it might always land on the CEO/cofounder(s), or if the startup is operating at scale, it could be someone in the C-suite based on the type of issue.

3. **Document a communications strategy for each code.** The red, yellow, and green codes can help you decide what's important to communicate, if at all. Code greens may require just letting relevant team members know what's happening, yellow may require communicating to key stakeholders like customers or partners, and code reds could require broad communication (public apologies, board updates, etc.). At DigitalOcean we had an issue that turned out only to impact a few dozen out of our thousands of customers. It was deemed to be a code yellow because we had a work-around until we could fix the problem in an upcoming release. By sizing the hole, we used our code yellow communication plan, which was to notify just the impacted customers about the issue instead

of issuing a broader announcement that may have alarmed the customers that were not impacted.

4. **Conduct a retrospective after any code green, yellow, or red crisis** to learn from what happened and continue to improve the crisis-management process.

While you can't prepare for every possible scenario, it's good to have a process in place. By taking the time to agree on levels of crises and how to respond to each, you can have an appropriate response to each and avoid overreacting, which can be distracting and waste time.

PART III

OPERATIONS TOOLBOX

Legal Matters

- Engage a lawyer who specializes in startups and, if needed, your specific business domain.
- Form a legal entity before money begins to exchange hands.
- Hold the bar when it comes to ethics and legal requirements as you are immersed in running your company.
- Work with an accountant to help you navigate tax laws, and with other experts if you operate all or part of your venture outside of the United States.
- Work with your lawyer to create contracts and agreements. When asked to use a third party's paper, don't be afraid to push back if terms are confusing and/or unfavorable.
- Understand the nuances between patents, trademarks, and copyrights and how they're relevant to your work.

Financial Matters

- Be aware of how your relationship with and emotional connection to money affects your approach to financial matters in your venture.
- It's vital to have conversations about money with your personal partner, if you have one, cofounders, and key stakeholders before you start a new venture or as soon as possible if you've already started.
- Know what to expect in the basic financial management of a startup.

Fundraising

- Not every venture needs to, should, or can take investor capital. If you do, understand that once you are on the fundraising hamster wheel, it's super hard to get off.

- If you plan to fundraise, determine if your business is venture-backable. Investors will want to see measurable evidence that there is a problem to solve, how your startup will differentiate in the market, and that you have a strong team and business model.
- There are many different types of dilutive and nondilutive forms of capital available to most startups.
- Funding happens in rounds. The most common types of funding rounds are pre-seed, seed, and priced rounds.
- Investors can be helpful beyond their money. They can help with hiring; marketing, sales, and partnerships; product development; and financial matters.
- Do backdoor checks on potential investors as you would for hiring employees.
- Protect yourself from bad actors by knowing your rights and leveraging legal counsel when structuring any deal.

Go-to-Market Strategies
- Know the difference between branding and brand awareness to fill the funnel with potential buyers.
- Have a content strategy for things like your website, social media, and other external channels.
- A product-led growth strategy leverages the company's product(s) as their primary driver of customer acquisition, expansion, and retention.
- Pricing intersects with sales and marketing as you figure out what customers are willing to pay for your product.
- A launch event can be an effective way to drive sales and promote your venture.

A Tale of Two Stools
- As your startup scales, you will juggle the interplay between the engineering, product, and design (EPD) teams and the product, sales, and support (PSS) teams.

- Build a process to ensure all functions are aligned in the two types of three-legged stools: EPD and PSS.

Communication Strategies

- As your team expands, you'll have different types of communication of the same issue, depending on the audience.
- Adopt best practices for board meetings as soon as your board is formed.
- When in a conflict situation, consider that there may be more going on than you realize. You can often get to the root cause of conflict by taking a compassionate approach.
- Brené Brown's *painting done* and *clear is kind* are tools that will help you mitigate conflict.
- Don't delay difficult conversations. Lean into them and get help when you need it.
- Use the code red, yellow, green framework to manage crises when they arise (because they probably will!).

Part IV

WORKING AT SCALE

One sunny afternoon in 2011, I was strolling through the vast, one-hundred-acre VMware campus in Palo Alto, California, with one of the company cofounders, Scott Devine. As we walked, people we didn't know kept saying hello to us. It was sort of awkward and sort of cool. We stood for a moment and scanned the windows of the five different buildings on campus where we could see people inside working at their desks and teams having lively meetings in conference rooms. Scott turned to me and said, "What do all these people even *do*?" At that point, the company had over ten thousand employees based in dozens of countries around the world. We were visiting from our much smaller office in Cambridge, Massachusetts, which I had grown from three people in 2005 to about 250 employees, and Scott and I were consistently struck with the enormity of it all whenever we visited the mother ship. Scott put his hand up to shade his face as he looked at the expanse of buildings, gorgeous plantings, and our community-adored turtle pond and said, "If you had told me that our little project back at Stanford would have resulted in a company at scale like this, I don't think I would have believed you."

Scott had been a PhD student at Stanford when he, his advisor Mendel Rosenblum, and two of his PhD candidate friends began to develop what became VMware's first virtual machine. What started as a thesis topic in the lab became a commercial solution, VMware Workstation. The five cofounders left the research lab at Stanford in 1998 to work in several sketchy spaces including a small office in a space above a purported crack house and an eventual upgrade to an office space over the much-loved Village Cheese House in Palo Alto's Town & Country Village, complete with a leaky roof and spotty internet connections. It was rumored that the founders each cleared tens of millions in cash when the company was acquired by EMC in 2003 for $625 million.

EMC allowed VMware to operate with autonomy as part of the acquisition. With a fresh infusion of cash and a big corporation behind us, scale was priority one. When I first met the VMware team in Palo Alto in 2004, we had two major products (Workstation and ESX), and various small teams were scattered across a half dozen or so buildings in Palo Alto as they waited for their new campus to be completed. The company employed a couple hundred people, mostly engineers, when I joined and by the end of my first month as an employee, I knew almost everyone by first name. By the time I left in 2013, we were over fifteen thousand people worldwide, our third CEO, Pat Gelsinger, had just come on board, we had many products, were completing our twenty-first startup acquisition, and were listed as a publicly traded company on the New York Stock Exchange.

I had experienced a lot of growing pains firsthand as we scaled at Akamai, but VMware's scale was next level. Experiencing both ventures' challenges and successes as they expanded also prepared me to help DigitalOcean and many of the companies I have since worked with when it comes to all things scale. Startup evolution and scale result in many twists and turns in the journey of entrepreneurship. In the earlier months and years, the initial idea will likely shift or a new epiphany from ongoing product-discovery work will incite a whole new problem to solve that causes the business to pivot and, ideally, you'll reach PMF. As the business scales, founders and leaders begin to realize there are key activities they no longer need to do or want to do, or there are things they prefer to do that they no longer have time for, such as the CEO who still likes to code. There are also challenges with employees who miss the old days when they could be nimble and work freely with few processes and had far less at stake if they screwed up and, of course, there are also hard times, successful and not-so-successful exits, and other aspects of a scaling business for which many founders are ill-prepared.

In this final part of the book, I'll share models I have developed to help founders and their teams approach their businesses at scale through exit. I'll start in Chapter 16 by guiding you through the changes that inherently come with scaling. I'll help you figure out how to balance staying in the details and delegating so you can focus on the bigger picture, and how to build trust while empowering your team to take ownership of critical work. In Chapter 17 we'll look at the many hats founders wear, how to determine which you should keep on and which to pass on to others, and how to prioritize your mental health as startup life competes for your energy and time. Chapter 18 covers the brass tacks of exits: their most common configurations, how to navigate them, and what the financials tend to look like. It then offers guidance on how to transition—whether that's becoming a joiner after a recent acquisition, stepping down as a company leader and handing the keys over to someone else to drive, or in some cases, leaving your venture altogether.

16.

BUILDING TO SCALE

There is a fine line between preparing for every if-then-else statement and having the right scaffolding in place to ease the transition toward a scaling organization. All three of the early-stage companies I joined were at the "Oh shit we're scaling" point without a plan. The excitement of scaling swiftly from a few founders to dozens or hundreds of employees comes with a lot of organizational and technical debt, and typically, no one sees it coming. You may need to fix things like cultural norms and hiring practices that may require layering in new leaders and the recalibration of everyone's titles and salaries. If you are building technology, the spaghetti code and good-enough designs you did early on may require total rewrites or overhauls of the earlier versions of your product. Operational processes will have to be tweaked to run at scale, and decisions become harder to make with more moving parts and stakeholders to please.

Whether you are preparing for future scale (good for you for planning ahead!) or you're in the thick of it now and playing catch-up (better now than never!), it's good to be aware of the common challenges that will stretch your organization. This chapter will help you prepare for and navigate these growing pains.

BALANCING THE HOW WITH THE WHAT

In 2024, Y Combinator founder Paul Graham wrote a controversial post on his personal blog explaining founder mode versus manager mode.[1] He suggested that notable founders like Brian Chesky (Airbnb) and Steve Jobs (Apple) scaled their hugely successful ventures because they maintained the role of founders and didn't succumb to the pressure they felt from their board and others to step out of the day-to-day details of their ventures to serve as (gasp!) managers. It's unrealistic to suggest that the modes are binary and that entrepreneurs should stay in founder mode without full context of what it takes to operate a startup. Rebecca Greene, CTO and cofounder of AI company Regal.io, which is a cloud contact center for customer engagement, responded to Graham's post by saying, "Concluding that founders should act like the most famous eccentric founder/CEO on the planet who built the most iconic company at the highest valuation is a bit . . . easy? Oh shit, why didn't I think to be more like Steve Jobs and Apple!?" Most founders—and the joiners who work with them—will thrive when they learn how to balance founder *and* manager mode as their ventures scale.

I have been lucky enough to work in the trenches as a joiner with several different founders who brilliantly balanced founder and manager modes—from early stages through post-IPO. These founders knew how to dive into the details without it feeling like micromanagement. They were able to do this because:

- They built a psychologically safe culture.
- They had the emotional intelligence (EQ) and empathy to build trust, collaborate, and foster the growth of their team members.

- They had seasoned coaches and senior employees to both support and mentor them as they developed as leaders.

I have covered how to think about and build many of these traits throughout this book, but sometimes, despite best planning and efforts, it takes working through these challenges to build the muscle to differentiate and navigate the various situations that require founder mode versus manager mode. The boat metaphor is one of my favorite ways to envision how roles shift as startups scale. This is usually in three phases:

Phase I—the Rowboat: In the early days, the venture is like a rowboat in the fog with a few people rowing together toward a destination that is fuzzy in the distance. The water may be rough at times and no one really knows where they will end up or who they'll see when they arrive. Everyone is immersed in the *how* by doing whatever they can to get there, learning new skills as they go and trying to get to a clear destination, or the *what*.

Phase II—the Motorboat: As the venture scales, at around fifteen to twenty people when there's evidence of product-market fit, it will feel more like a midsize motorboat. It's speeding toward a destination that may be a little clearer and with a team (marketing, sales, engineering, etc.) ensuring there's enough gas to get there (the product), supplies to serve the team (operations), and people waiting for them who know they are arriving and what to expect (your customers). This is the pivotal moment when the best founders start to shift from solely focusing on the *how* to toggling between the *how* and the *what*; when they begin to let go of being involved in every detail and allow their team to start to work independently. They are still involved in many details and perhaps manage a team or two themselves directly. For example, founders may be running sales during this phase both to stay close to customers and to get a handle on what the sales playbook is for their venture before they hand it off to a more seasoned sales leader (and to inform themselves on who that leader needs to be before they start a search).

Phase III—the Cruise Ship: This is when the venture starts
to scale with dozens or more employees, has established
product-market fit, and has a roadmap to broaden reach
in new verticals, geographies, and/or product offerings. At
this stage, founders serve as captains at the bridge of a ship.
They are deciding where the boat is headed and by when
(the *what*) and looking at a dashboard to track whether
their crew (engineering, sales, etc.) is getting the boat where

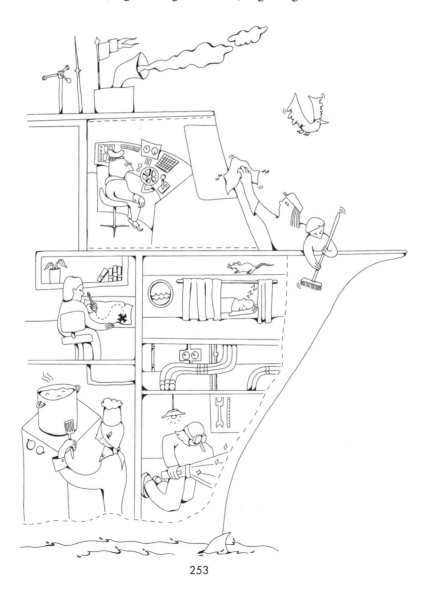

it needs to be, and on time (their crew has or is mastering the skills necessary to handle the *how*). There's a chef and galley crew to make meals for everyone (human resources), and a radio team communicating with the mainland (marketing), etc. This phase is often referred to as the "messy middle"[2] and tends to be the hardest transition point for leaders as they start to let go of the day-to-day, and still jump in where necessary, but must trust their teams and leaders to execute because it's just not scalable to do "all the things" in founder mode.

HUB AND SPOKE

As the venture scales from rowboat to motorboat, letting go while trusting and empowering the team to do their jobs can be a challenge if you are used to being in the know on everything going on. There is both the curiosity of "What is everyone doing?!" as Scott felt when he observed the masses of people at VMware's Palo Alto headquarters, to a sense of insecurity that all of these people just can't operate or care about the business as deeply as you do. This can result in a lack of clarity around hierarchy and roles.

One of the most common ways this lack of clarity manifests is when the CEO-founder serves as a "hub" between all their direct reports. This usually happens for one of two reasons. Either teams are made up largely of generalists, such as full-stack engineers or marketing professionals who can get the basics done but rely on founders for all decisions, or because the CEO-founder wants to stay in the loop (FOMO). The result is a hub-and-spoke situation that creates communication issues and productivity bottlenecks. Frankie was a classic CEO-founder of a post–series A software startup with a team of around thirty people made up of small engineering, support, and sales teams. They had unwittingly developed a hub-and-spoke situation. They met weekly with each of their team leaders one-on-one and coordinated activities between each meeting such as telling marketing about upcoming product releases instead of having the product leader talk with the marketing leader. Frankie's intent was to both optimize everyone's time and to develop strong working relationships with each of their leaders while staying informed on each functional area of the business. However, in doing so, they had created two major leadership challenges:

1. **Their leaders did not collaborate with each other.** Frankie ran a weekly leadership meeting, but they had very little interdisciplinary teamwork muscle. Frankie was serving as the go-between for each of these teams and because of this, each leader had created a dependency on Frankie for every decision per functional area, creating bottlenecks and slowing down much of the day-to-day operations. These teams' leaders also felt a lack of agency and autonomy to run each of their functional areas without Frankie's involvement.

2. **There were trust issues and holding back of information.** Frankie had developed an unfortunately common bad habit of talking about each leader to the others. They would explain to a head of product that the head of engineering was overwhelmed by too many new product ideas or tell their head of finance that they were dissatisfied with the performance of their head of HR. It wasn't meant as gossip—they thought they were serving the team well by trying to assuage concerns—but this behavior created uncertainty and doubt for each leader. *If Frankie is saying that about them, what are they saying about me?* Frankie had created a psychologically unsafe environment for their team.

After a number of leaders quit because of these issues, I worked with Frankie to shift their behavior to fully engage the power of their team. Frankie adopted my WE (work efficaciously) framework, which

I developed to break the hub-and-spoke model by shifting to a more collaborative model.

The WE framework uses the metaphor of driving cars. I'll use Frankie's situation as an example:

Step 1—Get out of the driver's seat: I asked Frankie to imagine they slid over to the front passenger seat of a car and one of their team leaders got behind the wheel. Assuming this leader is an experienced and qualified driver, what information did Frankie need to give them to drive to a specific destination? This is a great opportunity to use "painting done" as discussed in Chapter 9. Frankie role-played an upcoming customer visit for this exercise: They would say to their engineering leader, "We are driving from Boston to New Hampshire and need to be there for a customer meeting at 2 p.m. You will be doing a technical demo of our latest product feature so we can get their feedback on whether this feature can integrate into their current system." In this example, Frankie is clear about the *what* (driving to New Hampshire to arrive by 2 p.m.), *why* (to get customer feedback on something technical), and *who* (the engineering leader).

Step 2—Move to the back seat of the car: I then ask Frankie what would happen if several others had to visit the customer site (an engineer, a designer, and a sales rep) without her and the others and must coordinate to be prepared and arrive on time. They set up the same situation as above, but instead of hub-and-spoke and working with each person individually to organize the trip, I asked them to foster teamwork. Frankie said, "Please work together to figure out what you will each need to be prepared and figure out whether you all can carpool to save business expenses. Let me know if you have any questions." This change in behavior encouraged the team to work together to plan for this customer visit. By doing this, Frankie was still involved but had effectively moved to the back seat of the car: conveying trust, giving their team agency, and fostering teamwork and collaboration.

Step 3—Get out of the car: As leaders learn to work together more without a hub-and-spoke model, you will find more opportunities to step outside of the car, which Frankie was able to do in many—but not all—situations. This is level "WE"! Frankie still met with each leader for professional development and domain-specific discussions, but Frankie stepped out of the cross-functional hub role they had once embraced.

You don't have to implement the WE framework all by yourself. In fact, this is a great opportunity to co-create a plan to get there with your team. To avoid the fight-or-flight response discussed in Chapter 15, be transparent that you wish to move in that direction and ask your team to serve as your accountability partner as you try to move away from hub-and-spoke and more toward WE. A good measure for when the team has reached level WE is when you become an optional attendee in meetings and are brought in when your opinion or a strategic decision is needed. This can feel like being a symphony conductor; each functional area of your business operates well with experts like the string or horn section of an orchestra, but they need you to bring them together to play beautiful music. Your team appreciates you as their leader and knows you trust them to do what they do best. At WE level, you are feeling less FOMO or a lack of control and finding some relief that the team has it covered so you can focus on other, more strategic, activities. And the best part is, as you do this with *your* team, they will likely follow suit with theirs (now or in the future as your startup scales)—leading to greater efficiency across your organization.

It's hard to strike a balance between when to be super engaged and when to delegate to or coach a team or individual. Sometimes, the work is getting done, but not the way you would do it, and that's okay. Sometimes, though, especially at fast-growing startups, you just *have* to get into the weeds (founder mode). These questions can help you figure out when to stand back, when to coach, and when to step in:

- Is the work itself getting done without me and/or are metrics being met without compromising quality or breaking important guidelines?
- What are the consequences of the work not being closely managed by or completed by me?
- Is this an opportunity for me to coach someone who has demonstrated potential?
- Am I the domain expert and/or more experienced in this area, or are they?

THE VPE<>CTO FORK

In the early days of a technology startup, the CTO (who is often also a cofounder) is commonly the chief cook and bottle washer for all things technical. There tend to be two types of CTOs that evolve as a company grows:

The Evangelist: The shameless promoter of your product, this CTO is out on the road meeting existing customers and partners, and marketing your product. They understand industry trends and the ecosystem. They are the ultimate voice of the customer.

The Expert: Often a domain expert or technical guru, this CTO is heads down with your engineering or research team. They code, sit in code reviews, and mentor junior engineers. They may be designing your underlying architecture or perhaps innovating for the future. They enjoy meeting customers, but they prefer internal discussions about customer needs with product, sales, and support teams.

In the early days of a startup, either of these two CTO types can cover both roles, but at scale, the role can outgrow the person. Lost velocity in releasing new products/features, attrition or morale issues, fragile code, or lack of innovation are the symptoms indicating that you may need to "fork" and bring on a head of engineering or vice president of engineering (VPE). A great VPE will be process-oriented, great at hiring and coaching the team, and isn't afraid to get their hands dirty (can code if needed). They are also comfortable challenging the status quo and not just continuing to build what the cofounders started. They can manage cleaning up technical debt and can be a strategic thinker. Really good VPEs kill things sooner than a CTO or CEO may like for the sake of velocity and execution.

It can take a lot of soul-searching for a founding CTO to realize they're not serving the company well. They may worry about where they will fit in once a VPE is on board, but when partnered with a great VPE, they can thrive as strong individual contributors or leaders of a research team. Whatever you decide, as with any people-related decision noted in this book, don't drag it out. Get advice and coaching help if you need it. I've seen startups lose months if not years of productivity because they didn't want to hurt feelings by telling their CTO that the role had outgrown them. This can be done with compassion and kindness, but it must get done.

FOUNDER SEPARATION ANXIETY

It can seem like just yesterday that you were a team of five, sharing a one-room coworking space. There was an open flow of communication in the room, and unless someone was wearing headphones to signal they were "in the zone," anything was fair game to chat about among the founders and joiners. In these early days, the whole team knew where you were with sales, fundraising, and how customers were feeling about your product, and everyone was part of making most important decisions for the business. You saw each other's work on your screens or perhaps, if all remote, you were in a nonstop thread in a group-messaging tool with very few separate channels. It was intimate and cool . . . for some, intoxicating.

Even as the team grows from five to twenty-five, there is this sense of deep connection between early employees and the founders of the business. However, as your startup continues to grow beyond twenty-five or so employees, there becomes less intimacy, and managers may be hired between early employees and the founders; called "layering." This situation can create separation anxiety for early hires that manifests in different ways—from temper tantrums in meetings to disengagement and generally bad behavior—and can be the root of cultural issues, or worse, unwanted attrition of early employees or newer hires struggling to get their footing with this cultural change. I've been the manager layered over employees who used to report to the founder, and it was not only hard to build their trust in my leadership, but I also had to manage up to ensure the founder didn't undermine my authority with the team.

Most early team members will adjust to the scale of the business, the layering of leaders above or below them, and being less plugged in to the more strategic aspects of the business. However, some will struggle with this phase of growth, feeling less "in the know," less valued as a founder's trusted advisor, or a loss of prestige because they no longer report to the CEO, even if their title hasn't changed. They may also find themselves being scolded for going around their new manager's back to get a founder's decision or opinion on an idea. Even finding time to just chat with the founders can become a challenge as the startup scales and they are busy with other activities like board work and fundraising. "They don't have time for me anymore" is a common sentiment. There is a sense of abandonment or loss of power. And you may feel it too. It's not just shifting from the *how* to the *what* as you bring in more specialists. You may miss when you knew every little detail about what was happening in the company and who was doing it. You may lament that you cannot have casual conversations with more junior employees about the business as you once did.

A scaling business is not a fit for some employees and founders. Early stage may be their sweet spot and a transition may be necessary. However, for those in it for the long haul, you can mitigate challenges during this growth phase with these strategies to manage founder separation anxiety:

- **Normalize this situation with the team.** Once you close that series A or secure a big new customer that is going to cause a growth spurt, manage expectations. "Good news, we're growing! But this means we are going to be shifting how we work and some of us will be less in the know than we used to be." This can be a great opportunity to ask the team what they need during this growth phase and where they are feeling the biggest gaps. Address what you can but accept that you may not be able to honor all of their asks right away, if at all.

- **Make sure you are accessible to the entire organization** in both structured and unstructured ways. Create open office hours and skip-level or small-group meetings for team members other than your direct reports. Be clear that this time is to chat or bounce ideas around, not for making decisions. Newer employees will appreciate this time to get to know founders better, hear origin stories, or perhaps even share their first impressions about your company. These are invaluable opportunities to build connections.

- **Routine all-company or full-team off-sites** are critical—especially if you have an all-remote team—to create more opportunities to forge relationships, share information, and learn from each other.

- **Set boundaries when early employees have new bosses.** Be open to listening to their ideas/complaints, but coach them on how to express their concerns with their new bosses instead of offering to talk to them on their behalf or (worse) commiserating with them.

- **Be mindful of perceptions that come from special relationships between founders and early employees.** It is not unusual for early employees to form personal relationships with founders outside of work. Late-night beers or weekend family BBQs may have become routine. With a larger team, consider how these special out-of-work connections reflect on your leadership. Optically, it can infer special treatment or that some employees are privy to strategic business details. You don't need to end these friendships, but you should set clear boundaries about not talking about the business when you get together outside of work.

These simple efforts should result in early team members better adjusting to the growing separation between them and the founders and having less anxiety about their roles in the business. Not all early employees may stick around as the venture scales, but these tactics should mitigate some attrition and will likely contribute to fostering a healthy culture of transparency, trust, and respect among team members.

PRODUCT EVOLUTION AND WHAT'S NEXT

Scaling from a small team to bigger teams and adding management layers to improve how your organization operates goes hand-in-hand with scaling your product portfolio to attract more customers and grow revenue. This starts with asking the first question, "What's next?" But often missed is the second question, "Will we have to change what we do with that next thing?" Just like your team has to adjust to these bigger teams and layers, you will need to adjust your operations to handle product-portfolio expansions. VMware got its start as a developer tools product. Our "what's next" came in the form of an innovation that allowed virtual machines to move from one physical server to another without downtime. This new capability unlocked a whole new way for us to sell enterprise software and required a change to our business and operational models from just selling a developer tool to a full suite of enterprise products. Our marketing and sales team had to rebrand and retool the sales playbook, our support team needed new skills to support a different type of customer, and this expansion created a whole new set of opportunities for us to do business development, strategic partnerships, and acquisitions. It was an inflection point for the business and gave us a roadmap of what became many new products and features released in the following years.

There can be a paradox of choice when you have many new ideas and options to choose from to expand your business. Fear of picking the wrong next thing can lead to peanut buttering—a metaphor inspired by the "Peanut Butter Manifesto,"[3] which I use to explain that situation where you are thinly spreading all your resources across several ideas hoping something will stick and making a mess along the way. Wombi Rose and John Wise founded the greeting card startup Lovepop in 2014. After getting a big marketing boost from being on the popular TV show *Shark Tank* in 2015, they began to think about their "what's next." They had a healthy direct-to-consumer business selling their unique brand of pop-up cards via e-commerce and in kiosks in shopping malls and train stations. Their "what's next" list included everything from expanding sales through retail stores like Walmart and online stores like Amazon to creating their own brick-and-mortar retail stores. They were also thinking about promotional merchandizing and wholesale models as well as many new ideas for the cards themselves. Each effort would have required different distribution models, capital costs, and a variety of new employee skills. Had it not been for a great team of advisors and their board, they may have tried to do too many of those all at once, made a mess, and put the startup at risk. Peanut butter! They ended up prioritizing the construction of their own retail stores and had at least seven up and running by 2022. Reflecting on this decision, Wombi said, "We have continued to learn from experience that at every turn we would have been better off applying more focus."

Sometimes, instead of peanut buttering, you can get stuck in build mode on your one-and-only product. You keep creating new features for your software product or colors or flavors of the same consumer product to show customers and/or investors you are working hard and earning their money, but these efforts are not moving the needle for the business in a meaningful way. Startups stuck like this have fallen into the build trap[4] and have lost their customer-discovery juice as we discussed in Part I. Remember, customer-discovery work is forever! Customers' needs evolve, markets change, new entrants come in. Just building upon what you already have can put your startup at risk.

You may not be stuck in the build trap, but you could be struggling to innovate and come up with new product ideas or ways to expand into new market segments. To avoid this conundrum and plan for "what's next," set up a culture of innovation. Having a culture of innovation means three things:

- There is a psychologically safe environment to float new ideas and to celebrate both the wins and the failures.
- There is funding set aside to ensure new ideas can incubate and flourish (or be killed).
- There are the right people and processes in place to foster innovation.

At VMware, I ran an annual event to gather engineers from across the company to foster innovation. The event started in 2005 as a small, half-day brainstorming session with a couple dozen of our engineers and evolved to a three-day, fourteen-hundred-person internal conference as the company scaled. The R&D Innovation Off-site (RADIO) is an integral part of VMware's culture of innovation and continued to run for almost two decades. You can start to build a culture of innovation early on at your startup by:

- Having a couple hackathons a year for teams to work on new ideas together
- Attending conferences to get new ideas or going to research talks at universities
- Organizing customer ride-alongs to have employees hear what customers are saying (or complaining) about your product. This can be done by going on actual customer visits or by listening in on calls/recordings of customer meetings.
- Going on field trips to manufacturing sites or labs for physical product companies
- Scheduling monthly in-person meetings or phone calls between team members that don't typically work with each other. Imagine the innovative ideas that could come from an engineer meeting with a sales or support rep to learn about customer pain points or how a particular part of the product is designed.

Having a process for "what's next" ensures the company doesn't become complacent and continues to work with urgency to stay ahead in the market. At VMware, Diane Greene used to always remind us that if we didn't watch our backs, we could be displaced by competitors. She discouraged us from copying what the competition was doing and encouraged us to innovate. When Scott Devine and I wanted to explore putting virtualization on mobile devices in early 2007—when Android was still a lab experiment and smartphones were just coming to market—Diane gave us the go-ahead to spin up a skunk works project with an MIT researcher and a Harvard PhD student to see what we could innovate. Even when our architecture board questioned whether mobile devices would ever have enough computational power to support our complex technology, they still encouraged us to innovate and forge ahead. Not only did we get the project done, but it led to VMware's first mobile virtualization product and my first (and only!) US patent.[5]

Not everyone is comfortable with the growing pains that come with scaling. Some founders and joiners decide that once they have moved from a rowboat to a speedboat or cruise ship that the company is bigger than they prefer. And sometimes, a company outgrows many of its early hires as it scales. Reboot.io founder and professional coach Khalid Halim refers to this as "the law of startup physics" to explain that while humans grow linearly, companies grow exponentially. When this happens, more experienced hires will likely need to come on board.[6] If you are there already, take stock of what's working and what's not. Are you struggling to balance the *what* and the *how?* Are you fostering innovation? Slogging through the peanut butter and not getting much done? Stuck in the build trap? If the answer to any of these is yes, consider some of the suggestions above to ensure you are set up to scale, or get help from a coach that has experience with scale. Don't go it alone; you don't have time. You're scaling!

17.

BALANCING HATS
AND MENTAL HEALTH

Startup founders and joiners wear many hats that they don't always willingly put on and take off as the business scales. One moment you are managing finances and the next you are making critical product decisions. As a quarter-end nears, you are leading sales, and as the company expands (or contracts) you're running HR. Joiners are often in player-coach mode, doing hands-on work while overseeing team members. There can be tremendous stress that can impact your mental health when you try to wear too many hats at once or struggle to decide which hats to wear, which hats to remove, and which hats to hand off to someone else—if someone else even exists! Your tendency to wear too many hats can not only create a bottleneck for team members but can also lead to you getting too into the weeds, causing a lack of empowerment and undermining the talent brought in to scale the business as discussed in Chapter 16.

Megan Chinburg was a newly promoted vice president of engineering for a startup just after the business had raised their series

A. She had joined a year prior wearing the hat of a player-coach to manage a team of eight employees while doing a few technical projects herself. As a VP, her new hats included overseeing two engineering managers and a dozen engineers as well as project-management duties and working with cross-functional teams like sales and support. Megan enjoyed wearing these new hats, but after a few months, she became overwhelmed with her workload and had almost no time to focus on the technical projects she enjoyed. Through coaching, we identified a number of projects on her to-do list that she realized she no longer had to do herself and could delegate to someone on her team, or hire someone to do. She also learned how to manage up and asked the CEO-founder to support her while she took a few hats off, pausing projects that were less critical. This allowed her the time and space to get others on her team up to speed on the activities she delegated and to hire a few more people. Not only did these efforts free her up enough to work on an AI project she'd been putting off, but by delegating a few responsibilities, she also empowered her team. By balancing her hats, Megan was able to serve her company and focus on her, and her team's, professional growth.

Megan was fortunate that the founder she worked for was able to recognize all the hats she was wearing and gave her space to better calibrate her work. However, many founders are so consumed with juggling their own hats that they may not appreciate how their calibrations are impacting their teams. A common sentiment from first-time founders is "How is it we have so many more people, but nothing feels like it's getting done?" It is at this point in a scaling startup when it is important to take a step back, assess who is wearing what hats, and give yourself and your teams time to assimilate to scale. This doesn't mean slowing down or calming the sense of urgency common in most startups; rather, it's about teams having a chance to form, storm, and norm before they can perform.[1] You can't just hand off hats and add new people without a bit of a dip in performance, called the employee J-curve[2] (see figure), and if you add lots of people all the time, it's often

THE PRODUCTIVITY J-CURVE

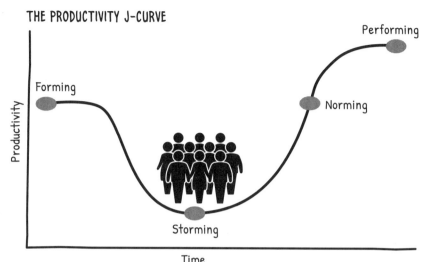

Source: Tuckman's Stages of Team Development (1965)

hard for a startup to ever reach a performance peak. Measured growth is always best for long-term growth.

As your startup scales, you may realize that no matter how much training, coaching, or mentoring you get, it's not about delegating and wearing new hats. You may realize you don't enjoy the hats you are wearing at all. This is usually when the company is at level-three (cruise ship) scale and you find you are spending most of your time in what I call the "adminisphere" (strategy and people leadership) and very little time in founder mode. But this sentiment can creep in earlier once you realize that there is more to a startup than just creating a product and raising capital.

A founder once called me elated to share that he found a way to carve out a day a week to code. He was a CEO of a seed-stage, pre-PMF company with ten employees. As CEO, instead of coding, he should have been focused on customer discovery and developing a marketing strategy while also considering his next funding round as they continued to burn cash. However, he was amazingly talented as an engineer and coding not only gave him joy and purpose but also allowed him to avoid the necessary, and not so fun for him, strategic elements of running his business. It took many months of coaching and his board's encouragement before he conceded that he preferred to be in a technical role rather than having to wear the operational and strategic hats of a CEO. He transitioned to being the company's CTO and brought in a seasoned CEO to run the venture by his side. Not every founder is as self-aware as this one, and unless you embrace the role and get proper coaching, you run the risk of burning out, creating a toxic culture, or, alas, quitting, being fired, or even closing up the business.

In this chapter we'll take a look at the common hats worn by founders and their first hires. I'll also share a framework I've created to allow you to assess which hats are most important for you to wear and what you'll need to do to get the right hats onto the right people.

THE HATS

Before deciding which hats to wear and when, you should first identify which hats (categories) are available to wear. These are the most common categories that are usually divided among cofounders and/or first hires:

Strategy: Determining the company's true north, near-term direction, and making critical decisions about things like fundraising, revenue, and human capital. Strategizing also includes defining and communicating *why* the company is doing what it does, which is as important as where it is going. CEOs rarely take off this hat.

Product: What the company produces. In the earliest stages of a venture (rowboat and maybe motorboat) the person wearing the product hat may be responsible for customer discovery, design, building, shipping, and support. Wearing a product hat also includes prioritization and tradeoff decision-making for features, new products, and services. Many startup CEOs and/or CTOs are product people, and this is usually the first hat to put on and the hardest hat to take off—if ever.

Culture and Process: As discussed in Chapter 7, if the culture doesn't work, then the processes won't work either. Creating high-performing, inclusive, and diverse teams goes well beyond what workflows, policies, and procedures are in place. Culture and process is how the team communicates, operates, and evolves as a living organism. Some founders are natural culture builders and systems thinkers, but if these are not strong suits, culture and process is definitely a hat that should be worn by someone else on your team with these propensities.

Talent and Development: As noted in Part II, who you hire and how you develop the team will determine whether the venture can scale successfully. As companies grow, there will always be tradeoffs on when to promote from within, when to hire more experienced talent, and when it's time for some team members to move on. CEOs often wear this hat more often than others, but many have COOs or strong HR leaders on their teams who wear this hat permanently.

Other Functional Areas Like Marketing, Sales, Support, and Finance: Brand identity, closing deals, supporting customers, and managing cash flow all require high founder engagement. Some founders are very functionally oriented, which can derive huge benefits for the business as long as there are capable leaders on the team wearing other hats.

Depending on the type of business you are in, there could be other hats to wear for domain-specific areas, such as clinical hats for a life-sciences business or a data-science hat for an AI-centric startup. Figure out which ones are important in your organization, which ones are clearly being worn by someone already, and which ones need owners. Next, we'll discuss what to do once you've taken inventory of all the hats and who is or is not wearing them.

THE HAVE-TO-DOS, WANT-TO-DOS, AND GOOD-ATS

Any key member of a scaling startup ideally wears only a few hats at a time. These select hats are the things that *have* to be done. It's great when these prioritized hats also happen to be hats you want to wear and require skills that you believe you are good at, but that is not always the case—especially if your venture is super early-stage. Similarly, there can be things you are good at and want to do, but the business needs you to do other things (like the CEO who loved to code). There are also times when something has to be done and you want to do it but lack the skill to do it well. When this happens, you may need to get some additional training or hire a specialist to do it instead of you (take the hat off!).

If your company has the cash runway to hire more people, you can usually move swiftly to swap or delegate hats with the support of your leadership team as Megan did. However, for the fledgling teams who can't fund these improvements, it is even more important to make hard choices about which hats to wear or take off . . . even if that means letting some things slide or not executing perfectly. The tradeoffs can be hard, and it is extremely common for founders to become so paralyzed about which hats to wear that the company's performance suffers more than if they had just picked a few hats to focus on and moved forward.

To combat this hat-wearing conundrum, I have created an assessment chart to help anyone juggling all the hats. Here's how the assessment works with an example from a CEO who completed it as part of our coaching session.

	Put a Y or N in each column for each category.				
CATEGORY (HAT)	HTD	WTD	GA	ACTIONS	MEASURES
PRODUCT					
PEOPLE					
ACCOUNTING					
STRATEGY					
SALES					

1. **Identify the primary categories (hats) you wear today.** This can be done together with personal hats (mother, caregiver, volunteer, etc.) or two different charts—one for work and one for nonwork hats.

2. **Reflect on the hats identified and assess your have-to-dos (HTDs), want-to-dos (WTDs), and good-ats (GAs) today.** Y for yes and N for no. This assessment is subjective and requires a large dose of humility—what "good at" means to you may be viewed differently by others (team, investors, partner, etc.). If unsure, ask for candid feedback from your team and/or investors.

3. **Define the actions you plan to take to change your Ys to Ns or vice versa.** For example, if talent development is something you have to do or want to do, but you're not good at it, what steps will you take to improve? Hire a coach? Take a course? Read a book? Or, like accounting, for example, you may not have to do it or want to do it, so the action may be to hire a bookkeeper.

4. **Decide how you'll measure your actions.** How will you know you have effectively achieved your goals? Will employee satisfaction or retention numbers improve and, if so, by when? If

you are hiring a bookkeeper, when would they come on board and how will you know you've officially taken that hat off?

Here is an example of a completed chart from the CEO I worked with:

Put a Y or N in each column for each category.					
CATEGORY (HAT)	HTD	WTD	GA	ACTIONS	MEASURES
PRODUCT	Y	Y	Y	N/A	N/A
PEOPLE	Y	N	N	Coaching	Successful Hires Lower Attrition by Q3-24
ACCOUNTING	N	N	Y	Hire Bookkeeper	Taxes Complete & Accurate for 2024
STRATEGY	Y	Y	N	Coaching	Strategy Presentation to Board & All Company Q1-25
SALES	Y	Y	Y	N/A	N/A

The CEO prioritized product, people, strategy, and sales as the hats they have to wear. Here's how they thought about these and the other hats:

- As a former engineer, product is their area of expertise and, at their startup's stage, it's a hat to keep on.
- Both people (hiring, culture, etc.) and strategy were important hats for this CEO to wear, but they felt their skills in both areas could be improved and decided to work with me as their coach to develop those skills.
- Even though they are good at accounting, they didn't enjoy that work and knew it could easily be handed off to a bookkeeper.
- Finally, this CEO felt they still needed to be involved in sales, enjoyed that work, and was good at it so, would keep that hat on for now.

Anyone can do this exercise and should revisit it every six to twelve months—especially if you are at an early-stage startup that is evolving quickly. This can be done as a diverge<>converge exercise in a team where each person works on their hat assessment separately then reviews them together to achieve alignment and help each other calibrate hats.

NO RECIPE IS PERFECT

The balancing hats exercise is one approach to bring some sanity to a role as your venture scales, but there's no perfect algorithm, and while one might aim to wear only a few hats at a time, there will be times when more hats will have to be worn. You may even find that once you've mastered a new skill, the hat you previously didn't want to wear is actually one you enjoy wearing more than expected. Another approach is a balance-wheel exercise where you identify your current efforts in percentage slices of a pie, the sizes of which are relative to your efforts on each. Then, you make a new wheel that depicts what you want your slices of the pie to look like. This can include personal needs—like time with family and friends—and even thinking time, which many people who work in startups lament over not having enough of. This type of exercise can help you calibrate your efforts toward that second wheel.

Over my almost nine years at VMware, I would pause once a year (usually in January) and do the balance-wheel exercise. I would assess the percentage of time I spent on things I was doing and then create a new version for what I wanted to do in the coming year. Like when we were massively scaling our Cambridge office in the early years, I was serving as the de facto head of HR for our one-hundred-plus employees. While I love people stuff, I was not spending enough time on technical work that had to get done, I loved to do, and was good at! So, I got more HR support for our growing office. That was the year I dug into the mobile-virtualization project that brought me joy and was fruitful for the business. Win-win!

No matter how you decide to assess and prioritize your hats, the balancing process will likely mitigate stress and potential burnout, which I will touch on next.

MENTAL HEALTH, TIME OUTSIDE OF WORK, AND SAYING NO

The number-one statement my coaching clients say when we start a session is, "I am so overwhelmed." Starting or joining a new venture can be an exhilarating experience, but it can also be incredibly demanding and stressful. When jumping onto this roller coaster, it's crucial to be aware of the potential impact on your mental health and take proactive steps to safeguard your well-being. The first step is to be honest with yourself and acknowledge the stress. Just saying not only to yourself but to your cofounder, your partner, or coach "I am stressed out" is a step in the right direction. This is a perfectly normal feeling in startup land! Once you acknowledge the stress, then do something about it. Below are a few tips, but I encourage anyone on this journey to work with a startup-savvy coach and/or therapist (most of my clients have both) to help you manage the stress.

Important: This section is not a substitute for medical advice, diagnosis, or treatment. If you find yourself struggling with anxiety, depression, addiction, or other mental health issues, seek professional help. Also, coaches are not therapists, and if they are properly trained (there are a lot of untrained coaches out there) they know where the boundaries are and may advise you to seek clinical help.

Tips to manage stress in startup land:

- **Accept imperfection:** Winston Churchill purportedly said "Perfection is the enemy of progress," echoing Voltaire's belief from Chapter 3 that perfection is counterproductive. And perfectionism can be a major source of stress. Accept that not everything will go as planned and that mistakes and setbacks are totally normal for a startup.

- **Set boundaries:** When you are trying to get to PMF, have employees who need to get paid, and have investors on your back, work can take over your life—especially if you are working remotely from home, where there's no clear delineation between an office and living space. Even if you are madly in love with what you are doing and all you want to do is eat, sleep, and breathe your startup, establish working hours and communicate when you are and are not available to your team and key stakeholders.

- **Make time just to think:** I encourage my coaching clients to carve out two to three hours *per week* to write or to go for "thinking walks." One client does his best thinking in a local gym's sauna, another while walking her dog. Carving out this time is not checking out on your startup, but rather investing in it by giving yourself time to process "all the things."

- **Practice self-care:** There is empirical evidence[3] that mindfulness and regular exercise can reduce and improve mental health and emotional well-being. Exercise can also help with sleep and promote brain health. Carve out time to do whatever you can to move your body and get your heart rate up every day. Meditation practice can help manage stress and improve mental clarity. Even a few minutes a day can make a significant difference. Also, as discussed in Chapter 1, journaling is an effective way to process everything in your head. Even fifteen minutes a day of journaling can help relieve stress.

- **Pursue nonwork activities:** Hobbies or spending time with loved ones can help your brain take a break from startup life. Elizabeth Lawler and her second-time tech company cofounder (who is also her husband), Kevin Gilpin, took this idea to the max by deciding to build an entire automobile from scratch in their garage on weekends as a forcing function for them to both do something fun together with their children and to work with their hands to get away from the computer screen. Not only did they successfully build the car, but they went on to get their pilot's licenses and build an airplane together. Thousands of rivets into it, Elizabeth says, "It gives us an opportunity to accomplish something as a family that isn't the family business of a venture-backed startup. Building a startup is something everyone participates in, including your kids because they see the late nights and weekends. It is important to have something else you can also do as a family." It's no wonder Elizabeth and Kevin had one successful exit and went on to build a second startup together—they found their secret sauce!

- **Prioritize friends and family:** Kait, who we met in Chapter 2, missed receiving an award for her startup at a conference because she stayed home to nurse her baby that morning. While accepting the award in front of a live audience would have been a good marketing opportunity for her startup, the true award was that time with her daughter that she'll never get back. You don't have to have kids to prioritize this time. Another founder I work with regularly schedules brewery tours with his twin brother to make sure they are intentional about connecting over their shared love of craft beer.

- **Hire a strong team (and fire B players):** The most common form of stress I hear from my coaching clients is dealing with employee issues. As discussed in Chapter 9, coach where you can, but also trust your gut if you feel someone isn't able to perform well. The cycles in your head deciding whether to fire someone are better used to find their replacement!

- **Set realistic goals and celebrate wins:** Ambitious goals are important at a startup but, as discussed in Chapter 5, they should also be realistic and achievable. Unrealistic expectations can lead to disappointment, frustrated team members, and increased stress. Recognize and celebrate victories—even the small ones—along the way. This helps maintain motivation and a positive outlook.

- **Foster open communication:** The entrepreneurial journey has many highs and lows. Being mentally prepared for this can help you navigate the emotional turbulence, but once you're in it, it can be hard to recognize (or admit to yourself) that you are struggling. There are founders who have shared their mental health issues publicly to destigmatize things like ADHD and depression. Others have created a culture where team members feel comfortable discussing mental health and stress at work. Open communication can lead to collective problem-solving and support.

- **Say no and accept the unknown:** As the startup and your career progress, there will be many opportunities to meet interesting people, speak at events, or be interviewed by the press. There are also a million things to learn and know about. We are inundated with information online, and it's impossible to stay on top of everything. Humans cannot do or know everything. Period. Come up with a list of criteria that would make you say yes to something or require you get up to speed on something new, and hold to it as much as you can. The slider tool developed by Rob Thomsett for product prioritization[4] can be a useful way to decide whether to do almost anything. Simply identify no more than five criteria that would allow you to decide a go or no-go. For example, if you are deciding whether to participate in a pitch competition, the criteria could be *visibility, financial upside potential, effort to participate*, and whether it will be *fun to do*. You would then plot a dot along a continuum for each of these criteria. The slider tool for this may look like the example on the next page.

Only you can decide how close each dot must be to the right or over the center line to make a call, but by visualizing it this way, you will likely give yourself the perspective you need to decide what to do.

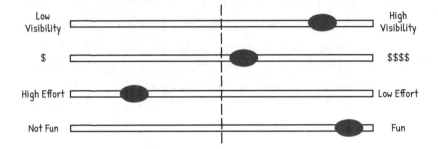

- **Find or build a support group:** Like-minded groups of empathetic founders, joiners, or investors are vital in the startup community. You may find this group in school, an accelerator program, a community within your home city, or a virtual community like my nonprofit Good For Her for women founders. These groups can be a lifeline when you may have limited support outside of your cofounder or a personal partner who may not fully empathize with startup life.
- **Ask for help:** Being self-aware and asking for help is a superpower. No matter how capable and experienced you are, you can't possibly know everything, and it's likely someone in your network (investors, peers, former coworkers, professors, etc.) may have the answers you need when you are feeling stuck. Or, perhaps they are empathetic to your situation and can commiserate or even brainstorm solutions with you with a fresh perspective.

There is a common saying that starting a new venture is a marathon, not a sprint, and prioritizing your mental health during that marathon is not a luxury but a necessity for sustained success. A healthy and balanced founder or joiner is more likely to lead and scale a healthy and successful startup. Take care of yourself, stay mindful of your mental health, and embrace the journey with self-compassion.

18.

EXITS AND TRANSITIONS

The startup journey often culminates in a significant decision point: the exit. Whether through a sale, merger, or initial public offering (IPO), exits are pivotal moments that set the stage for the future trajectory of the business. Equally important are transitions, which often accompany exits, but can also happen pre-exit as the venture scales. Transitioning leadership of one's venture to a new leader—or acquiring company—can be one of the most emotionally intense challenges for founders, as it involves not just handing over the reins but also could result in redefining the company culture and vision. I'll never forget the day that we found out that Diane Greene was no longer our CEO at VMware. Many of us "OGs" of the company couldn't imagine how we would maintain our lead in the industry and amazing culture of innovation without her at the helm. To her credit, she had built a solid business and organizational culture that withstood not only her transition out of the business, but the three wildly different CEOs who followed her before the company was acquired by Broadcom in

2023 for $69 billion. According to Ali Tamaseb's research, among all the unicorns founded in the past decade or so, 35 percent were not led by the original founder as the CEO.

Ultimately, successful exits and transitions are not merely about financial gain but also about preserving the legacy of the founders while ensuring the long-term sustainability of what you created. Despite all your best efforts, you may find the role of founder, or founder of your particular venture, is not for you. Your investors may also decide it's time for a new leader for any number of reasons, from poor financial performance to clashes about company strategy. Regardless of why you leave a venture, transitions can take an emotional toll and leave you feeling anything from charged up to go after the next thing to feeling grief for the loss of what once was. Let's discuss how these situations may play out and what to expect if and when you face an exit and/or transition.

EXITS

Most ventures start with an expectation of some sort of exit in the future for financial returns. Because an average of only 1 percent of startups exit via an IPO, mergers and acquisitions (M&A) are the most common outcome unless the venture fails and has to shut down. There are many ways M&A deals play out, but the most common for startups are:

1. **Acquisition of a whole organization to operate independently from the larger organization.** These are sometimes referred to as "bolt-ons." EMC did this when they bought VMware so we remained platform agnostic (critical in the data center space) and operated as an independent subsidiary.
2. **Acquisition of a whole organization to fully integrate and operate within the larger organization.** These acquisitions

are sometimes called "tuck-ins" and are often done to take advantage of proprietary products, talent, and/or customers. When VMware bought the network virtualization startup Nicira for $1.26 billion in 2012, we were not just acquiring a talented team, but this was a classic buy-versus-build decision to flesh out our product offerings. Post-acquisition, Nicira employees became VMware employees and integrated their technology and operating practices with ours.

3. **Acquisition of just the IP and/or customers (sometimes with a partial team).** There are many startups you may have never heard of that had small teams but great IP and/or customers that were of value to a larger company. For example, before Travis Kalanick founded Uber, Akamai acquired his tiny startup, Red Swoosh, in 2007 for its file-sharing capabilities. Sometimes there is a financial upside for founders, employees, and investors for these types of acquisitions, but not always. More often they are a full or partial "acquihire" (next point).

4. **Acquiring the team only (acquihire).** Smaller startups with few customers and limited revenue or IP may be acquihired into a larger company for their expertise. The company essentially hires a team and these individuals are then integrated into the larger organization. The startup itself is shut down, and other than salaries and equity associated with the acquiring company, there is usually no additional financial gain for founders, their employees, or their investors.

5. **Mergers.** Two entities join forces to become a new entity, such as when Sirius Satellite Radio and XM Satellite Radio merged to create a single entity called SiriusXM to consolidate resources, reduce costs, and strengthen negotiating power with content providers and automakers. These types of deals are tricky and can trigger antitrust issues, such as when startups DraftKings and FanDuel—two of the largest daily fantasy

sports companies in the United States—attempted to merge in 2016, but the merger was called off by the Federal Trade Commission.

6. **Private equity (PE).** These investments do not represent a complete exit in the same way that an acquisition or IPO does, but they still provide pathways for liquidity (cash off the table for founders, key team members, and investors) and are often seen as strategic exits for startups looking to enhance their growth or capitalize on their success. It is not uncommon for a PE firm to put in their own leadership team to scale the venture and for the founders and some loyal joiners to exit the business after closing the deal.

Your experience with any of these types of exits can vary from transaction to transaction and can depend on many different situations. The most common challenges for the founders and their teams fall into the following five areas:

- **Being bought versus sold.** A "hot" company with lots of acquisition interest for a great valuation is likely a venture that was bought. A venture that is running out of cash and/ or struggling to get traction is a venture that is sold. Being bought can, although not always, result in a financial boon for founders, investors, and early employees. The team could also end up in a larger company with great jobs, salaries, and benefits. Being sold, on the other hand, may not have a major financial outcome and in some cases only a small percentage of key employees are retained in the transaction.
- **Acquirer's M&A experience.** Even a great purchase of a venture for a high valuation can be a rough transition if the acquiring company has little or no experience with M&A. This may result in unclear expectations, such as when the acquired team's roles in the bigger venture are vague or not

well matched with their former roles. Or, the acquirer doesn't appreciate that the new team members need time to assimilate before they can be productive. These acquisitions can be deemed a failure before they've been given a chance. In the more than two dozen M&A deals I have personally been part of, it's taken an average of six months to fully integrate an acquired team, and the more complex the deal (people, IP, customers, etc.), the longer it takes.

- **Organ rejection.** The acquisition process itself was fine, but the cultures between the two organizations are wildly different. It could be that the fast, nimble startup culture can't adjust to the slower, more bureaucratic big-company culture or that each venture approaches functional areas from engineering to manufacturing to sales in wildly different ways. I experienced this firsthand at VMware in 2008 when we acquired a roughly twenty-person venture in France to augment our growing mobile virtualization team. At least a year, thousands of airline miles, and hundreds of croissants later, we finally figured out our cultural and operational differences and established a strong working rapport.

- **Strategic/covert behavior.** There is a lack of transparency or even malicious intent about the real reason an acquisition was made. For example, the acquired company being told that the entire startup is valuable, but then once the deal is closed finding out that they were acquired simply to take a competitor out of the market. Some team members may still find homes at the acquiring company, but most of these teams often get laid off and their IP is put on the shelf.

- **Golden handcuffs.** Depending on how the deal is structured, you may have an earn-out period (the average is two years) and certain noncompete or IP restrictions that could make it difficult to leave the company that acquired your venture—without walking away from a lot of cash—or start something new right away when you leave without litigation. So be sure to get legal counsel about your earn-out and talk with other founders who had successful exits before signing any acquisition deal.

I am not going to provide an acquisition playbook here, but I do think it's important for anyone in startup land to understand how they may play out. First, most acquisitions are not massive, and many have less-optimal outcomes for the founders if they were heavily diluted by investors. The popular navigation app Waze was acquired by Google for approximately $1.1 billion in 2013. Despite the large acquisition price, they had several funding rounds, which significantly diluted the founders' equity. It was rumored that the founders each owned between 2 and 6 percent of the company at the time of the acquisition. This meant that their financial take from the deal was far less than one might infer from the headlines. Sadly, in standard startup terms, even if each founder made twenty million dollars (a lot of money for most people!), they certainly didn't get anything close to the acquisition value. I've also worked with several startups that sold for tens of millions of dollars but still less than the total capital they raised, which resulted in zero financial upside for the founders or their employees; and in these cases, investors recouped only a small portion of their original capital investment.

Even if you have a huge financial outcome and/or land at a bigger company that you are thrilled to be part of and in a role you are delighted to be in, there will be a lot of internal feelings that may not be visible to others. If your goal was to get to an IPO, then you may feel you never reached your goal. Or, perhaps the outside world, family, and friends are saying "Well done!" because the headlines say your venture exited for hundreds of millions of dollars, but you actually made little-to-no money, had to lay off some of your team as part of the acquisition (survivor's guilt), or perhaps you never made the impact on an industry or the world that you had hoped for.

Even with a big financial outcome, you may also struggle to find your place in the world post-acquisition. There's nothing like the high of starting that first thing without a clue about what you are doing and, despite all odds, getting it to success. This can be a real motivator for you to start your next startup, and, with newfound cash, you may be less worried about failure and be willing to take more risks! But, you may find that you don't have the same motivation you had the first time when you were eager to prove that you could pull off starting and growing a new venture. Making enough money in the exit may make you less hungry. The financial freedom to spend time with family and friends after a hard grind on your startup for many years can be liberating but can also impact how you think about your identity. You will always be the founder of your company (a hat you'll never remove), but it could take a while to figure out your purpose if you are no longer running your startup. And these situations don't just happen to founders. Joiners I have worked with at successful startups often jump from job to job after that first big one because they just don't feel the same juice they felt the first time. Conversely, I knew exactly what that felt like at Akamai and was lucky enough to repeat it twice at VMware and DigitalOcean. A startup joiner trifecta!

Further, if you land at an acquiring company you may find it hard to get as excited and motivated or even struggle with your identity as a "regular employee." The pace of a larger organization can be frustrating or, especially for founders, you may not like the lack of control and decision-making power that you once had at your startup. That said, I have seen many exits go well for all involved. Post-IPO or healthy acquisitions can give you the opportunity to pay off debt, start families, buy homes, become philanthropists, invest in startups yourself, and, perhaps, start a new venture. And if you end up as an employee at the acquiring company, you may get to realize amazing opportunities not only in your professional growth but with your products. Anything is possible!

TRANSITIONS

It's hard to imagine in the early days of your startup that you will transition to something else one day. When or how you leave your venture is a big unknown, and how you will actually feel when it happens is hard to predict. Seth Sivak was the CEO of Proletariat, which he started with Joe, whom we met in Chapter 6, and three other cofounders (yes, there were five of them!). For over a decade, these cofounders scaled their startup to over a hundred people and released several popular video games until an opportunity arose in 2022 that made an exit through acquisition the right choice for the business. As we learned in Chapter 6, Joe decided to do another startup instead of joining the acquiring company, Activision Blizzard ("Blizzard"). However, a big part of the deal was contingent on Seth and the other three cofounders joining Blizzard as executives.

Joe and Seth each entered a period of transition quite different from the other. Without a lot of time to reflect on his decade-long journey before jumping into his new role at Blizzard, Seth had to swiftly learn how to adapt to a corporate environment, with more bureaucracy, that operated at a slower pace than a startup. He was also no longer where the "buck stopped" and had to work with a leadership team that made all the big calls he was used to owning at Proletariat. Joe was able to take a bit more time to reflect and consider what he wanted to do next and catch up with his family before deciding he wanted to start another venture. That said, he had to go back to fundraising, forging a relationship with a new cofounder, and building a team and a product from scratch. Both of them, however, shared the transitioning experience. They would always wear the Proletariat founder hat (or as Seth says, "It's more like a tattoo"), but, when one has put their heart and soul into a startup from day one, any type of transition can be jarring if not traumatic.

Transitions can also be the result of founders wanting a role change from leader to individual contributor, like the CEO mentioned in Chapter 17 who preferred to code. Some founders (or their boards) decide a more experienced leader would be appropriate to take the business to the next level and some are just ready for something new. In the case of Jon Stein of Betterment—an online B2B investment-management platform—he wanted both to bring in the experience and go after his next thing. Betterment had raised hundreds of millions of dollars, secured billions of assets under management, and had over a half a million customers when, in 2020, Stein decided to look for someone from outside the financial services industry to take Betterment to the next level. "Industry insiders often lack the perspective needed 'to disrupt services in a more customer-focused direction,'" he said in a *Wall Street Journal* article announcing his transition out of Betterment.[1] Jon later shared with a group of my students in 2024 how he not only maintained his belief that it was important to have a new leader with experience and a fresh perspective to take what he had started to the next level, but also how he missed the earlier stages of a new venture when he had a bigger stake in the outcome and more ability to shape the future. "As a company grows, and raises so much money, there are so many stakeholders, so many employees, so many customers, depending on things being a certain way. It's nice to start again with a blank sheet of paper, and full agency. I've never done well with having a boss."

Sometimes a transition is abrupt due to clashes with a board or, in rare cases, an egregious activity. But in most cases, transitions are thoughtful shifts managed with intention. By transitioning with intention, you are more likely to come out on the other side with more clarity, less stress, and a higher likelihood of success—in whatever way you define success. When you are in the process of transition, such as stepping down from your role, preparing to leave your startup, or your startup is about to be acquired, set aside time to reflect on what happened since you stepped onto this roller coaster. Consider the impact of the transition and what lies ahead. You may want to journal your thoughts using these prompts:

- What are the highlights and lowlights from your experience?
- What have you learned as . . . a leader, partner, employee, peer, innovator, businessperson? What specific skills have you developed or mastered?
- What are you more aware of about yourself? How have you evolved and who have you become along the way?
- What do you wish to leave behind or want to teach others?

If your transition involves others, such as cofounders or partners, consider conducting a group reflection process in addition to your individual process. While each team member played a role in your efforts, it is almost always how the team worked together that led to where you are now. Consider these prompts for that conversation:

- What are the highlights and lowlights of the work you did together?
- What are you most proud of as a team?
- What were key learnings for everyone?
- What do you wish for each other to encourage your paths forward?

Finally, commit to each other. This may be very tactical like committing to getting together once a quarter for beers or a family gathering. Or, it could be committing to supporting each other in your journeys going forward (networking, job reference, a place to crash when one of you are in town, etc.). Transition of any kind can be very emotional, which is why working through it with intention can be so helpful. Every single human goes through transitions at various stages in their lives. It's constant and we are wired to be resilient and adaptive throughout. During one transition in my life, I said to my coach Jerry Colonna, "It hurts," to which he replied, "If it hurts it means you're growing." So, embrace transitions, learn from them, and grow!

PART IV

WORKING AT SCALE TOOLBOX

Building to Scale

- To balance founder mode and manager mode, founders need to create a psychologically safe culture, build trust, foster growth, and bring on seasoned employees both to support and mentor them as they develop as leaders.

- As the venture scales, you might struggle with letting go, trusting the team, and empowering them to do their jobs. This can manifest as a hub-and-spoke dynamic. Use my WE (work efficaciously) framework to move to a more collaborative model.

- Scaling can cause founder separation anxiety as teams grow and many individuals no longer work directly with the founder(s).

- Setting up a culture of innovation can help you figure out "what's next." Create a psychologically safe environment to float new ideas and to celebrate both the wins and the failures, set aside time and resources to allow new ideas to incubate (or be killed), and make sure there are the right people and processes in place to foster innovation.

Balancing Hats and Mental Health

- If you find yourself wearing too many hats, it's time to take a step back, assess who is wearing what hats, and give yourself and your teams time to assimilate to scale.

- Use the balancing hats assessment to pinpoint your have-to-dos, want-to-dos, and good-ats.

- The balance-wheel exercise can also help you assess and prioritize your hats.

- When jumping onto the startup roller coaster, it's crucial to be aware of the potential impact on your mental health and take proactive steps to safeguard your well-being.
- If you're stressed or overwhelmed, do something about it. Work with a startup-savvy coach and/or therapist to help you manage the stress.
- Use the sliders tool to help you decide whether to take on something new or let it go.

Exits and Transitions

- Acquisitions are the most common outcome for startups that don't go public or simply fail.
- After an exit you may struggle to find your place in the world.
- Founders and joiners who land at an acquiring company can find it hard to get as excited and motivated or even struggle with their identity as a "regular employee."
- Whatever your exit situation, by transitioning with intention, you are more likely to come out on the other side with more clarity, less stress, and a higher likelihood of success—in whatever way you define success.

EPILOGUE

Building and operating a startup can be a thrilling journey filled with unique challenges and opportunities. As we've explored throughout this book, the key pillars of a successful startup are product, people, operations, and working at scale. By synthesizing the insights from these core areas, you can prepare for and navigate the complexities of the startup landscape and steer your venture toward a successful outcome—whatever "success" means to you!

My experiences and those of my clients and students are a collection of perspectives that should give you a good sense of what to expect and how to navigate the journey. However, everyone who's been in the crazy world of startups has their own stories to tell. Even those who were in the trenches with me through the many personal experiences I share in this book could have a different take on how the story played out. I do not profess that my ideas are the only way to think about things, rather just one way to consider how you approach startups. Whether you are a founder, joiner, or an investor, embrace each experience as a learning opportunity. Stay curious, remain adaptable, and never lose sight of your passion and purpose. Remember that success is how *you* define it. By focusing on building a great product and optimizing operations at scale, you are setting the foundation for a thriving venture. However, people are complicated, and if you don't cultivate a strong company culture and manage your mental health, the product and operations just won't matter. As founders and for early joiners, a big part of your success will come from not being thwarted but rather excited by all that comes before you and taking care of yourself and others along the way.

Remember, startup life is f'ing hard. If any of the stories within these pages make you bristle, you may want to pause and consider whether startup life is right for you. And if you join a startup for the first time, one experience will not represent all startups. Each startup is different and highly dependent on many variables. When executed poorly, you could impact people and/or the world in negative ways. It is my hope that the lessons from this book will inspire you to achieve great things and do so in a responsible way.

All that said, I've been on this roller coaster for three decades and it's been a hell of a ride. It can be *so* cool to join a startup or start something from scratch, be your own boss, and make an impact. And of course there's the possibility of financial rewards. The impact I was able to make, the vast quantity of things I've learned, and the amazing people I've been able to work with have been well worth the effort. Whether you are already in it or are about to start the journey, I hope you enjoy it as much as I have!

ACKNOWLEDGMENTS

If you had told me when I was an awkward and rebellious teenager that I would become a nerdy tech executive, educator at Harvard, and book author, I would have never believed you. My career path has been an organic zigzag of opportunities that has been an amazing ride so far. And I never could have enjoyed it as much as I have without so many brilliant and supportive humans in my life.

One thing that was certain for me from age six onward was that I would be a mom, and I won the lottery when it comes to children! Abigail, Amelia, and Eliza, you are my everything. You have brought so much joy into my life even during the toughest of times. You sat quietly in the back seat of the car while I was on endless business calls, and joined me on so many work trips and events that you became friends with my teammates. You gave me thoughtful perspectives on everything from what outfits to wear as a keynote speaker to creative solutions for technical and management challenges. You have been a constant source of good humor and straight talk, sharing your perspectives on the world, offering opposing views, and keeping me in check as I adapted to the constant changes in social norms and practices as the years have passed. I can't thank you enough for your endless patience and understanding during this journey. Your love, support, and honest feedback ensured this book would be thoughtful and inclusive. I adore all three of you equally and completely. I am so lucky to be your mom.

An extra shout-out to Amelia, for bringing this book to life through her incredible illustrations. Your talent and creativity have added a unique and beautiful dimension to this project. It has been a joy to collaborate with you.

I am forever grateful to my agent, Sylvie Carr, who approached me to write a book even though it was never on my bingo card. You saw my potential and encouraged me to go for it. Thank you for believing in this project from the very beginning! Your vision and persistence made this book possible, and I am profoundly grateful.

A huge thank you to the entire team at Basic Venture for their expertise and fortitude as my word count kept going up throughout the publishing process. (It's hard to pack three decades of experience into short form!) Also, to my editor, Maria Gagliano—your keen insights, patience, and tireless dedication have elevated this book beyond what I thought possible. I am deeply grateful for your expertise and commitment to ensuring this book achieved our goal of a practical and easy-to-read resource to anyone in the startup ecosystem. Also, a special shout-out to Aarushi Jain, who dedicated her time (and graduate school credits!) as a reader, researcher, protagonist chaser, and supporter of this project.

To my mentors and coaches—Tom Eisenmann, Kim Scott, Jerry Colonna, and Lillian Abrams—your guidance and wisdom have shaped not only this book but also my life and career. I am so lucky to have your support and counsel, and this book reflects lessons I've learned from each of you.

To my wonderful friends and experts who signed up to be readers—Finula Darwin (who was in the trenches with me at Akamai and has been my BFF ever since!), Seth Sivak, Lauren Davis, Ed Goldfinger, Steve Ranere, and Bryce Roberts—thank you for your thoughtful feedback. I'm so lucky to have you in my corner.

A heartfelt thank you to the many founders, joiners, investors, students, alumni, and Good For Her members I have worked with, coached, and invested in over the years and whose stories are within these pages. I am truly grateful for your generosity and willingness to be vulnerable so that others can learn from your experiences.

To my family, friends, and colleagues who supported and encouraged me during this project—thank you from the bottom of my heart. This book wouldn't exist without your belief in me and your contributions along the way.

Finally, I would like to express my deepest gratitude to my late father, George, whose unwavering support, wisdom, and belief in what I could achieve continue to guide and inspire me every day. Though you are no longer here, your influence is present in every word of this book.

GLOSSARY

These are common terms used in the book or in the field and should be part of any startup stakeholder's lexicon.

409A valuations—The fair market value of the common stock of a private company as valued by a third-party appraiser. Startups need 409A valuations to grant employees stock options on a tax-free basis.

A/B test—Testing two versions of a hypothesis to understand which fits better with the intended audience.

acquihire—When a venture is sold to a larger entity for its team and not for its products or services. This occasionally includes its intellectual property as well, although usually just for "parts" and integrated into the purchaser's products.

annual recurring revenue (ARR)—The amount of revenue a business will garner per year.

beachhead—The starting market from where you are in a good strategic position to capture adjacent markets.

business-to-business (B2B)—A venture that creates products or services that solve problems for other businesses.

business-to-consumer (B2C)—A ventures that creates products or services that solve problems for consumers.

buyer persona—Not always the user of the solution, they hold the purse strings. This persona is most common in B2B businesses.

For example, the head of HR may buy a candidate-tracking system for their recruiters.

conversion rate—The average number of conversions per ad or other sales interaction, shown as a percentage. Conversion rate is calculated by simply taking the number of conversions and dividing that by the number of interactions that can be tracked to a conversion during the same time period.

customer acquisition cost (CAC)—Measures how much an organization spends to acquire new customers. It is the total cost of sales and marketing efforts, as well as property or equipment, needed to convince a customer to buy a product or service.

directly responsible individual (DRI)—The person who is ultimately responsible for a decision or making sure a project or task is completed.

direct-to-consumer (DTC)—A business that sells its products directly to consumers, typically online through its websites or mobile applications.

diverge<>converge exercise—Breaking down a thinking process into two phases: divergence and convergence. In the divergence phase, generate ideas to broaden possibilities, and in the convergence phase, eliminate or streamline the ideas to converge on the best solution.

equity dilution—A decrease in the percentage of ownership that existing shareholders have in a company. It occurs when a company issues new shares of stock to investors, which increases the total number of outstanding shares. This means that each existing shareholder's percentage of ownership is reduced.

fear of missing out (FOMO)—A slang term referring to anxiety that an exciting or interesting event may currently be happening elsewhere, often aroused by social media posts.

hypothesis testing—Validating assumptions to make informed decisions about potential solutions (more details in Chapter 3).

ideal customer profile (ICP)—Detailed description of the persona that will most benefit from your product (more details in Chapter 3).

initial public offering (IPO)—A private company selling shares of its stock to the public for the first time. Also known as "going public."

legal redlining—A process of reviewing and editing legal documents, such as contracts, by making markings to indicate changes. The term comes from the practice of using a red pen to make annotations, but other colors or annotations can be used in digital documents.

lifetime value (LTV)—A metric that estimates how much revenue a customer will generate for a business over the course of their relationship. Also known as customer lifetime value (CLV or CLTV) or lifetime customer value (LCV).

minimum viable product (MVP)—The most basic solution a business can offer to begin to iterate with its target personas.

net promoter score (NPS)—A metric invented by Fred Reichheld that measures customer loyalty and satisfaction. It's calculated by asking customers how likely they are to recommend a company or product to a friend or colleague on a scale of 0 to 10. The resulting score is a number between -100 and 100, and anything over 80 is considered world-class.

pivot—A strategic decision to change a startup's direction or focus in response to market conditions, experiments, or other external factors. It involves making significant adjustments to the business model, product offering, target market, or overall strategy.

product-market fit (PMF)—When customers are buying, using, and telling others about the company's product in numbers large enough to sustain that product's growth and profitability (more details in Chapter 2).

product roadmap—An outline of the vision, priorities, and progress of a product over the foreseeable future.

RACI model—A managerial tool that helps define roles and responsibilities in a project or process. While there is no named inventor, the RACI matrix has been used since the 1950s.

release—Making an enhancement/modification of a product available to customers.

restructuring—A strategic company decision that can involve layoffs. A startup may restructure to become more efficient and cut costs or to change or eliminate functions and roles to make room for new hires.

software as a service (SaaS)—A type of software delivery and licensing in which software is accessed online via a subscription, rather than bought and installed on individual computers.

stock option—A form of equity compensation that allows someone to buy a specific number of shares at a preset price. Most startups include them as part of a compensation plan for prospective employees and offer options as a form of compensation for advisors and independent board directors.

strike price—The price employees will pay to purchase a share of your startup's stock when they exercise a stock option.

target persona—A fictional archetype(s) a business builds its solution for (more details in Chapter 1).

total addressable market (TAM)—The market segment that will potentially buy a product or service.

upselling—Persuading an existing customer to buy products/services over and above what they are currently purchasing.

user experience (UX)—A user's perception of utility, ease, and efficiency of a product.

willingness to pay (WTP)—The maximum amount a user is ready to pay for an offering (more in Chapter 3).

word of mouth (WOM)—A marketing strategy that encourages consumers to share positive experiences with a product or service with others. It can happen organically through casual conversations between friends and family, or it can be intentionally created by a business.

RESOURCES

BOOKS

Money and Finances

David A. Duryee and Tracy A. Bech, *60 Minute CFO: Bridging the Gap Between Business Owner, Banker, and CPA* (Best Seller Publishing, 2017).

Brad Feld and Jason Mendelson, *Venture Deals: Be Smarter than Your Lawyer and Venture Capitalist* (Wiley, 2019).

Morgan Housel, *The Psychology of Money: Timeless Lessons on Wealth, Greed, and Happiness* (Harriman House, 2021).

Leadership

Brené Brown, *Dare to Lead: Brave Work. Tough Conversations* (Whole Hearts, Random House, 2018).

Jerry Colonna, *Reboot: Leadership and the Art of Growing Up* (Harper Business, 2019).

Carol S. Dweck, *Mindset: The New Psychology of Success* (Random House, 2006).

Amy Edmondson, *Right Kind of Wrong: The Science of Failing Well* (Simon Element/ Simon Acumen, 2023).

Frances Frei and Anne Morriss, *Unleashed: The Unapologetic Leader's Guide to Empowering Everyone Around You* (Harvard Business Review Press, 2020).

Patty McCord, *Powerful: Building a Culture of Freedom and Responsibility* (Silicon Guild, 2018).

Kim Scott, *Radical Candor: Be a Kick-Ass Boss Without Losing Your Humanity* (St. Martin's Press, 2019).

Product and Design

Meredith Broussard, *More than a Glitch: Confronting Race, Gender, and Ability Bias in Tech* (The MIT Press, 2023).

303

Nir Eyal, *Hooked: How to Build Habit-Forming Products* (Penguin, 2014).

Rob Fitzpatrick, *The Mom Test: How to Talk to Customers and Learn if Your Business Is a Good Idea When Everyone Is Lying to You* (CreateSpace, 2013).

Elizabeth Goodman, Mike Kuniavsky, and Andrea Moed, *Observing the User Experience: A Practitioner's Guide to User Research* (Morgan Kaufmann, 2012).

Chip Heath and Dan Heath, *The Power of Moments: Why Certain Experiences Have Extraordinary Impact* (Simon & Schuster, 2017).

Jake Knapp, John Zeratsky, and Braden Kowitz, *Sprint: How to Solve Big Problems and Test New Ideas in Just Five Days* (Bantam Press, 2016).

Don Norman, *The Design of Everyday Things*, rev. ed. (Basic Books, 2013).

Caroline Criado Perez, *Invisible Women: Data Bias in a World Designed for Men* (Abrams Press, 2019).

Melissa Perri, *Escaping The Build Trap: How Effective Product Management Creates Real Value* (O'Reilly Media, 2018).

Strategy and Operations

John Doerr, *Measure What Matters: How Google, Bono, and the Gates Foundation Rock the World with OKRs* (Portfolio, 2018).

Brad Feld, Matt Blumberg, and Mahendra Ramsinghani, *Startup Boards: A Field Guide to Building and Leading an Effective Board of Directors*, 2nd ed. (Wiley, 2022).

Dave Gerhardt, *Founder Brand: Turn Your Story Into Your Competitive Advantage* (Lioncrest, 2022).

Martin Gonzalez and Joshua Yellin, *The Bonfire Moment: Bring Your Team Together to Solve the Hardest Problems Startups Face* (Harper Business, 2024).

Ben Horowitz, *The Hard Thing About Hard Things: Building a Business When There Are No Easy Answers* (Harper Business, 2014).

W. Chan Kim and Renée Mauborgne, *Blue Ocean Strategy: How to Create Uncontested Market Space and Make the Competition Irrelevant*, expanded ed. (Harvard Business Review Press, 2015).

Geoff Smart and Randy Street, *Who* (Ballantine Books, 2008).

Scale and Personal Growth

Pema Chodron, *Comfortable with Uncertainty: 108 Teachings* (Shambhala, 2002).

Marshall Goldsmith and Mark Reiter, *What Got You Here Won't Get You There: How Successful People Become Even More Successful*, rev. ed. (Hachette Books, 2007).

Matt Higgins, *Burn the Boats: Toss Plan B Overboard and Unleash Your Full Potential* (William Morrow, 2013).

Claire Hughes Johnson, *Scaling People: Tactics for Management and Company Building* (Stripe Press, 2023).

Startup Research

Tom Eisenmann, *Why Startups Fail: A New Roadmap for Entrepreneurial Success* (Crown Currency, 2021).

Ali Tamaseb, Dean Temple, et al., *Super Founders: What Data Reveals About Billion-Dollar Startups* (PublicAffairs, 2021).

PODCASTS FOR ENTREPRENEURS

bossbabe
The Goal Digger
Handcrafted
How I Built This
Planet Money
Reboot
Side Hustle Pro
Startup Grind
The Tim Ferriss Show
This Week in Startups

FILMS

The Beanie Bubble, a 2023 AppleTV+ docudrama, and *Beanie Mania*, a 2021 Max documentary, about the craze for Beanie Babies.

Dilemma, a 2020 Netflix docudrama exploring the negative effects of social media.

The Dropout, a 2022 Hulu docudrama, and *The Inventor: Out for Blood in Silicon Valley*, a 2019 Max documentary, about Theranos founder Elizabeth Holmes.

Fyre: The Greatest Party That Never Happened, a 2019 Netflix documentary featuring Billy McFarland, the event's organizer.

Generation Hustle, a 2021 Max documentary series exploring the "lengths young people will go to for fame, fortune, and power."

Inventing Anna, a 2020 Netflix miniseries, and "How Con-Artist Anna Sorokin Ripped Off the New York Elite and Became a Star," *60 Minutes Australia*, aired April 18, 2021, about fake heiress Anna Sorokin, also known as Anna Delvey.

The Social Network, a 2010 Max docudrama about the founding of Facebook, and *The Social Super Pumped: The Battle for Uber*, a 2022 Netflix miniseries based on Mike Isaac's book of the same name dramatizing the rise and fall of former Uber CEO Travis Kalanick.

WeCrashed, a 2021 AppleTV+ miniseries, and *WeWork: Or the Making and Breaking of a $47 Billion Unicorn*, a 2021 Hulu documentary, about WeWork founders Adam and Rebekah Neumann.

NOTES

INTRODUCTION: WELCOME TO STARTUP LAND

1. The year 2000 problem, commonly known as the Y2K problem, refers to potential computer errors related to the formatting and storage of calendar data for dates in and after the year 2000. Many software programs represented four-digit years with only the final two digits, making the year 2000 indistinguishable from 1900. Computer systems' inability to distinguish dates correctly had the potential to bring down worldwide infrastructures for computer-reliant industries.

2. Todd Leopold, "The Legacy of Danny Lewin, the First Man to Die on 9/11," CNN.com, September 11, 2013.

CHAPTER 2: WHY DISCOVERY MATTERS

1. Josh Howarth, "What Percentage of Startups Fail?," *Startup Failure Rate Statistics (2024)*, Exploding Topics, November 3, 2023, https://explodingtopics.com/blog/startup-failure-stats.

2. Tom Eisenmann, *Why Startups Fail: A New Roadmap for Entrepreneurial Success* (Crown Currency, 2021).

CHAPTER 3: THE ART OF DISCOVERY

1. Rob Fitzpatrick, *The Mom Test: How to Talk to Customers and Learn if Your Business Is a Good Idea When Everyone Is Lying to You* (CreateSpace Independent Publishing Platform, 2013).

2. Abbie Griffin and John R. Hauser, "The Voice of the Customer," *Marketing Science* 12, no. 1 (February 1993): 1–27, https://pubsonline.informs.org/doi/10.1287/mksc.12.1.1.

3. *The Wonderful Wizard of Oz* is a 1900 children's novel written by author L. Frank Baum and illustrated by W. W. Denslow. It is about a Kansas farm girl named Dorothy who ends up in the magical Land of Oz after she and her pet dog Toto are swept away from their home by a cyclone. Readers come to learn that a lot of the magic in Oz is not magic at all, but rather a complex system managed by a

not-so-powerful or ominous wizard hiding behind a curtain within his castle. It is used as a metaphor in the United States to suggest that what you see as magic may be an illusion.

4. The MaxDiff is a long-established theory in mathematical psychology with very specific assumptions about how people make choices.

5. Todd Jackson, host, In Depth, episode 64, "Airtable's Path to Product-Market Fit—Co-Founder Andrew Ofstad on Building Horizontal Products," First Round Review, August 18, 2022, 46 min., https://review.firstround.com/podcast/airtables-path-to-product-market-fit-co-founder-andrew-ofstad-on-building-horizontal-products/.

CHAPTER 4: THE CUSTOMER JOURNEY

1. The jobs-to-be-done framework was developed by Tony Ulwick and began as his patented process called Outcome-Driven Innovation (ODI), a framework focused on identifying outcomes that customers seek, as opposed to products they want.

CHAPTER 5: SETTING THE VISION AND A PLAN

1. DigitalOcean stock began trading on the New York Stock Exchange on March 24, 2021.

2. George T. Doran, a consultant and former director of corporate planning at Washington Water Power Company, first used the acronym SMART in 1981.

3. Jimit Bagadiya, "60+ Instagram Statistics Marketers Need to Know in 2024," SocialPilot, September 10, 2024, https://www.socialpilot.co/instagram-marketing/instagram-stats#:~:text=Instagram%20has%20over%202%20billion,visited%20website%20in%20the%20world.

4. DA, "OpenTable: Restaurant Reservations Made-Easy," HBS Digital Initiative, March 23, 2020, https://d3.harvard.edu/platform-digit/submission/opentable-restaurant-reservations-made-easy/.

CHAPTER 6: THE COFOUNDER COURTSHIP

1. Jason Greenberg and Ethan R. Mollick, "Sole Survivors: Solo Ventures Versus Founding Teams," SSRN Electronic Journal, January 13, 2018, http://dx.doi.org/10.2139/ssrn.3107898.

2. Tomio Garon, "Ditch the Venture Model, Say Founders Who Buy Out Early Investors to Make a Clear Break," Wall Street Journal, July 17, 2018, https://www.wsj.com/articles/ditch-the-venture-model-say-founders-who-buy-out-early-investors-to-make-a-clear-break-1531827001.

3. HumanFirst was acquired by clinical trials giant ICON plc in 2024.

4. Greenberg and Mollick, "Sole Survivors."

CHAPTER 7: ESTABLISHING A KICK-ASS ORGANIZATION FROM DAY ONE

1. Luis Villa, "Tidelift Values, Inside and Out," Tidelift, February 7, 2019, https://blog.tidelift.com/tidelift-values-inside-and-out.

2. Frances Frei and Anne Morriss, *Unleashed: The Unapologetic Leader's Guide to Empowering Everyone Around You* (Harvard Business Review Press, 2020).

3. Jessica Bennett, "What if Instead of Calling People Out, We Called Them In?," *New York Times*, November 19, 2020, https://www.nytimes.com/2020/11/19/style/loretta-ross-smith-college-cancel-culture.html.

4. *Forming, storming, norming,* and *performing* are the stages of group development in psychologist Bruce Tuckman's model that describes the phases teams go through as they grow and mature.

CHAPTER 9: SEPARATION

1. "Developing Brave Leaders and Courageous Cultures," BreneBrown.com, Dare to Lead Hub, https://brenebrown.com/hubs/dare-to-lead/.

CHAPTER 10: LEGAL MATTERS

1. Patrick Hanlon, "Zirtual Crashed but Can Its Brand Still Fly?," *Forbes*, August 16, 2015, https://www.forbes.com/sites/patrickhanlon/2015/08/16/zirtual-crashed-but-can-its-brand-still-fly/.

2. Marc Andreessen, "The Pmarca Guide to Startups, Part 5: The Moby Dick Theory of Big Companies," Pmarchive, June 27, 2007, https://pmarchive.com/guide_to_startups_part5.html.

3. SAFE stands for simple agreement for future equity. See "Safe Financing Documents," Y Combinator, accessed November 20, 2024, https://www.ycombinator.com/documents.

CHAPTER 12: FUNDRAISING

1. Eric Paley and Joseph Flaherty, "Overdosing on VC: Lessons from 71 IPOs," TechCrunch, October 15, 2016, https://techcrunch.com/2016/10/15/overdosing-on-vc-lessons-from-71-ipos/.

2. Dana Kanze, Laura Huang, Mark A. Conley, and E. Tory Higgins, "We Ask Men to Win and Women Not to Lose: Closing the Gender Gap in Startup Funding," *Academy of Management Journal* 61, no. 2, April 20, 2018, https://journals.aom.org/doi/10.5465/amj.2016.1215.

CHAPTER 13: GO-TO-MARKET STRATEGIES

1. "The Golden Circle," SimonSinek.com, https://simonsinek.com/golden-circle/.

2. The term "dogfooding" originated from a 1970s Alpo dog food commercial where actor and singer Lorne Greene claimed to feed Alpo to his own dogs. The

phrase "eating your own dog food" became a metaphor for using the products you were promoting. The term gained popularity in the tech industry in 1988 when Microsoft manager (and future CEO of VMware) Paul Maritz sent an email titled "Eating Our Own Dogfood," where he encouraged his team to use the company's product more.

3. Dave Gerhardt, *Founder Brand: Turn Your Story Into Your Competitive Advantage* (Lioncrest Publishing, 2022).

4. I highly recommend the docudrama *WeCrashed*, a 2021 AppleTV+ miniseries, or *WeWork: Or the Making and Breaking of a $47 Billion Unicorn*, a 2021 Hulu documentary, to get a full sense of how a founder's brand can impact the success or failure of a venture.

CHAPTER 16: BUILDING TO SCALE

1. Paul Graham, "Founder Mode," PaulGraham.com, September 2024, https://paulgraham.com/foundermode.html.

2. Scott Belsky, *The Messy Middle: Finding Your Way Through the Hardest and Most Crucial Part of Any Bold Venture* (Portfolio, 2018).

3. This manifesto is articulated in a memo, available at https://sriramk.com/memos/garlinghouse-peanut-butter.pdf.

4. Melissa Perri, *Escaping the Build Trap: How Effective Product Management Creates Real Value* (O'Reilly Media, 2018).

5. Lawrence S. Rogel, Julia B. Austin, Scott W. Devine, and Srinivas Krishnamurti, Controlling usage in mobile devices via a virtualization software layer, US Patent 8219063, filed May 14, 2009, and issued July 10, 2012.

6. Khalid Halim, "Hypergrowth and The Law of Startup Physics," interview in Management, *First Read*, n.d., https://review.firstround.com/hypergrowth-and-the-law-of-startup-physics/.

CHAPTER 17: BALANCING HATS AND MENTAL HEALTH

1. Psychologist Bruce Tuckman came up with the memorable phrase "forming, storming, norming, and performing" in a 1965 paper in which he described the path teams follow on their way to high performance. Later, he added a fifth stage, "adjourning" (also known as "mourning"), to mark the end of a team's journey. See Bruce Tuckman, "Developmental Sequence in Small Groups," *Psychological Bulletin* 63, no. 6 (1965): 384–399, https://psycnet.apa.org/record/1965-12187-001.

2. Team performance curve was first outlined in Jon R. Katzenbach and Douglas K. Smith, *The Wisdom of Teams: Creating the High-Performance Organization* (Harvard Business Review Press, 1992).

3. Ru Liu, Rashid Menhas, and Zulkaif Ahmed Saqib, "Does Physical Activity Influence Health Behavior, Mental Health, and Psychological Resilience Under

No

the Moderating Role of Quality of Life?," *Frontiers in Psychology* 15 (March 2024), https://doi.org/10.3389/fpsyg.2024.1349880.

4. Rob Thomsett, *Radical Project Management* (Prentice Hall, 2002).

CHAPTER 18: EXITS AND TRANSITIONS

1. Anne Tergesen, "Betterment CEO Jon Stein Steps Down: Investment-Advice Firm Chief to Be Succeeded by Former ViacomCBS Executive Sarah Kirshbaum Levy," Finance, *Wall Street Journal*, December 8, 2022, https://www.wsj.com/articles/betterment-ceo-jon-stein-steps-down-11607445001.

INDEX

Julia Austin is a seasoned operator who has served in leadership roles at several technology startups. She is on the faculty at Harvard Business School and is faculty cochair of the Arthur Rock Center for Entrepreneurship. As a certified executive coach, Austin works exclusively with startup founders. She is an angel investor, serves on startup boards, and advises many founders through her work with several accelerators. She has three daughters and lives in New York City.